THE

RHETORIC OF ARISTOTLE.

THE
RHETORIC OF ARISTOTLE.

A TRANSLATION

BY

Sir RICHARD CLAVERHOUSE JEBB,

O.M., Litt.D.,

late Regius Professor of Greek in the University of Cambridge,

EDITED

WITH AN INTRODUCTION

AND WITH SUPPLEMENTARY NOTES

BY

JOHN EDWIN SANDYS, Litt.D.,

Fellow of St John's College, and Public Orator

Cambridge :
at the University Press
1909

CAMBRIDGE
UNIVERSITY PRESS

University Printing House, Cambridge CB2 8BS, United Kingdom

Cambridge University Press is part of the University of Cambridge.

It furthers the University's mission by disseminating knowledge in the pursuit of
education, learning and research at the highest international levels of excellence.

www.cambridge.org
Information on this title: www.cambridge.org/9781107448162

© Cambridge University Press 1909

First published 1909
First paperback edition 2014

A catalogue record for this publication is available from the British Library

ISBN 978-1-107-44816-2 Paperback

Cambridge University Press has no responsibility for the persistence or accuracy of
URLs for external or third-party internet websites referred to in this publication,
and does not guarantee that any content on such websites is, or will remain, accurate
or appropriate.

PREFACE

MORE than thirty years have passed since I had the privilege of revising and editing for the Syndics of the University Press the *Commentary* on Aristotle's *Rhetoric*, which was left in a nearly finished form by the late Mr Edward Meredith Cope, formerly Senior Fellow and Tutor of Trinity. It was under the advice of two other distinguished Fellows of that College, Mr Munro and Mr Jebb, that Mr Cope's brother did me the honour of inviting me to revise and complete the work, and it has now fallen to my lot to prepare for the press another posthumous work connected with the same subject, the *Translation* of the *Rhetoric* left in manuscript by one of the admirable scholars above mentioned, the late Sir Richard Jebb.

From memoranda found in various parts of the manuscript, it appears that the translation was begun 'about August 20, 1872,' that the first two Books were finished on March 22, and the third on May 26, 1873. Thus, in the period of its preparation, it falls between the date of the translation of the *Characters of Theophrastus* (1870), and that of the publication of *The Attic Orators* (1876). The first two Books of the *Rhetoric* were among the set subjects for the Classical Tripos of 1874 and 1875, and, as an Assistant Tutor of Trinity, Mr Jebb lectured on all three Books during the academical year 1872–3, and again in 1873–4. The lectures were open to members of other Colleges, and among those who attended them was one of the present Syndics of the Press, who still retains a vivid recollection of the clear and vigorous English in which the text was then rendered. It was with a view to this course of lectures that a considerable number of original and selected notes was written out, followed (in the case of Book I) by a second draft subsequent to the publication of Cope's *Commentary* in 1877. The manuscript contains very few notes on Book III.

The whole of the translation was copied out for the press by an amanuensis; and the editor has had before him the original draft, written out with perfect clearness by the translator himself, as well as the transcript. At an uncertain date, a proof of the first twelve pages was prepared, but this proof remained uncorrected, and, owing probably to the pressure of other duties in an increasingly busy life, the printing was never resumed. The translation has been carefully revised by the editor; a few accidental omissions of single clauses or whole sentences have been supplied, and some other unimportant oversights have been corrected. It may be added that a certain amount of uniformity has been introduced into the various transliterations of Greek names, in which the translator shows, during the progress of his work, an increasing preference for the forms in k, such as Perikles and Iphikrates, and similarly in the case of the word 'epideiktic.' A brief analysis, partly founded on the translator's own memoranda, has been prefixed to the translation, besides being printed in slightly varying language in the margin of the successive portions of the text, and, necessarily, in a still briefer form in the head-lines of the pages. References to the sections of each chapter in the Oxford Variorum edition of 1820, and to the pages of Bekker's Berlin edition of 1831, have been placed in the margin and at the head of the pages, so that any passage can be easily found, while the translation can readily be used side by side with Mr Cope's *Commentary* (in which the Oxford sections are indicated) as well as with the critical editions of Bekker, Spengel, and Roemer.

As the commentaries of Spengel and of Cope are accessible to scholars and to students, it has not been deemed necessary to indulge in any large amount of explanatory annotation. Almost all, however, of the translator's few notes on Book III are here printed, with a selection from those on Books I and II. These notes are distinguished by the initials of the translator. For all the rest the editor is responsible. In the latter, the sources of Aristotle's numerous quotations are indicated, and the literary or historical allusions briefly explained; any variations in the text, so far as they affect the translation, are noticed; and, in some few cases, alternative renderings or alternative opinions as to the author's meaning have been added. The editor has also supplied an Introduction on the general subject of the treatise, in which the translator's own references to that subject, in the course of his *Attic Orators*, have been specially kept in view. The Introduction is followed by an Analysis of each of the successive chapters, while reference to the contents of the work is further facilitated by the Index.

J. E. SANDYS.

MERTON HOUSE, CAMBRIDGE,
November, 1908.

*The Treatise on Rhetoric is a magazine of intellectual riches....
Nothing is left untouched, on which Rhetoric, in all its branches, has
any bearing. The author's principles are the result of extensive
original induction. He sought them, if ever man did seek them, in
the living pattern of the human heart. All the recesses and windings
of that hidden region he has explored: all its caprices and affections,
—whatever tends to excite, to ruffle, to amuse, to gratify, or to offend it,
—have been carefully examined. The reason of these phænomena is
demonstrated, the method of creating them is explained.... The whole is
a text-book of human feeling; a storehouse of taste; an exemplar of
condensed and accurate, but uniformly clear and candid reasoning.*

EDWARD COPLESTON'S *Reply* (Oxford, 1810), p. 26 f.

INTRODUCTION

EVEN in the heroic age, long before the rise of any theory
Greek eloquence in praehistoric times. of rhetoric, the practice of oratory is brilliantly
exemplified in the Homeric poems. The eloquent
speaker is there regarded as a divine being[1]; the
elders of Troy are able orators[2], while, on the side of the
Greeks, the speech of the aged Nestor 'flows sweeter than
honey,'[3] and words 'fall like flakes of snow' from the lips of
Odysseus[4]. By the side of beauty of physical form, and
soundness of intellectual sense, the Homeric triad of human
excellences includes the god-given power of discourse. The
oratory of that age is represented as an extraordinarily brilliant
type of natural eloquence, an eloquence approaching the
modern ideal simply because its great examples are to be
found in the region of debate, while the greatest of all (as the
answer of Achilles to the envoys in the First Book of the *Iliad*,)
take the form of reply. But the distinction of being a 'speaker
of words,' as well as a 'doer of deeds,'[5] was reserved for the
kings and the nobles ; the voice of the people found utterance
only in the terse animadversions of the Homeric *tis*, the un-
named and hardly recognised representative of the multitude ;
and the first condition of civil eloquence, the right of the
commoner to speak his mind on affairs of State, was still
wanting[6].

---

[1] *Od.* viii 173.   [2] *Il.* iii 150.   [3] *Il.* i 249.
[4] *Il.* iii 222.   [5] *Il.* ix 433.
[6] Cp. Jebb's *Attic Orators*, I cviii–cxi ; and *Essays and Addresses*, 130–133.

x   *Origin of Greek Rhetoric*

In historic times, men of political power, such as Solon,
Eloquence of early Greek statesmen. Peisistratos and Kleisthenes, have the credit of being able speakers, for the times in which they lived[1]; but it was not until the expulsion of the tyrants and the establishment of democracy in 510 B.C., that civil eloquence could really flourish in Athens[2]. Between this date and the outbreak of the Peloponnesian war, the two foremost Athenian orators were Themistokles[3] and Perikles[4], but the fame of their eloquence rests on tradition alone. In the case of Perikles, although the historian supplies us with the purport of three of his speeches, a few striking metaphors, such as those preserved in the *Rhetoric*[5] of Aristotle, where Ægina is called the 'eye-sore of the Peiræus,' and where the State that has lost its young heroes in war is compared with 'the year that is reft of its season of Spring,' are almost all that has descended to posterity. His eloquence, like that of his political precursors, was apparently of a purely practical type, uninfluenced by the theoretical treatment of the art which was soon to reach Athens from another quarter[6].

While the home of eloquence was Athens, the native land
Origin of Greek rhetoric. of rhetoric was Sicily. It was there that, 'after the fall of the tyrants,' that is, after the expulsion of Thrasydaios by the Agrigentines (in 472) and of Thrasybulos by the Syracusans (in 466), the establishment of a democracy and the requirements of a new order of things, with its claims for the restitution of confiscated goods, and its suits for succession to property, aroused a distinct demand for professional instruction in the art of speech. Among the clever and disputatious Sicilians this demand was supplied by
Korax and Tisias. one Korax, who is said to have reduced the practice of speaking to a formal shape by drawing up a rhetorical treatise, which was the first of its kind. Before the time of Korax and his pupil Tisias, though many

---

[1] Cicero, *Brutus*, 27.
[2] *Brutus*, 45.
[3] Thuc. i 138; Cic. *Brutus*, 28.
[4] Thuc. i 139 § 4; *Brutus*, 44.
[5] III x 7.
[6] Cp. Introduction to Cicero's *Orator*, pp. ii–iv, ed. Sandys.

speakers had expressed themselves with care and precision, and had even written their speeches, no one had composed by rule of art.

Such is the story of the origin of Greek rhetoric, as given by Cicero[1], on the authority of Aristotle. The story was doubtless derived from the work in which Aristotle collected all the treatises on rhetoric which preceded his own[2]. The loss of this work has been only in part made good in modern times by the *Artium Scriptores* of Spengel (1828), in which the scattered fragments of the earlier rhetorical treatises are collected and discussed. Korax is said to have divided all speeches into five parts, proem, narrative, arguments (ἀγῶνες), subsidiary remarks (παρέκβασις), and peroration[3]. In indicating the sources from which arguments might be derived, he confined himself to the illustration of a single topic, the argument from probability. The stock example of this is the case of assault, when a strong man is charged with attacking a weak man, in the absence of witnesses. The use of such an argument, as shown by Aristotle, might easily degenerate into the merest quibbling[4]. This topic is quoted by Aristotle from the 'art' of Korax, to whose pupil, Tisias, it is ascribed by Plato[5]. It was doubtless the common property of both.

To the school of Korax and his pupil is due the early definition of rhetoric as the 'artificer of persuasion,'[6] 'a definition which is at once immoral and inadequate; immoral, because it makes persuasion at any price the object of rhetoric; inadequate, because it is equally applicable to other things,—for example, to bribery.'[7] In the familiar story of the lawsuit between Korax and his pupil for the recovery of his fee, the pupil begins with the inquiry: 'Korax, what did you undertake to teach me?' 'To persuade anyone you please.' 'If so, I now persuade you to receive no fee; if not, you have failed to teach me to persuade you: in either case, I owe you

---

[1] *Brutus*, 46.   [2] συναγωγὴ τεχνῶν.
[3] Walz, *Rhet. Gr.* iv 12.
[4] *Rhet.* II xxiv 11; Jebb's *Attic Orators*, I cxxi.
[5] *Phaedrus*, 273 A B.
[6] πειθοῦς δημιουργός, Proleg. in Hermogenem, p. 8.
[7] Introduction to Cicero's *Orator*, p. v.

nothing.' Korax retorts with a similar dilemma: 'If you persuade me, I have taught you the art; if not, you have failed to
persuade me to remit the fee: in either case, you are bound to
pay.' Whereupon the court dismisses the case with the con-
temptuous proverb: κακοῦ κόρακος κακὸν ᾠόν[1]. It is not the
subtlety of the new art that is expressed by this story, but
rather its 'grotesque unpopularity.'[2] The technical treatise
ascribed to Tisias was probably only an expansion of that of
his master, which it appears to have superseded.

The teaching of Korax and Tisias was transmitted to the
foremost representative of the Sicilian school, the
Gorgias.   link between the rhetoric of Sicily and that of
Athens, Gorgias of Leontini. 'The foremost man of his age
in rhetorical skill,' he appeared at Athens for the first time in
427, as the leading envoy of his native city, when 'the clever
Athenians, with their fondness for eloquence, were struck by
the foreign air of his style, by the remarkable antitheses, the
symmetrical clauses, the parallelisms of structure, the rhyming
terminations, and the other similar figures of speech, which
were then welcomed because of their novelty.'[3] He returned
to report the result of his mission, and he probably revisited
Athens not long after. The greater part of his declining years
was spent in Thessaly, and it was there that he is said to
have counted among his pupils the famous rhetorical teacher,
Isokrates. The frequent employment of metaphor gave a
poetic colouring to the style of Gorgias[4], while his use of rare
and foreign words imparted a novel and striking character to
his speeches. He has been recognised as 'the founder of
artistic prose.'[5]

'Beauty of speech'[6] was the special aim, and the cultivation
of a semi-poetical type of prose the main purpose, of the Sicilian
school represented by Gorgias and his pupils.
Pôlos.   Among these the impetuous Pôlos, 'colt by name
and colt by nature,'[7] is familiar to us from the *Gorgias* of

---

[1] Walz, *Rhet. Gr.* iv 13 f, v 215 f; Introd. to *Orator*, p. vi.
[2] Jebb's *Attic Orators*, I cxxiii.
[3] Diodorus, xii 53; cp. *Attic Orators*, I cxxiii–cxxviii.
[4] *Rhet.* III i 9.   [5] *Attic Orators*, I cxxviii.
[6] εὐέπεια (of Pôlos), Plato, *Phædrus*, 267 C.   [7] *Rhet.* II xxiii 29 n.

Plato, while from an obscure passage of the *Phædrus* it has been inferred that he not only invented a number of technical terms, but also borrowed others from his friend Likymnios[1], whose 'art of rhetoric' supplies Aristotle with examples of needless nomenclature in the form of new names for the different parts of the speech, such as 'speeding on,' which he apparently applied to the straightforward course of uninterrupted narrative, and 'aberration' and 'ramifications,' to digressions from it[2].

Likymnios.

Another pupil of Gorgias, named Alkidamas, insisted on the importance of acquiring a capacity for extemporaneous speech. Of the two declamations bearing his name, the one that is almost certainly genuine is an attack on the composers of elaborately written discourses most prominently represented by Isokrates[3]. His deliberative orations included a speech in which he pleaded for the freedom of the Messenians, a speech twice quoted in the *Rhetoric*[4]. In an extant fragment of his 'art of rhetoric' he partly anticipates Aristotle's definition by describing this art as the '*faculty of persuasion.*'[5] Aristotle quotes from his pages a considerable number of examples of faults of taste due to his fondness for strange words or poetic compounds, and for the inordinate use of epithets and metaphors. Modern critics of style would certainly be less severe than Aristotle in denouncing his metaphorical description of the *Odyssey* as 'a fair mirror of human life.'[6]

Alkidamas.

The use of foreign words and poetic compounds is a fault of taste exemplified by Lykophron[7], a rhetorician belonging to the middle of the fourth century[8]. Another rhetorician, Polykrates, who flourished about 390, and is best known through his 'Accusation of Sokrates' and his 'Defence of Busiris,' is only definitely named in the *Rhetoric*

Lykophron.
Polykrates.

---

[1] *Phædrus*, 267 C, with Thompson's note.   [2] III xiii 5.

[3] περὶ τῶν τοὺς γραπτοὺς λόγους γραφόντων, in Appendix to Antiphon, ed. Blass, 1871.

[4] I xiii 2 ; II xxiii 1.

[5] δύναμις τοῦ ὄντος πιθανοῦ, Proleg. in Hermog. in Walz, *Rhet. Gr.* vii (1), 8.

[6] III iii. See, in general, Vahlen, *Der Rhetor Alkidamas*, Vienna, 1864; Blass, *Attische Beredsamkeit*, II (1892) 364 ; Brzoska in Pauly-Wissowa.

[7] III iii 1-2.   [8] Blass, *Att. Ber.* II 364.

as the author of a trivial encomium on mice, and of a lauda-
tion of Thrasybulos[1]; but he is also sometimes supposed to be
the author of a panegyric on Paris, anonymously quoted in
several passages[2].

In contrast with the 'beauty of speech' cultivated by the

Protagoras.

Sicilians, 'correctness of speech'[3] was the aim of
the Greek school represented by Protagoras,
Prodikos, Hippias and Thrasymachos.   Thus Protagoras was
apparently the first to give special attention to elementary
points of grammar and philology, to distinctions of gender in
nouns[4], to the classification of modes of expression, to the
criticism of poetry and to speculations on language and
etymology[5].   He is also noted for the Commonplaces which
he caused his pupils to commit to memory, while his Dialectic
is famous for its undertaking to make the weak cause the

**Prodikos.
Hippias.**

stronger[6].   Prodikos concerned himself with
questions of etymology and with distinctions
of synonyms[7].   Hippias included grammar and
prosody among his many accomplishments, while he also
aimed at a correct and elevated style[8].   In the opinion of

**Thrasy-
machos.**

Aristotle's pupil, Theophrastos, Thrasymachos of
Chalkêdôn opened a new epoch in the prose style
of Greece by blending the elaborately artificial style of writers
like Thukydides with the simple and plain style subsequently
represented by Lysias[9].   Aristotle himself, in treating of
rhythm in prose, tells us that the rhetoricians, from Thrasymachos downwards, made use of the pæan[10].   His treatise
on pathos is the theme of an elaborate allusion in the

Theodôros.

Phædrus[11], and is definitely mentioned in the
Rhetoric[12].   Lastly, Theodôros of Byzantium,

---

[1] II xxiv 3, 6.
[2] II xxiii 5, 8, 12; xxiv 7.   See, however, Blass, II 371.
[3] ὀρθοέπεια (of Protagoras), *Phaedrus*, 267 c.
[4] *Rhet.* III v 5.
[5] Cope in *Cambridge Journal of Cl. and Sacred Philology*, iii 48–52.
[6] *Rhet.* II xxiv 11.
[7] *ib.* iii 57; Plato, *Prot.* 337 A, 340 A, 358 A D, etc.
[8] Plato, *Hipp.* I, 285 C D; II, 368 D; Cic. *De Or.* III 127.
[9] Dion. Hal. *Dem.* c. 3; cp. Jebb's *Attic Orators*, I cxiii–cxvi; II 423.
[10] III viii 4.   [11] 267 C.   [12] III i 7.

whom Aristotle couples with Tisias and Thrasymachos as one of the most important contributors to the development of rhetoric[1], introduced some novel terms for the subdivisions of a speech.   Plato satirically describes them as the 'niceties of his art,'[2] while Aristotle denounces them as absurd and unnecessary[3].

The 'art of Kallippos,' possibly one of the earliest pupils of
Kallippos.   Isokrates[4], is described by Aristotle as including
Pamphilos.   the topic of consequence[5], and that of possibility,
which was also contained in the 'art' of another early rhetorician, Pamphilos[6].   Aristotle complains that the earlier writers of 'arts' (such as those above-mentioned) had confined themselves to the Forensic branch of rhetoric[7]; and the same complaint had been made, half a century previously, by Isokrates[8].

The most independent, and the most distinguished, of the
                pupils of Gorgias was the great rhetorician,
Isokrates.   Isokrates (436—338).   During part of his early
career (403—393), he was a professional writer of forensic speeches,—a fact which he affected to ignore at a later date. About 392 he opened a school of rhetoric near the Lyceum. In that school he professed to teach the art of speaking, or writing, on large political subjects, as a preparation for advising or acting in political affairs,—the pursuit, in fact, of journalism, as a preparation for parliament.   He describes this art as his 'philosophy,' his theory of culture, and he now casts contempt on the forensic rhetoric of his earlier career. The fame of his school extended over the whole of the Hellenic world, and, apart from public men such as Timotheos and Leôdamas, his pupils included the future orators, Isæos, Lykurgos, and Hypereides.   His style is marked by a smoothness due to the avoidance of 'hiatus'; he is recognised by Cicero as the earliest artist in the rhythm proper to prose[9], and by Dionysios of Halikarnassos as the master of an ample and

---

[1] *Soph. El.* 183 *b* 32.
[2] τὰ κομψὰ τῆς τέχνης, *Phaedrus*, 266 D.
[3] III xiii 5.   [4] *Antid.* 93.   [5] II xxiii 14.
[6] *ib.* 21.   [7] I i 10.
[8] *In Sophistas*, 19; cp. Jebb's *Attic Orators*, II 133.   [9] *Brutus*, 32.

luxuriant type of period which 'leads one on' like a winding river[1]. He is the creator of a standard type of literary rhetorical prose[2].

In considering Aristotle's relations to Isokrates, we have

Aristotle's relations to Isokrates.
to distinguish between the two periods of Aristotle's residence at Athens, the earlier period of 367 to 347, and the later period of 335 to 322.
Isokrates died three years before Aristotle's return to Athens, so that any personal relations between them must belong to the first of the above periods and probably to its latter part. To Aristotle, according to some later authorities, the popularity of the school of Isokrates appeared undeserved, and his indignation at the rhetorician's undue regard for mere beauty of diction, to the neglect of the essentials of the art, led to his determining on setting up a rival school in which rhetoric should be studied in a more philosophical manner. Parodying a line from a tragic poet,—''twere shame to keep silence and suffer *barbarians* to speak,' he is said to have exclaimed,—''twere shame to keep silence and suffer *Isokrates* to speak.'[3]   He is also said to have sneered at the bundles of the rhetorician's forensic speeches that were hawked about by the booksellers[4].

Notwithstanding the 'feud' between Aristotle and Isokrates during Aristotle's first residence at Athens, both were inspired with Macedonian sympathies.   Moreover, the artificial style of Isokrates lent itself readily to citations illustrating rhetorical forms of expression.   Hence in the *Rhetoric*, which belongs to Aristotle's second period of residence at Athens, there is no author that is more frequently quoted; there are as many as ten citations in a single chapter[5].   But, although Aristotle

Demosthenes.
was at Athens during the delivery of the *First Philippic* (351) and the *Three Olynthiacs* (349), he never illustrates a single rule of rhetoric from any of the

---

[1] *Dem.* 4.

[2] See, in general, Blass, *Att. Ber.* II esp. 101–213; Jebb's *Attic Orators*, II 36–79; Introd. to Cicero's *Orator*, xvi–xxiii.

[3] αἰσχρὸν σιωπᾶν Ἰσοκράτην δ' ἐᾶν λέγειν. Cp. Cic. *De Or.* III 141; Quint. iii 1, 14.

[4] Dion. Hal. *De Isocr.* 18.   [5] III ix.

speeches of Demosthenes. To Demosthenes he ascribes an isolated simile, which is not to be found in his published speeches[1], while he cites the saying of a minor orator, to the effect that the policy of Demosthenes was the cause of the disasters of Athens, as an example of fallacious reasoning[2]. He illustrates the metaphorical use of βοῆσαι from an obscure contemporary of Demosthenes[3], though he might have found a better illustration in Demosthenes himself[4]. Aristotle, who lived as a foreigner at Athens, and had close relations with Philip and Alexander, may well have felt a sense of delicacy in exemplifying the precepts of rhetoric from the speeches of the great opponent of Macedonia[5].

The two dialogues of Plato specially concerned with the criticism of rhetoric are the *Gorgias* and the
Plato.
Phædrus. In the former he declares that rhetoric, so far from being an art, is only a happy knack acquired by practice[6], and Gorgias and his pupil are taken to task as representatives of the current rhetoric of the day. In the *Phædrus* we find a treatise on rhetoric thrown into a dramatic form. Here, as before, the writer ridicules the popular manuals of the art, but, instead of denouncing rhetoric unreservedly, he even draws up an outline of a new rhetoric founded on a more philosophical basis, resting partly on dialectic, which aids the orator in the invention of arguments, and partly on psychology, which enables him to discriminate the several varieties of human character in his audience, and to apply the means best adapted to produce the 'persuasion' which is the aim of his art[7]. The hints thrown out by Plato in the *Phædrus* are elaborately expanded in the first two Books of the *Rhetoric* of Aristotle, which deal with the means of producing persuasion. In the first Book these are classified, while the second includes '(1) a careful analysis of the affections of which human nature is susceptible and also of the causes by which such affections are

---

[1] III iv 3.   [2] II xxiv 8.   [3] III x 7.
[4] xix 92, 129.
[5] *History of Classical Scholarship*, i (1906) 81 f.
[6] 463 B, 501 A.   [7] Thompson's *Phædrus*, p. xiv.

called forth; (2) a descriptive catalogue of the various modifi-
cations of the human character and the sort of arguments
adapted to each.'[1]   The first two Books, dealing with the
invention of arguments, are followed by a third, which is
occupied with style and with the arrangement of the several
parts of the speech, the subject of delivery being touched
upon in such a way as to show that its adequate treatment is
still in the future.   While Plato regards rhetoric with contempt, and describes dialectic as the crown or 'coping-stone
of all the sciences,'[2] and rhetoric as only 'the shadow of a part
of politics,'[3] Aristotle insists, at the very outset of his work,
that 'rhetoric is the counterpart of dialectic,' and a branch of
dialectic and of politics[4].   In his logical works he has dis-
covered the Syllogism, and has invented logic: in the *Rhetoric*
he declares that the rhetorical counterpart of the Syllogism is
the Enthymeme, that is, 'a syllogism drawn from contingent
things in the sphere of human action.'[5]

In the third Book we are told that 'the commencements of

Theodekteia.   periods have been enumerated in the *Theodekteia.*'[6]
This may be reasonably regarded as a reference
to a work on rhetoric written by Aristotle himself in the
earlier part of his career, probably while he was still carrying
on his rhetorical school.   It derives its name from the author's
pupil Theodektes[7].

Among the works once ascribed to Aristotle is the *Rhetorica*

Rhetorica ad   *ad Alexandrum*, the spuriousness of which was
Alexandrum.   divined by Erasmus.   It has been assigned by
Victorius and by Spengel to the authorship of Anaximenes
(*c.* 380—320)[8].   The latest event mentioned in its pages be-

---

[1] Thompson, p. xx.   The knowledge of human nature displayed in the first 17
chapters of this book finds its parallel in many passages of Shakespeare quoted in
Joseph Esmond Riddle's *Illustrations of Aristotle on Men and Manners*, Oxford,
1832.

[2] *Rep.* 534.   [3] *Gorg.* 462.   [4] I i 7; iv 5.
[5] I ii 8 n.   [6] III ix 9 n.   [7] Cope's *Introd.* 55–67.
[8] *Anaximenis ars rhetorica*, ed. Spengel (1847); Cope, *Introd.* 401–464; Blass,
Att. Ber. II 378–399; Brzoska in Pauly-Wissowa, *s.v.* Anaximenes; P. Wendland
(Berlin, 1905); and W. Nitsche, *Dem. u. Anaximenes* (*ib.* 1906).   The commentary
of Didymos on Demosthenes, first published by Schubart and Diels in 1904, preserves the tradition that the pseudo-Demosthenic speech (*Or.* XI) πρὸς τὴν
ἐπιστολὴν τὴν Φιλίππου, was composed by Anaximenes.

longs to 340 B.C., but the exact date of its publication is unknown. It is never quoted in the *Rhetoric*, but it has some superficial points of resemblance with that treatise. Its moral purpose, however, is totally distinct. There is no extant work that gives us a clearer view of the sophistical type of rhetoric, which makes success at any price the aim of the art.

Aristotle's definition of rhetoric.

There is no definition of rhetoric, but the writer is clearly in sympathy with the sophistical tradition which makes rhetoric the 'art of persuading,' whereas Aristotle defines it as 'the faculty of observing or discovering in every case the possible means of persuasion.'[1]

In the course of the *Rhetoric* Aristotle refers to the *Politics*,

References to his other works.

and to his *Treatise on Poetry*, as well as to his *Analytics* and his *Topics*[2]. The *Treatise on Poetry* was, to all appearance, mainly written after the first two Books of the *Rhetoric*[3], but before the third[4]; the reference to the former in Book I[5] may have been added by Aristotle himself at a later date.

Aristotle may possibly have begun the *Rhetoric* before his

Date of the 'Rhetoric.'

second residence in Athens. The reference to 'the *Attic* orators' and to the 'orators *at Athens*' prompts the suspicion that these passages were written while the author was still absent from Athens, but they are also consistent with a sense of aloofness from Athenian politics which was natural in a Macedonian resident at Athens. As a whole, the work is best assigned to the period of his second residence (335—322). In the second Book he mentions an embassy sent by Philip and his allies asking the Thebans for permission to pass through their territory into Attica[6]. This embassy belongs to the year 338,—shortly before the battle of Chæronea[7]. He also mentions the 'Common Peace.'[8] This has been identified with the peace which all the Greeks (with the exception of the Lacedæmonians) made with Alexander after the death of Philip in 336[9]. If 336

---

[1] I i 14; ii 1, 7.   [2] See *Index*.
[3] *Poet.* c. xix (on διάνοια), ἐν τοῖς περὶ ῥητορικῆς κείσθω.
[4] *Poet.* mentioned in III i 13; ii 2, 5, 7.   [5] I xi 29.
[6] II xxiii 6.   [7] Spengel, *Specimen Comment.*, 1844.   [8] *ib.* 18.
[9] Spengel, *Specimen Comment.*, 1839. His general conclusion in 1851 was that the work might be assigned to *c.* 330.

was the date of its completion, the author was then 48
years of age, and a new interest is added to his own statement
that 'the mind is in its prime *about* the age of 49.'[1]

While Anaximenes was the author of 'the best practical
treatise on rhetoric that has come down to us in
Greek,' Aristotle stands alone in the philosophic
treatment of the subject.   Yet 'the school of
Aristotle...produced not a single orator of note except Deme-
trius Phalereus; the school of Isokrates produced a host.'
'Isokrates, though inferior in his grasp of principles, was
greatly superior in the practical department of teaching.'
'Aristotle's philosophy of rhetoric proved comparatively
barren, not at all because rhetoric is incapable of profiting
materially by such treatment, but because such treatment can
be made fruitful only by laborious attention to the practical
side of the discipline.   Had Aristotle's *Rhetoric* been composed
a century earlier, it would have been inestimable to oratory.
As it was, the right thing was done too late.'[2]   Nevertheless,
it was Aristotle, not Isokrates, who 'fixed the main lines on
which rhetoric was treated by most of the later technical
writers.'[3]

(margin: Anaximenes. Isokrates. Aristotle.)

It was the opinion of Niebuhr that the *Rhetoric* was
one of those works of which the 'first sketch'
belongs to the early period of the author's
life, while it has continued to receive additions
and corrections down to its close[4].   Brandis, who was at
first inclined to accept this view, afterwards saw nothing
to suggest an early period of composition, or a long and
desultory elaboration; on the contrary, the regularity and
uniformity with which the plan was carried through, indicated a continuous and uninterrupted application; he
accordingly regarded it as *ein Werk aus einem Gusse*[5].

(margin: Modern criticisms: Niebuhr. Brandis.)

Similarly, Sir Alexander Grant has observed
that the first part of the work bears marks of
having been in the author's mind for many years before it

(margin: Grant.)

---

[1] II xiv 4; cp. *History of Classical Scholarship*, i 81.
[2] *Attic Orators*, II 431.
[3] *Greek Literature* in Cambridge *Companion to Greek Studies*, p. 139.
[4] *Roman Hist.* i note 39 (Cope, *Introd.* 40 f).
[5] *Philologus*, iv 1, 8 f.

was reduced to writing. 'The outlines of its arrangement are characterised by luminous simplicity, the result of long analytic reflection; the scientific exposition is made in a style which is, for Aristotle, remarkably easy and flowing; and each part of the subject is adorned with a wealth of illustration which indicates the accumulations of a lifetime.'[1]

Turning from these general characterisations to some of the more special criticisms of the condition in which the work has come down to modern times, we note that it has been

Roemer.

urged by Roemer[2] that the present text is made up of two editions of the treatise, and that it consists of a combination of a longer and a shorter recension.

Hirzel.

The 13th and 14th chapters of the First Book have been attacked by Rudolf Hirzel[3].

It had previously been pointed out by Spengel[4] and

Spengel.
Vahlen.

Vahlen[5] that the last nine chapters of the Second Book, on logical proofs, ought really to have preceded the first seventeen, which deal with proofs con-

Cook Wilson.

nected with the feelings and the character; while Professor Cook Wilson[6] has argued against the genuineness of the 25th and 26th chapters of that Book.

The author's original plan may well have been limited to the first two Books[7], and some confusion of expression may be noticed in the last paragraph of Book II owing to the subsequent addition of a third Book. The genuineness of that

Cope.

Book has been attacked by Sauppe[8] and Rose[9], and defended by Spengel[10], by Cope[11], and by

---

[1] *Aristotle* (1877), 77 f.   [2] Pref. to Teubner text, ed. 2, 1898.

[3] *Abhandl. d. sächs. Ges.* xx (1900) 11.

[4] Munich Acad. 1851, 32–37.   [5] Vienna Acad., Oct. 1861, 59–148.

[6] *Trans.* Oxford Philol. Soc., 1883–4, pp. 4 f, criticised by Susemihl in Bursan's *Jahresb.* xlii 38 f.

[7] The list of Aristotle's works in Diogenes Laërtius includes τέχνης ῥητορικῆς ᾱ β̄, περὶ λέξεως ᾱ β̄, the latter apparently referring to the two parts of Book III, also described as περὶ λέξεως καθαρᾶς ᾱ (Rose, *Fragm.* p. 14).

[8] 1863; *Ausg. Schr.* 354 f.   [9] *Ar. Pseud.* 137 (cp. Zeller, 78, 1; 74, 2 E.T.).

[10] Ed. 1867, ii 354, 'tertius liber, quem nostratium quidam temere et inepte Aristotelis esse negant, si quis alius ingenuus philosophi nostri foetus est.'

[11] *Introd.* 1867, p. 8, 'If the third book of the Art of Rhetoric did not proceed from the pen of Aristotle, all evidence of authorship derived from resemblance of style, manner, method, and diction, must be absolutely worthless.'

Diels[1], who shows that it fits into its proper place as the immediate precursor of the rhetorical works of Aristotle's pupil, Theophrastos. The numerous *lacunæ* in all three Books alike, as well as the confusion in the arrangement of the contents of the whole work, are explained by Marx[2] on the supposition that the work was prepared by a pupil of Aristotle from imperfect notes of his master's lectures. Errors in the text, such as Hêgêsippos for Agêsipolis[3], and γνώμη for μνήμη[4] in a well-known passage of Isokrates, are attributed to the lecturer's indistinctness of utterance[5]; while the last six chapters of the work are regarded as a report of a lecture in which Aristotle attacked a lost treatise on the several parts of the speech, which had been put forth by some unknown pupil of Isokrates.

J. E. S.

Diels.
Marx.

[1] Berlin Acad. 1886, iv 1–37.   [2] *Ber. d. sächs. Ges.* 1900, 241–328.
[3] II xxiii.   [4] III vii.
[5] Aristotle was τραυλὸς τὴν φωνήν (Diog. Laërt. v i).

ANALYSIS

BOOK I

RHETORIC is an Art. Hitherto, the essence of this Art has been neglected for the accidents, and the Deliberative branch for the Forensic. The master of Dialectic will be the true master of Rhetoric. Rhetoric is useful, because it is (1) corrective, (2) instructive, (3) suggestive, and (4) defensive. It is not concerned with any single or definite class of subjects, but is the counterpart of Dialectic. Its function is not to persuade, but *to discover the available means of persuasion in each case.* It has a fallacious branch, but those who pursue this branch are not, as in Dialectic, called by any distinctive name; they are in either case called 'rhetoricians' (i).

Rhetoric being defined as 'the faculty of discerning in every case the available means of persuasion,' we proceed to the subject of proofs. These are either (1) 'artificial' or (11) 'inartificial.' Artificial proofs are (1) ethical, (2) pathetic, (3) logical. (1) Ethical proof is wrought, when the speech is so spoken as to make the speaker credible; (2) pathetic, when emotion is stirred in the audience by the speech; (3) logical, when a truth, or an apparent truth, has been demonstrated by the means of persuasion available in each case. (The faculty of rhetoric has two elements, corresponding respectively to (1) dialectical skill, and (2) political science.) Logical proof is either (*a*) deductive, proceeding by means of Enthymeme, i.e. 'rhetorical syllogism,' or (*b*) inductive, proceeding by means of Example, i.e. 'rhetorical induction.' Rhetoric must address itself to *classes*, not to individuals; its subjects are *contingent*; and its premisses must be *probabilities*. Every premiss of the enthymeme is either a 'probability' or a 'sign.' The 'probable' and the 'sign' (whether fallible or infallible) are thereupon defined; and a distinction drawn between enthymemes proper and not proper to Rhetoric (ii).

There are three species of Rhetoric, deliberative, forensic, and epideiktic, differing in their elements, their times, and their ends (iii).

The topics of Deliberative Rhetoric are five in number:—ways and means, war and peace, defence, commerce, and legislation (iv). The deliberative speaker exhorts, or dissuades, with a view to the happiness of the persons addressed; the elements of happiness are good birth, the possession of goodly and numerous offspring, wealth, good repute, honour, health, happy old age, troops of friends, good fortune, and virtue (v). He appeals to the interest of his audience; interest is a kind of 'good'; we must therefore define and analyse things 'good' (vi). But the question will arise, which of two 'good' things is 'better'; hence we must treat the topic of degree (vii). The greatest aid towards giving good counsel is to be found in discriminating the four forms of government,—democracy, oligarchy, aristocracy, monarchy, and the institutions and interests peculiar to each (viii).

The Epideiktic branch of Rhetoric is concerned with Virtue and Vice in their popular conceptions. ('Praise' expresses moral approbation, while 'encomium' is concerned with actual achievements.) Of all the topics that of amplification is most useful in the Epideiktic branch of Rhetoric; examples to the Deliberative; and enthymemes to the Forensic (ix).

Forensic Rhetoric has for its elements, accusation and defence, and, for its end, justice or injustice. We must therefore begin by analysing injustice, and inquiring into the motives and aims of wrong-doing. Actions are either voluntary (arising from habit, reason, anger, or lust), or involuntary (from chance, nature, or force). All things that men do of themselves are good or apparently good, pleasant or apparently pleasant; the former has been discussed under Deliberative Rhetoric; let us now speak of the latter (x). Then follows a popular definition of pleasure, and an analysis of things 'pleasant' (xi). From the motives of wrong-doing we pass to the characters which dispose men to do wrong, and which expose men to suffer wrong (xii). Wrongs are classified (*a*) in reference to law, either special or universal; or (*b*) according as the wrong is done to the individual or the community. The definition of an offence often raises a legal issue. It is needful, therefore, to define and distinguish the principal offences. In contrast to the written rules of right and wrong are the unwritten. The latter are of two kinds: (1) those that refer to acts that merit public praise or disgrace, public honour or dishonour; (2) those that are supplementary to the written law, and are concerned with things 'equitable' (xiii). The topic of degree is next applied to wrongs, with a view to distinguishing the different degrees of wrong (xiv).

The Inartificial Proofs proper to Forensic Rhetoric are derived from Laws, Witnesses, Contracts (or other documents), Torture, or Oaths (xv).

BOOK II

A good impression of *the speaker's character* may be produced by means of his speech. He should make his audience feel that he possesses intelligence, virtue, and good-will. We must therefore analyse (*a*) the virtues, and (*b*) the moral affections. The *virtues* have, in fact, been already analysed in I ix. In regard to each of the *moral affections*, we have to discern (1) its nature; (2) its antecedents; and (3) its objects (i).

Analysis of the *affections*:—anger (ii) and mildness (iii); friendship and enmity (iv); fear and boldness (v); shame and shamelessness (vi); gratitude (or favour) and ingratitude (vii); pity (viii) and indignation (ix); envy (x) and emulation (xi).

In appealing to the affections or feelings, the speaker must take account of the general *character of his audience*; according as they are young or old, rich or poor, etc. Hence we must analyse the character of youth (xii), old age (xiii), and middle age (xiv); also that of good birth (xv), wealth (xvi), power, and good fortune (xvii).

A brief retrospect is here followed by an introduction to the analysis of the '*universal' classes of argument* which are applicable to all special premisses derived from special branches of knowledge (xviii).

These classes of argument are (1) the topic of the possible and impossible; (2) the topic of fact past and of fact future; (3) the topic of degree; (4) the topic of amplification and depreciation (xix).

The *proofs common to all branches of rhetoric* are example and enthymeme. There are two kinds of example, involving the use of either historical or artificial parallels, the latter including fables (xx). A maxim, or general statement concerned with objects of action, is an incomplete enthymeme (xxi). Then follow general precepts on the enthymeme. (1) The rhetorical reasoner must not draw his con-clusion from points that are too remote; (2) he must leave out those propositions which his audience can readily supply; (3) he must know the special facts from which enthymemes can be derived in each subject. Enthymemes are of two kinds:—demonstrative, and refuta-tive (xxii). Then follows an enumeration of twenty-eight heads of argument from which enthymemes can be constructed; the 'demonstrative' enthymeme is almost exclusively treated, but the 'refutative' can be inferred from it (xxiii).   Next succeed ten topics of apparent, or sham, enthymemes (xxiv).   An argument may be refuted, either by opposing enthymeme to enthymeme, or by bringing an objection against a particular point (xxv).   The Book ends with supplementary criticisms, apparently meant to correct errors made by previous writers on rhetoric.   (1) 'Amplification and depreciation' are not a mere topic of an enthymeme; they form one of the 'common topics' of c. xviii.   (2) 'Destructive' enthymemes are not different in *kind* from 'constructive.'

This may suffice for the *inventive* province of rhetoric,—the way to find arguments, and the way to refute them (xxvi).

BOOK III

We have next to speak of *diction*, or style, and first of the art of delivery, which has not yet been touched, except by Thrasymachos in his work *on Pathos* (i).

Diction in regard to single words (or *diction proper*) has for its principal merits, clearness and appropriateness, the latter including the due use of accepted terms, of proper terms, and of metaphors (ii). Faults of style are next classified under four headings, with examples of each :—(1) poetic varieties of compound words, (2) rare or archaic words, (3) inordinate epithets, and (4) unsuitable metaphors (iii). The simile (which is a metaphor with a term of resemblance prefixed) is too poetical to be often available in prose; examples of its use are, however, quoted from Plato and the orators.   Similes can readily be converted into metaphors (iv).

Diction with regard to composition (properly σύνθεσις) has for its primary requisite idiomatic purity, dependent on the proper use of connecting particles, the use of special and not general terms, the avoidance of ambiguity, and the observance of gender, and of number.

In every case a composition should be easy to read, easy to deliver; it should avoid solecisms arising from a neglect of symmetry; it should also avoid long parentheses (v).

Dignity of style is aided by the use of (1) the description, instead of the name, (2) suitable metaphors and epithets, (3) the plural instead of the singular number, by (4) the repetition of the article, (5) the use of conjunctions and other connective words, and (6) of description by means of a series of negations (vi).

Propriety of style depends on its appealing to the feelings of the hearer, and on its being characteristic of the speaker, and proportionate to the subject (vii).

Prose must have *rhythm*, but not *metre*. The rhythm must not, however, be too precise. The heroic measure is too grand; the iambic, too common; the trochaic, too comic. There remains the pæan, the 'first pæan' (– ᴗ ᴗ ᴗ) suiting the beginning, and the 'fourth pæan' (ᴗ ᴗ ᴗ –) the end of the sentence (viii).

The style must be either running and unbroken in its chain, or compact and periodic. The period may have one or more members. It must be neither curt nor long. The period of more than one member may be either simply divided, or antithetical. 'Antithesis' implies contrast of sense. When the members are equal, this is 'parisôsis'; when their first or last syllables are alike, 'paromoiôsis,' or, when the terminations alone correspond, 'homoioteleuton' (ix).

Pointed sayings depend on the use of metaphor, antithesis, and actuality, i.e. on 'setting things before the eyes' (x). Those words 'set a thing before the eyes' which describe it in an active state,—a device often employed by Homer. A striking effect is secured by using a metaphor which involves a touch of surprise. The hearer has the pleasure of learning something new; hence also the pleasure given by riddles. Then follow some remarks on similes and on hyperbole (xi).

There is a difference between the literary and the combative style (and, in the latter, between the deliberative and the forensic). It is necessary to know both. The literary style is the most precise; the combative, best fitted for delivery; this fitness depends on the expression of character, or on the expression of emotion. The deliberative style is like drawing in light and shade; it is meant to produce its effect at a distance, and will not bear looking at closely. The forensic admits of greater finish. The epideiktic is best suited for writing; its proper function is to be *read*. The chapter ends with criticisms on various superfluous classifications of style under the headings of 'sweetness' and 'magnificence' (xii).

Style having now been discussed, both generally and particularly, it remains to speak of *arrangement*. There are only two essential parts of a speech:—*statement* and *proof*. The received four-fold division applies strictly to the forensic branch alone; if we are to add any parts to *statement* and *proof*, they can be only *proem* or exordium, and *epilogue* or peroration (xiii).

Proem. In an epideiktic speech, the proem need not be closely connected with the sequel. It is like the prelude in music, which is linked on to the key-note of the main theme. In a forensic speech, the proem is comparable to the prologue of a tragedy or of an epic poem. The contents of a proem come usually under one of two heads, (1) exciting or allaying prejudice, (2) amplification or detraction. In a deliberative speech, a proem is comparatively rare, for the subject is already known and needs no preface (xiv). The various forms of argument for 'exciting or allaying prejudice' are next enumerated (xv). ('Amplification' and 'detraction' have already been treated in II xix.)

Narrative, in relation to the three branches of rhetoric. In the epideiktic branch, it should be broken up and diversified. In the forensic, the narrative of the defendant can usually be shorter than that of the plaintiff. In joining issue with the plaintiff, the defendant ought not to waste time over unnecessary narrative. In the deliberative branch, there is least need of it (xvi).

Proofs. These must have reference to one of four possible issues :—(1) fact, (2) harmful quality, (3) legal quality, (4) degree. Example (or 'rhetorical induction') is best suited for deliberative rhetoric; enthymeme (or 'rhetorical syllogism') for forensic. Proof is harder in deliberative, since it deals with the future. The forensic speaker, again, has the law as a mine of argument (xvii). Interrogation of the adversary may be used within certain limitations, to enforce an argument (xviii).

Epilogue. Its aim is (1) to prepossess the audience in our favour, (2) to amplify or extenuate, (3) to excite emotion, and finally (4) to recapitulate the facts.

ARISTOTLE'S RHETORIC

BOOK I

RHETORIC is the counterpart of Dialectic,—since both are 1354 a
Rhetoric is an Art. concerned with things of which the cognizance is, in a manner, common to all men and belongs to no definite science. Hence all men in a manner use both; for all men to some extent make the effort of examining and of submitting to inquiry, of defending or accusing. People 2 in general do these things either quite at random, or merely with a knack which comes from the acquired habit. Since both ways are possible, clearly it must be possible to reduce them to method ; for it is possible to consider the cause why the practised or the spontaneous speaker hits his mark; and such an inquiry, all would allow, is the function of an art.

Now hitherto the writers of treatises on Rhetoric have 3 constructed only a small part of that art; for **Hitherto, the essence of this Art has been neglected for the accidents.** proofs form the only artistic element, all else being mere appendage. These writers, however, say nothing about enthymemes, which are the body of proof, but busy themselves chiefly with irrelevant matters. The exciting of prejudice, of 4 pity, of anger, and such like emotions of the soul, has nothing to do with the fact, but has regard to the judge. So that if trials were universally managed, as they are at present managed in some at least of the cities, and for the most part in the best governed, such people would have nothing to say. All the world over, men either admit that the laws ought 5 so to forbid irrelevant speaking, or actually have laws which forbid it, as is the case in the procedure of the Areiopagos; a wise provision. For it is a mistake to warp the judge by moving him to anger or envy or pity; it is as if a man, who was going to use a rule, should make it

6 crooked. Further, it is clear that the litigant's part is simply to prove that the fact is or is not, has occurred or has not occurred. Whether it is great or small, just or unjust, in any respects which the lawgiver has not defined, is a question, of course, on which the judge must decide for himself, instead of being instructed upon it by the litigant.

7 Now it is most desirable that well-drawn laws should, as far as possible, define everything themselves, leaving as few points as possible to the discretion of the judges; first, because it is easier to get a small than a large number of men

1354 b qualified by their intelligence to make laws and try causes; next, because legislative acts are done after mature deliberation, whereas judgments are given off-hand, so that it is hard for the judge to satisfy the demands of justice and expediency. Most important of all, the decision of the lawgiver concerns no special case, but is prospective and general; when we come to the ekklesiast and the dikast, they have to decide actual and definite cases; and they are often so entangled[1] with likings and hatreds and private interests, that they are not capable of adequately considering the truth, but have

8 their judgment clouded by private pleasure or pain. On all other points, then, we say, the judge ought to be given as little discretionary power as possible; but the question whether a thing has or has not happened, will or will not be, is or is not, must perforce be left in his hands; these things

9 the lawgiver cannot foresee. If, then, this is so, it is manifest that irrelevant matter is treated by all those technical writers who define the other points,—as what the proem, the narrative and each of the other parts should contain; for they busy themselves here solely with creating a certain mind in the judge,—but teach nothing about artificial proof, that

---

[1] συνήρτηται, printed in the text of the Venice ed. and preferred by Muretus. With the manuscript reading, συνῄρηται, the sentence could only mean: 'and, in their case, likings etc., are often *taken into account*'.

is, about the way in which one is to become a master of enthymemes.

It is for this reason that, though the same method applies 10 to public and to forensic speaking, and though the Deliberative branch is nobler and worthier of a citizen than that which deals with private contracts, they ignore the former, and invariably aim at systematizing the art of litigation.   In public speaking it is less worth while to talk about things beside the subject. Deliberative oratory is less knavish than Forensic, and embraces larger interests.   In a public debate, the judge judges in his own cause, so that nothing more is needful than to prove that the case stands as the adviser says.   In forensic speaking this is not enough ; it is important to win over the hearer. The judge's award concerns other men's affairs ; and if he views these in reference to his own interest, and listens in a partial spirit, he indulges the litigant instead of deciding the cause.   Hence it is that in many places, as we said before[1], 1355 a the law forbids irrelevant pleading : in the public assembly, the judges themselves take care of that.

And the Deliberative branch has been neglected for the Forensic.

It is manifest that the artistic Rhetoric is concerned 11 with proofs.   The rhetorical proof is a sort of demonstration, for we entertain the strongest persuasion of a thing when we conceive that it has been demonstrated.   A rhetorical demonstration is an enthymeme,—this being, generally speaking, the most authoritative of proofs.   The enthymeme again is a sort of syllogism, and every kind of syllogism alike comes under the observation of Dialectic, either generally or in one of its departments.   Hence it is clear that he who is best able to investigate the elements and the genesis of the syllogism will also be the most expert with the enthymeme, when he has further mastered its subject-matter and its differences from the logical syllogism.   Truth and the likeness of truth come under the observation of the same faculty.   (It may be added that men are adequately gifted for the quest of truth and generally succeed in finding it.)   Hence the same sort of

The master of Dialectic will be the true master of Rhetoric.

[1] § 5 *supra.*

man who can guess about truth, must be able to guess about probabilities.

It is plain, then, that the mass of technical writers deal with irrelevant matter ; it is plain, too, why[1] they have leaned by choice towards forensic speaking.

12   Rhetoric is useful, first, because truth and justice are

Use of the Art of Rhetoric. It is (1) corrective: naturally stronger than their opposites ; so that, when awards are not given duly, truth and justice must have been worsted by their own fault[2]. This is worth correcting. Again, supposing we had

(2) instructive : the most exact knowledge, there are some people whom it would not be easy to persuade with its help ; for scientific exposition is in the nature of teaching, and teaching is out of the question ; we must give our proofs and tell our story in popular terms,—as we said in the *Topics*[3]

(3) suggestive : with reference to controversy with the many. Further,—one should be able to persuade, just as to reason strictly, on both sides of a question ; not with a view to using the twofold power—one must not be the advocate of evil—but in order, first, that we may know the whole state of the case ; secondly, that, if anyone else argues dishonestly, we on our part may be able to refute him. Dialectic and Rhetoric, alone among all arts, draw indifferently an affirmative or a negative conclusion : both these arts alike are impartial. The conditions of the subject-matter, however, are not the same ; that which is true and better being naturally, as a rule, more easy to demonstrate and more con-

(4) defensive. vincing. Besides it would be absurd that, while

1355 b incapacity for physical self-defence is a reproach, incapacity for mental defence should be none; mental effort

13 being more distinctive of man than bodily effort. If it is objected that an abuser of the rhetorical faculty can do great mischief, this, at any rate, applies to all good things except virtue, and especially to the most useful things, as strength,

---

[1] διότι = ὅτι, 'that' (Cope).
[2] If those who have truth and right on their side are defeated, *their defeat must be due to themselves*, to their own neglect of Rhetoric (Cope).
[3] *Topica*, i 2.

health, wealth, generalship. By the right use of these things a man may do the greatest good, and by the unjust use, the greatest mischief.

It appears, then, that Rhetoric is not concerned with any 14

Summary:—
The province
of Rhetoric.
single or definite class of subjects but is parallel to Dialectic: it appears, too, that it is useful; and that its function is not to persuade, but to discover the available means of persuasion in each case, according to the analogy of all other arts. The function of the medical art is not to cure, but to make such progress towards a cure as the case admits; since it is possible to treat judiciously even those who can never enjoy health. Further

Its fallacious
branch—how
related to the
fallacious
Dialectic.
it is clear that it belongs to the same art to observe the persuasive and the apparent persuasive, as, in the case of Dialectic, to observe the real and the apparent syllogism. For the essence of Sophistry is not in the faculty but in the moral purpose: only, in the case of Rhetoric, a man is to be called a rhetorician with respect to his faculty, without distinction of his moral purpose; in the case of Dialectic, a man is 'sophist' in respect to his moral purpose; 'dialectician' in respect, not of his moral purpose, but of his faculty.

Let us now attempt to speak of the method itself—the mode, and the means, by which we are to succeed in attaining our objects. By way of beginning we will once more define the art, and then proceed.

ii. Let Rhetoric be defined, then, as the faculty of dis-
Definition of
Rhetoric.
cerning in every case the available means of persuasion. This is the function of no other art. Each of the other arts is instructive or persuasive about its proper subject-matter; as the medical art about things wholesome or unwholesome,—geometry, about the properties of magnitudes, arithmetic, about numbers,—and so with the rest of the arts and sciences. But Rhetoric appears to have the power of discerning the persuasive in regard (one may say) to any given subject; and therefore we describe it as having the quality of Art in reference to no special or definite class of subjects.

2   Proofs are either artificial or inartificial. By 'inartificial'
                    I mean such things as have not been supplied
Proofs:
I. Inartificial: by our own agency, but were already in exis-
II. Artificial.
                    tence,—such as witnesses, depositions under tor-
ture, contracts, and the like: by 'artificial' I mean such
things as may be furnished by our method and by our
own agency; so that, of these, the 'inartificial' have only
to be used; the 'artificial' have to be invented.

3   Of proofs provided by the speech there are three kinds;
1356 a Artificial   one kind depending on the character of the
Proofs—   speaker; another, on disposing the hearer in a
(1) ethical,
(2) pathetic,   certain way; a third, a demonstration or apparent
3) logical.   demonstration in the speech itself.

4   Ethical proof is wrought when the speech is so spoken as
1. Ethical   to make the speaker credible; for we trust good
proof.   men more and sooner, as a rule, about everything;
while, about things which do not admit of precision, but
only of guess-work, we trust them absolutely. Now this
trust, too, ought to be produced by means of the speech,
—not by a previous conviction that the speaker is this
or that sort of man. It is not true, as some of the technical
writers assume in their systems, that the moral worth of the
speaker contributes nothing to his persuasiveness; nay, it
might be said that almost the most authoritative of proofs
is that supplied by character.

5   The hearers themselves become the instruments of proof
2. Pathetic   when emotion is stirred in them by the speech;
proof.   for we give our judgments in different ways
under the influence of pain and of joy, of liking and of hatred;
and this, I repeat, is the one point with which the technical
writers of the day attempt to deal. This province shall
be examined in detail when we come to speak of the
emotions.

6   Proof is wrought through the speech itself when we have
3. Logical   demonstrated a truth or an apparent truth by
proof.   the means of persuasion available in a given
case.

These being the instruments of our proofs, it is clear that 7
they may be mastered[1] by a man who can
The faculty of Rhetoric has two elements, reason; who can analyse the several types of
Character and the Virtues, and thirdly, the
Emotions — the nature and quality of each
emotion, the sources and modes of its production.   It results
that Rhetoric is, as it were, an offshoot of Dia-
answering to (1) Dialectical skill; (2) Political Science. lectic and of that Ethical science which may
fairly be called Politics.   Hence it is that
Rhetoric and its professors slip into the garb
of Political Science—either through want of education, or
from pretentiousness, or from other human causes.   Rhetoric
is a branch or an image[2] of Dialectic, as we said at the beginning.   Neither of them is a science relating to the nature
of any definite subject-matter.   They are certain faculties of
providing arguments.

Enough has perhaps been said about the faculty of Dialectic and of Rhetoric and about their relation to each other.

3. Logical proof: With regard to those proofs which are wrought 8
by demonstration, real or apparent, just as in
Dialectic there is Induction on the one hand, and Syllogism 1356 b
or apparent Syllogism on the other, so it is in Rhetoric.   The
Example is an Induction.   The Enthymeme is a Syllogism;
the Apparent Enthymeme is an Apparent Syllogism[3].   I call
the Enthymeme a Rhetorical Syllogism[4] and the
either (a) deductive, by Enthymeme; or (b) inductive, by Example. Example a Rhetorical Induction.   All men effect
their proofs by demonstration, either with ex-
amples or with enthymemes; there is no third
way.   Hence, since universally it is necessary to
demonstrate anything whatever either by syllogism or by

[1] ταύτας [τὰ τρία] ἐστὶν λαβεῖν.
[2] ὁμοίωμα, the reading of the inferior MSS: ὁμοία, that of the best MS (retained by Spengel and Roemer).
[3] Spengel's addition of these words is confirmed by Dionysius of Halicarnassus, *Ad Ammaeum*, c. vi.
[4] " By *enthymeme*, Aristotle meant a rhetorical syllogism : that is, a syllogism drawn, not from the premisses (ἀρχαί) proper to any particular science—such, for instance, as medicine—but from propositions relating to contingent things in the sphere of human action, which are the common property of all discussion; propositions which he classifies as general (εἰκότα) and particular (σημεῖα); and accordingly

induction (and this we see from the *Analytics*[1]), it follows that Induction and Syllogism must be identical respectively with

9 Example and Enthymeme. The difference between Example and Enthymeme is manifest[2] from the *Topics*[3]. There, in reference to syllogism and induction, it has already been said that the proving of a proposition by a number of like instances, is, in Dialectic, Induction—answering to the Example in Rhetoric; and that, when certain things exist, and something else comes to pass through them, distinct from them but due to their existing, either as an universal or as an ordinary result, this is called in Dialectic, a Syllogism, as in Rhetoric

10 it is called an Enthymeme. It is clear that the Rhetorical branch of Dialectic commands both these weapons. What has been said in the *Methodica* holds good here also; some rhetorical discourses rely on Example, some on Enthymeme; and so, likewise, some rhetoricians prefer the one and some the other. Arguments from Example are not the less persuasive; but arguments in the form of Enthymeme are the

11 more applauded. The reason of this, and the way to use either, will be explained by and by[4]. Now let us define the things themselves more clearly.

First, the notion of persuasion is relative; some things being at once persuasive and credible in themselves, other things because they are supposed to be demonstrated by persons who are so. Again, no art considers the particular; thus the medical art considers, not what is wholesome for Sokrates or Kallias, but what is so for a certain sort of man

---

defines an enthymeme as 'a syllogism from probabilities and signs.' A misapprehension of Aristotle's meaning had, as early as the first century B.C., led to the conception of the enthymeme as not merely a syllogism of a particular subject-matter, but also as a syllogism *of which one premiss is suppressed*" (*Attic Orators*, ii 289 f, *q.v.*). Cope supported the former view in the text of *Introd.* 102 f, and reverted to the latter view in the note.

[1] *An. Pr.* ii 23; *An. Post.* i 1.

[2] 'Is manifest' (φανερόν)—*i.e.* may be inferred from the definitions of Induction and of the Syllogism in the *Topics*. Nothing is said in the *Topics* about Example or Enthymeme specially.

[3] *Top.* i 1, p. 100 A. 25 (syllogism): i 12, p. 105 A. 13 (induction).

[4] The cause and origin of them (so Victorius), and the mode of their employment, we will describe hereafter (ii 20-24). Cope, *Introd.* p. 155.

or a certain class.   This is characteristic of an Art, whereas

Rhetoric must address itself to classes, not individuals.

particulars are infinite and cannot be known. Hence Rhetoric, too, will consider, not what is probable to the individual, as to Sokrates or Hippias, but what is probable to a given class, just as Dialectic does.   Dialectic does not reason for *any* premisses—dotards have notions of their own—but from premisses which require discussion.   So does Rhetoric reason 1357 a

Its subjects are contingent things which men can influence.

only upon recognised subjects of debate.   Its 12 concern is with subjects on which we deliberate, not having reduced them to systems ; and with hearers who cannot grasp the unity of an argu-

ment which has many stages, or follow a long chain of reason- ing.   We debate about things which seem capable of being either thus or thus.   Matters which admit of no ambiguity, past, present, or future, are debated by no one, on that sup- position : it is useless.

Now, one may construct a syllogism and draw a con- 13

Its premisses must be pro- babilities.

clusion either from facts already reduced to syllogisms or from facts which have not been proved syllogistically, but which need such proof, because they are not probable.   The former of these pro- cesses is necessarily difficult to follow owing to its length ;— the umpire being assumed to be a plain man.   Reasonings of the latter kind are not persuasive, because drawn from pre- misses which are not admitted or probable.   Hence both the enthymeme and the example must deal with things which are (as a rule) contingent—the example, as a kind of induction, the enthymeme as a syllogism, and as a syllogism of few elements,—often, of fewer than the normal syllogism.   Thus,

One premiss of the enthy- meme may be suppressed.

if one of these elements is something notorious, it need not even be stated, as the hearer himself supplies it.   For instance, to prove that Dorieus

has been victor in a contest, for which the prize is a crown, it is enough to say that he has been victor in the Olympic games.   It is needless to add that in the Olympic contests the prize is a crown ; every one is aware of that.

The premisses of rhetorical syllogisms seldom belong to

14 the class of necessary facts. The subject-matter

Every premiss of the enthymeme is a Probability or a Sign. of judgments and deliberations is usually contingent; for it is about their actions that men debate and take thought; but actions are all contingent, no one of them, one may say, being necessary. And results which are merely usual and contingent must be deduced from premisses of the same kind, as necessary results from necessary premisses:—this, too, has been shown in the *Analytics*[1]. It follows that the propositions from which enthymemes are taken will be sometimes necessarily true, but more often contingently true. Now the materials of the enthymeme are Probabilities and Signs. It follows that Probabilities and Signs must answer to the Contingent and the Necessary truths[2].

15 The Probable is that which usually happens; (with a

The Probable defined. limitation, however, which is sometimes forgotten —namely that the thing *may* happen otherwise :) the Probable being related to that in respect of which it is probable as Universal to Particular.

16 One kind of Sign is as Particular to Universal; the other,

1357 b *Signs.* as Universal to Particular. The Infallible Sign is called *tekmêrion*; the Fallible Sign has no

17 distinctive name. By Infallible Signs I mean those which supply a strict Syllogism. Hence it is that this sort of Sign is called *tekmêrion*, for when people think that what they have said is irrefutable, then they think that they are bringing a *tekmêrion* (a *conclusive* proof)—as if the matter had been demonstrated and *concluded* (πεπερασμένον); for *tekmar* and *peras* mean the same thing ('*limit*') in the old language.

18 The Sign which is as a Particular to a Universal would be illustrated by saying, 'Wise men are just; *for* Sokrates was wise and just.' This is a Sign, indeed, but it can be refuted, even though the statement be a fact; for it does not make a syllogism. On the other hand, if one said—'Here is a sign that he is ill—he is feverish'; or, 'she is a mother, for

[1] *An. Pr.* i 8.
[2] See Cope's *Introduction*, p. 159.

she has milk,' this is a strict proof. This is the only conclusive sign (or *tekmêrion*); for this alone, if the fact be true, is irrefutable. Another Sign, which is as Universal to Particular, would be exemplified by saying—'This is a sign that he has a fever, he breathes quick.' But this, too, even though it be true, is refutable. A man may breathe hard without having a fever.

The nature of the Probable, of a Sign and of a conclusive Sign, and the nature of the difference between them have been explained sufficiently for our present purpose. In the *Analytics*[1] a fuller account of them has been given, and of the reason why some of them are inconclusive, while others are strictly logical. It has been said that an Example is an   19

The Example.   Induction, and the matters with which it is concerned have been stated. It is neither as part to whole nor as whole to part nor as whole to whole, but as part to part, as like to like. When both things come under the same class, but one is better known than the other, that better-known one is an Example. For instance, it is argued that Dionysios aims at a tyranny in asking for a body-guard; for Peisistratos formerly, when he had such a design, asked for a guard, and, having got it, became tyrant;—as did Theagenes at Megara; and so all the other cases known to the speaker become Examples in reference to Dionysios—as to whom they do not yet know that this was his motive for the request. All these cases come under the same general principle, that a man who aims at a tyranny asks for a body-guard.

Such, then, are the sources from which the professedly   20 demonstrative proofs are drawn. In regard to   **1358 a**

Distinction between enthymemes proper and not proper to Rhetoric.   enthymemes, there is an important distinction which has been almost universally ignored; a distinction which applies equally to the syllogisms employed by Dialectic. Some enthymemes belong properly to Rhetoric, as some syllogisms belong properly to Dialectic; other enthymemes are peculiar to other arts and faculties, either existent or still to be

---

[1] *An. Pr.* ii 27.

formulated. Hence, though the speaker does not perceive it[1], the more he handles his subject with technical appropriateness, the more he is passing out of the province of Dialectic and Rhetoric[2]. My meaning will be plainer when expressed more fully. Dialectical and Rhetorical syllogisms deal properly with the so-called topics (or common-places), by which I mean here the *Universal* topics applicable to Justice, Physics, Politics, and a variety of other subjects of all sorts. Take the topic of More or Less. This topic will not help us to make a syllogism or an enthymeme about Justice rather than about Physics or anything else, different though these things are in kind. *Particular* Common-places are those arising from the propositions relative to the several species and classes of things. Thus there are propositions about Physics from which it is impossible to make a syllogism or an enthymeme about Ethics,—and others again, about Ethics from which one cannot reason upon Physics ; and so in each case. The Universal Common-places will not make a man intelligent about any special class of things ; since they have no special subject-matter. As to the Particular Common-places, the more carefully a speaker picks his propositions, the nearer he will be unconsciously coming to a science distinct from Dialectic and Rhetoric ; for, if he lights upon special first principles, this will be no longer Dialectic or Rhetoric, but that science of which he has the first principles. Most enthymemes are based upon these Particular or Special Common-places ;—fewer upon the Universal. As in the *Topics*[3], then, so here we must distinguish, in regard to enthymemes, the Special Topics and the Universal Topics from which they are to be taken. By Special Topics I mean the propositions peculiar to any given subject ; by Universal Topics, those which are common to all. We will begin with the Special Topics. But first of all we must determine how many branches of Rhetoric there are,

21

The Universal Common-places.

The Particular Common-places.

22

---

[1] Omitting τοὺς ἀκροατὰς with Muretus and Spengel.
[2] Jebb's *Essays and Addresses*, 1907, p. 528.
[3] *Topica*, ix (*Soph. El.*), c. 9.

in order that, having done this, we may ascertain separately
the elements and the propositions of each.

iii. The species of Rhetoric are three in number, for the
*The three
species of
Rhetoric.* hearers of speeches belong to that number of
classes. The speech has three elements—the
speaker, the subject, and the person addressed; 1358 b
and the end proposed has reference to this last, that is, to the
hearer. Now the hearer must be either spectator or judge; 2
and, if judge, then of the past or of the future. The judge of
things future is (for instance) the ekklesiast; the judge of
things past, the dikast; the other hearer is a spectator
*Deliberative,
forensic, and
epideictic.* of the faculty. It follows that there must be 3
three kinds of rhetorical speeches, the deliberative, the forensic, the epideictic.

Now the elements of counsel are exhortation and dis-
*Their ele-
ments.* suasion; since both private advisers and speakers
in the public interest always either exhort or
dissuade. The elements of litigation are accusation and
defence; since the parties to a suit must be occupied with
one or the other of these. The elements of an epideictic
speech are praise and blame. The times which 4
Their times. belong to these classes severally are:—to the
deliberative speaker, the future; for he offers advice,
exhorting or dissuading, about things to be;—to the litigant,
the past; for the subjects of accusation on the one hand and
defence on the other are always things past;—to the epideictic speaker, properly the present; for all men praise or
blame in accordance with existing conditions, though they
often avail themselves also of reminiscences from the past
and conjectures about the future.

For these three classes there are three distinct ends, 5
Their ends. namely:—for the counsellor, utility or harm
(since the exhorter advises a thing as being
better, and the dissuader opposes it as being worse), and it is
in reference to this topic that he uses the subsidiary topics of
justice and injustice, honour and shame;—for litigants,
justice and injustice,—and these, again, use subsidiary topics
in reference to this one;—for those who praise or blame, the

honourable and the shameful; and these, too, refer their other topics to this standard.

6   That the end of each class is such as has been stated is shown by this fact, that the other points are sometimes not contested by the speakers. For instance, the litigant will sometimes not dispute that a thing has happened or that he has done harm; but that he is guilty of an injustice, he will never admit; else there would be no need of a lawsuit. Similarly, speakers in debate often give up all other points, but will not allow that they are advising an inexpedient course, or dissuading from one which is advantageous; while, as to showing that it is no injustice to enslave a neighbouring and perhaps unoffending community, they often give themselves no anxiety. In the same way panegyrists and censurers do not consider whether such an one's acts were

1359 a expedient or harmful; but often make it a ground of positive praise that, regardless of his own advantage, he did something or other noble. For instance they praise Achilles for coming to the rescue of his friend Patroklos, when he knew that he must die, though he might have lived. Now for Achilles such a death was nobler; but life was expedient.

7   It appears from what has been said that we must first ascertain the propositions bearing upon these topics. Now signs, fallible or infallible, and probabilities are the propositions of Rhetoric; for as, universally, a syllogism is formed of propositions, so the enthymeme is a syllogism formed of the above-named propositions.

8   And as there can be no performance, past or future, of impossible things, but only of possible; and since things, which have not occurred, cannot have been done, and things, which are not to be, cannot be about to be done;—it is necessary alike for the Deliberative, for the Forensic, and for the Epideictic speaker to have propositions about the Possible and the Impossible, and on the question whether a thing has

9 or has not happened, is or is not to be. Besides, since all men in praising or blaming, in exhorting or dissuading, in accusing or defending try to prove, not merely the above

facts, but also that the good or evil, the honour or disgrace,
the justice or injustice is great or small, whether they are
taken absolutely or in comparison with each other, it is plain
that it will be necessary to have propositions about greatness
or smallness, and about greater or less, both universally and
in particular cases ; as on the question which is the greater
or less good, the greater or less act of injustice—and so with
the rest.

These, then, are the subjects in which it is necessary to
ascertain the available propositions.   Next, we must examine
in detail each class of these subjects ; namely, those of
debate ; those of epideictic speaking ; and, thirdly, those of
lawsuits.

iv.   First, then, we must ascertain about what sort of goods
or evils the speaker in debate offers counsel, since
he does not do so about *all* things, but only
about such as may or may not come to pass.

The special
Topics of
deliberative
Rhetoric.

As to things, which *necessarily* are or will be, or 2
which cannot be or come to pass, no counsel can be given.
Nor, of course, can it be given about all contingent things ; 3
for there are some goods of the contingent class, both natural
and accidental, about which it is idle to offer advice.
Evidently, advice can be given only on such subjects as
admit of debate ; and these are such as can be referred to
ourselves, and which it rests with us to initiate.   For our
discussions are not carried beyond the point at which we
find that things are impossible for us to do.

Now, accurately to enumerate and classify the several 4
subjects on which men are wont to confer, and, further, to **1359 b**
give of them, so far as possible, a really precise account, is an
attempt which need not be made at present ; first, because
this is not the business of Rhetoric, but of a more intelligent
and more exact method ; next, because already Rhetoric has
had assigned to it many more than its proper subjects of
consideration.   In fact it is true, as we have said before[1], that 5
Rhetoric is made up of the science of logical analysis, and of
that political science which is concerned with morals ; and it

[1] ii 7.

has a resemblance, partly to Dialectic, partly to sophistical
6 reasoning. But, in so far as any one attempts to construct
either Dialectic or Rhetoric, not as faculties but as special
sciences, he will unconsciously abolish their very essence, by
shifting his ground and reconstructing them into sciences
dealing with particular subjects and not with words alone[1].
7 Even here, however, we must notice these points which it is
to our purpose to discriminate, though they still supply
matter for inquiry to political science.

Now it may be said that the chief subjects, about which
all men debate, and on which those who offer counsel speak,
are five in number:—Ways and Means; War and Peace;
Protection of the Country; Imports and Exports; Legislation.

8   He, then, who is to give counsel on Ways and Means,
must know the sources of the public revenue,
their nature and number, in order that, if any is
neglected, it may be added, or, if any is too small, it may be
increased; further, all the expense of the State, in order that,
if any is superfluous, it may be taken away, or, if any is too
large, it may be repressed; since, relatively to their actual
property, men become richer, not only by acquiring, but
by retrenching. A comprehensive view of these questions
cannot be obtained simply by experience in private affairs;
it is further necessary, with a view to giving counsel on these
things, to be acquainted with the discoveries of others.[2]

Ways and Means.

9   As to War and Peace, one must know how great the
power of the State actually is, and is capable of
becoming; also, the nature of the actual power,
and of that which may be acquired; further, what wars the
State has waged, and how. And these things must be known,

War and Peace.

---

[1] λήσεται τὴν φύσιν αὐτῶν ἀφανίσας τῷ μεταβαίνειν ἐπισκευάζων εἰς ἐπιστήμας
ὑποκειμένων τινῶν πραγμάτων, ἀλλὰ μὴ μόνον λόγων. Vater and Jebb, and Bonitz
in the *Index Aristotelicus*, connect εἰς ἐπιστήμας with ἐπισκευάζων, and not with
μεταβαίνειν. Cope prefers the latter construction: 'he will be unconsciously
effacing their real nature by passing over (in his attempt to reconstruct them) into
sciences of definite special subjects, instead of (confining himself to) those which
deal with mere words,' *Comm.* i 61; *Introd.* 174.

[2] ἱστορικὸν εἶναι κτλ., 'to be *inquisitive* as to the discoveries of others,' cp.
Cope, *Comm.* i 64.

not only in respect to one's own State, but in respect to its neighbours also, in order that it may keep peace with the stronger, and have the option of making war on the weaker. One must know, too, whether the power of the State is 1360 a like or unlike that of its neighbours ; for here, too, there is a possibility of advantage or loss. In regard to these points, again, one must have considered the issue, not only of one's own country's wars, but of the wars waged by other States too ; for like causes produce like results.

Further, in regard to the protection of the country, one 10
Defence.   must not be ignorant how it is guarded : one must know the strength and the species of the protecting force, and the sites of the forts ; but this demands acquaintance with the country, in order that, if the garrison be too small, it may be increased, or, if superfluous, withdrawn ; and that the important places may be especially watched.

Then, as to the food question, one must know how much 11
Commerce.   outlay is enough for the State; what sort of food is produced in the country or can be imported ; also what articles the citizens require to export or import, in order that treaties and pacts may be made with the right States ; for there are two classes of States towards whom our citizens must be kept blameless :—the stronger, and those useful for commerce.

For safety, it is necessary to have the power of enter- 12
Legislation.   taining all these questions ; but nothing is more necessary than to understand how to legislate, since on its laws depends the weal of the State. One must know, then, how many forms of government there are ; what things are good for each form ; and by what things, proper to it or adverse to it, each tends to be corrupted. When I talk of a polity being corrupted by things proper to it, I mean that all polities, except the best, are corrupted, both by relaxation and by tension. Democracy, for instance, is weakened, so that it must end in oligarchy, not only by relaxing but by over-straining : just as the aquiline and the snub-nosed type, which unbending brings to the right mean,

J.   2 may also be intensified to a point at which the very semblance of a nose is lost.

13   Now, with a view to legislative acts, it is useful to see what polity is expedient; not merely in the light of history, but by knowledge of actual foreign polities, and by seeing what form of government suits what sort of people. Evidently, then, books of travel are useful with a view to legislation, since from them one can ascertain the laws of the different nations; histories should be read with a view to giving political counsel. All this, however, is the business of Political Science, not of Rhetoric.

1360 b   These, then, are all the chief subjects with which the intending debater should be conversant. Let us now state again the premises, from which he must exhort or dissuade on these and on all other subjects[1].

v.   It may be said that all men, individually and in the *Analysis of* aggregate, have some aim, with a view to which *Happiness.* they choose or avoid; and this may be summa-
2   rily described as Happiness, with its parts. So, for the sake of illustration, let us ascertain what, speaking broadly, we mean by Happiness, and what are the elements of its parts; for Happiness and the things which tend to it, and the things adverse to it, are the subjects of all attempts to exhort or dissuade; since we ought to do those things which tend to create it or any one of its parts, or to increase that part; but we ought not to do those things, which corrupt, or hinder it, or produce its opposite.

3   Let Happiness, then, be prosperity combined with virtue; or independence of life; or that existence which, being safe,

---

[1] The connexion of the next three chapters is as follows: " The deliberative speaker exhorts or dissuades with a view to the *happiness* of the persons addressed. Hence we must consider the popular notions of happiness which prevail among men. Here follows a series of *popular* definitions of happiness, and a list of the elements which are generally regarded as constituting it (c. 5). The deliberative speaker appeals to *the interest*, τὸ συμφέρον, of those whom he addresses. The συμφέρον is a kind of ἀγαθόν. Hence we must consider what are ἀγαθά. A popular analysis and list follow (c. 6). But the question will arise 'of two good things, which is the *better*?' Hence we must treat the κοινὸς τόπος of μᾶλλον καὶ ἧττον, or 'degree' (c. 7)" (R. C. J.).

is pleasantest ; or a flourishing state of property and of body, with the faculty of guarding and producing this ; for it may be said that all men allow Happiness to be one or more of these things.

If, then, Happiness is this sort of thing, these must be 4 parts of it :—good birth, the possession of many friends, the possession of good friends, wealth, the possession of good children, the possession of many children, a happy old age ; further, the excellences of the body, as health, beauty, strength, great stature, athletic power ; also good repute, honour, good fortune, virtue. For a man would *then* be most independent, if he possessed both the personal and the external goods, since besides these there are no others. Personal goods are partly mental, partly bodily ; external goods are birth, friends, money, honour. Further, we think that he ought to have influence and good fortune ; for thus will his life be safest. So let us ascertain in like manner what each of these, too, is.

Good birth, then, means, for a nation or a city, that the 5 people is indigenous or ancient ; that its earliest
Good birth.
representatives were conspicuous as leaders, and that many of their descendants have been conspicuous for those things which excite emulation. The individual's good birth may be either on the father's or the mother's side ; it implies pure blood, and that (as in the case of the community) the founders of the line have been notable for virtue or for wealth or for something else which is honoured ; and that the family has many conspicuous members, men and women, young and old.

The possession of good children and the possession of 6 many children are terms of plain meaning. The
Goodly and numerous offspring.
community has these things, if the youth be numerous and good, first as regards excellence 1361 a of body, such as stature, beauty, strength, athletic power ; the moral excellences of a young man are moderation and courage. The individual has these blessings, when his own children are numerous and good, both female and male ; the bodily excellence of a woman being beauty and stature,—the

moral, moderation and an industry which is not sordid. The existence of all such conditions is desirable both for the individual and for the state, and in regard to women as well as to men ; for people among whom the state of women is low, as in Lacedæmon, have scarcely more than a half prosperity.

7   The elements of wealth are—plenty of money—the possession of territory and of farms,—further,

Wealth.

the possession of furniture, of cattle, and of slaves in great number, distinguished for their stature and beauty[1]; it being understood that all these things are[2] safe, worthy of a freeman, and useful. Those things are the more useful, which are the more productive ; those things rather befit a freeman, which tend to enjoyment. By productive things I mean those from which revenues come ; by things for enjoyment, such as yield nothing worth speaking of, except their use. The definition of secure possession is possession of things in such a place and manner, that the use of them depends on one's self :—the test of things being one's own, in one's having the power of alienating them ; by alienation I mean giving and selling. Universally, wealth consists in using rather than in possessing ; for wealth is the activity and the use of possessions.

8   Good repute consists in being respected by all men, or in being thought to have something which is

Good repute.

desired by all men, or by most, or by the good, or by the prudent.

9   Honour is a mark of good repute for beneficence. Those men are honoured justly and most, who have

Honour.

done benefits; not but that honour is paid also to a possible benefactor. A benefit has reference either to preservation or the other causes of being ; or to wealth, or to some one of the other goods, of which the acquisition is not easy, either generally, or in a given circumstance, or at a given time ; since many people get honour for things which

---

[1] πλήθει καὶ μεγέθει καὶ κάλλει vulgo; πλήθει καὶ κάλλει Roemer, following the text written by the first hand in the margin of the Paris ms.

[2] <οἰκεῖα> is inserted here from the context by Roemer, 'are <one's very own, and are> safe.'

look small; but the place and the moment account for it. The elements of honour are—sacrifices; records in verse or prose; privileges; grants of domain; chief seats; public funerals; statues; maintenance at the public cost; barbaric homage, such as salaams and giving place; and the gifts honourable among each people. The gift is the bestowal of a possession and a mark of honour: gifts, therefore, are desired both by the avaricious and by the ambitious, since for each it has what they want: it is a possession, which the 1361 b *avaricious* desire; and it brings honour, which the *ambitious* desire.

The excellence of the body is health,—this health meaning 10 that men are to be free from disease and to have the use of their bodies; for many people are healthy in the way in which Herodicus is said to have been, whom no one would count happy for their health, since they have to abstain from all, or nearly all, the things which men do. Beauty is different for each time of life : it is a youth's 11 beauty that his body should be serviceable for the toils of the race and for feats of strength, while he is also pleasant to look upon ;—so that the practices of the pentathlum are most beautiful, being formed at once for strength and for speed. The beauty of a man in his prime is that his body should be serviceable for the toils of war, while his aspect pleases and also strikes fear; the beauty of an old man is that his body should serve for the needful toils and be free from pain, through having none of those things which mar old age. Strength is the power of moving another as one likes, and 12 one must do so by drawing or pushing or lifting or pressing or compressing; so that a strong man is strong either in all or in some of these things. Excellence of size is a superiority 13 to the many in height and breadth, just so great as not thereby to make the movements slower. Athletic excellence 14 of body results from size, strength and swiftness[1]; for the swift man is strong. He who can throw his legs in a certain way and move them quick and far, is fit for running; he who

Health.

---

[1] καὶ τάχους, bracketed by Roemer. The next clause shows that it must have been omitted, as it adds the reason for its omission.

can compress and hold, for wrestling ; he who can drive with
a blow, for boxing ; he who can do both the last, for the
pancratium ; he who can do all, for the pentathlum.

15   Happy old age is old age which comes slowly, with
Happy old   painlessness; for a man has not a happy old age
age.   if he grows old, either quickly, or slowly indeed,
yet with pain.   It comes both from the excellences of the
body, and from good fortune : for, if a man is not free from
disease and is not strong, he will not escape suffering ; nor,
without good fortune [1], is he likely to have a long and painless
life.   There is, indeed, a distinct faculty of long life without
strength or health ; since many people live long without the
excellences of the body ; but precise discussion of these
matters is of no use for our present purpose.

16   The possession of many friends—the possession of good
Friendship.   friends—are plain terms, when ' friend ' has been
defined ; your friend being a person who tends to
do for your sake those things which he thinks good for you.
A man, then, who has many such well-wishers, has many
friends : he whose well-wishers are also worthy men, has good
friends.

17   Good fortune consists in those goods, of which fortune is
1362 a   the cause, coming to pass and belonging to us ;
Good fortune.   either all of them, or most, or the chief.   Fortune
is the cause of some things of which the arts also are causes,
and of many, too, which are *not* artificial,—as of those, for
instance, which Nature gives (though the gifts of Fortune may
be also contrary to Nature).   Thus Art may be the cause of
health, but Nature gives beauty and stature.—Generally, those
goods are the gifts of Fortune which are the objects of envy.
Fortune is also the cause of those goods which are beyond
calculation.   Suppose, for instance, that a man's brothers are
ugly, but *he* is good-looking : or that *he* found a treasure,
which everyone else had missed : or that the arrow hit the

---

[1] οὔτ' ἂν εὐτυχὴς, the reading of the Paris MS, was corrected by Muretus into
οὔτ' ἄνευ τύχης, where we should either omit οὔτε, with Hermolaus Barbarus, or alter
it into οὐκ, with Roth.   The former is the course adopted in this translation and in
Roemer's text.

man next him, and not *him* : or that he alone did not go to
a place which was his constant resort, while other people,
going once in a way, were killed. All such things are
counted pieces of good luck.

As to Virtue, since the topic of Praise has most to do 18
Virtue. with it, we must define it when we come to speak
of praise.

vi.   It is plain, then, what things, future or actual, should
be kept in view in exhorting, and what in dissuading—the
latter being the opposite of the former.   And since the aim
The end of   of him who gives counsel, is the expedient (for
counsel.   men debate, not about the end, but about the
means to the end ; while the means are those things which are
expedient in action); since, further, the expedient is a
good ;—it would seem that we must ascertain generally the
first principles of Good and of the Expedient.

Let Good, then, be defined as that which is desirable for 2
Good.   its own sake; or that, on account of which we
choose something else ; or as that which is
aimed at by all things, or by all sentient and intelligent
things ; or which would be their aim, if they got intelligence.
Again, all that intelligence would assign to each man, and all
the individual intelligence does assign to the individual, is
good for him ; and that is good for him,—having which he is
in a good case and independent.   The independent, again, is
good ; also that which tends to create or preserve such things
as these, and that on which such things attend, and everything that tends to prevent or destroy the opposites of these.
A thing may attend upon another in two ways—as a 3
concomitant, or as a *consequence*.   Thus, knowing attends as a
consequence on learning ; living attends as a *concomitant* on
being healthy.   And these things are productive of others in
three senses ; either as being healthy produces health, or as
food produces health, or as exercise is productive of health,
because, as a rule, it produces health.   These principles 4
settled, it follows that both acquisition of good things and
loss of evil things must be good : since freedom from the evil

attends, as a concomitant, on the latter, and possession of
5 good attends, as a consequence, on the former. Again, the
exchange of a smaller good for a greater, or a greater evil for
1362 b a smaller, is good: for, in proportion as the greater exceeds
6 the less, there is acquisition of good, or loss of evil[1]. The
virtues, again, must be good ; for, in respect of these, their
possessors are in a good state ; and the virtues tend to
produce and to do good things. What, and of what sort,
7 each virtue is, must be discussed separately[2]. Again, it follows
that pleasure is a good ; for all animals naturally aim at it.
So pleasant things, and beautiful things, must be goods ; for
the pleasant things are productive of pleasure, and, of the
beautiful things, some are pleasant, and others desirable for
their own sake.

8   To take one by one, the Goods must be these :—Happiness ; for it is desirable for its own sake and is independent,
9 and, on account of it, we choose many things ;—Justice,
Courage, Moderation, Magnanimity, Magnificence and the
other like habits of mind ; for they are moral excellences.
10 Health, Beauty, and such things ; for they are excellences of
the body, and productive of many things, as health is
productive both of pleasure and of life ; for which reason it is
thought the chief of goods, as being the cause of two things
11 supremely valued by the Many—pleasure and life. Wealth,
again :—for it is the excellence of possession, and a thing
12 productive of many others. A Friend and Friendship : for a
friend is desirable for his own sake, and productive of much
13 good. Honour, Reputation : for they are pleasant, and can
produce much else ; and are attended as a rule by the
existence of those things, for which men are honoured.
14 Power of speech or of action ; for all such things are
15 productive of goods. Further—Ability, Memory, Facility
16 in Learning, Quickness, and all such things : likewise, all the
Sciences and the Arts. And Life : for, though no other good

---

[1] Reading with the Paris MS, τούτῳ γίνεται τοῦ μὲν λῆψις, τοῦ δ' ὑπερβολή.
So Spengel. τοῦτο the reading of inferior MSS is accepted by Bekker, while τούτου
is preferred by Muretus, Vahlen and Roemer.
[2] c. ix *infra*.

should go with it, it is desirable for itself.   And Justice : for
it is something expedient in the common interest.

These, then, may be said to be the admitted goods ; and 17
from these the premisses of syllogisms must be taken in the 18
case of disputable goods.   That is good of which the opposite 19
is evil ; that, too, the opposite of which is expedient for our
enemies : for instance, if it is expedient for our enemies that
we should be cowards, clearly courage is most advantageous
for us.   And generally, the opposite of that which our 20
enemies desire, or at which they rejoice, seems advantageous.
This is the point of the verse—

' Surely Priam would rejoice, &c.'[1]

It is not always so, however ; but only as a rule : for there is
nothing to prevent our enemies' interest from being occa-
sionally the same as our own : whence the saying that evils
bring men together—when the same thing is harmful for **1363 a**
both.

Also that which is not in excess is good[2], and that which 21
is greater than it ought to be is evil.   That is good, too, for 22
which much toil or outlay has been incurred ; since already
it is an apparent good ; and such a thing is assumed as an
end, and as the end of many actions ; but the end must be a
good.   Hence the verse—

' They would leave a boast to Priam, &c.'[3]

and

''Twere shame, in sooth, to stay long and come back empty-handed[4].'

And so, again, the proverb about dropping the pitcher at the 23
door.

That is a good, too, at which many[5] aim, or which has the
prestige of being fought for : since that at which *all* aim was,
we agreed, a good ; and the many seem equivalent to ' all.'
That which is praised is a good ; for no one praises what is 24

---

[1] *Iliad*, i 255.
[2] οὗ μή ἐστιν ὑπερβολή, *i.e.* τὸ μέσον.   δ is suggested by Spengel and accepted
by Roemer.
[3] *Il.* ii 160.
[4] *Il.* ii 298.
[5] πολλοί : <οἱ> πολλοί is proposed by Spengel and accepted by Roemer.

not good. That, too, which enemies [and malevolent men][1] praise:—for the merit is now as it were admitted by all, when even the injured admit it: they can admit it only because it is manifest. In the same way those are worthless men, whom their friends censure and their enemies do not censure[2]. On this ground the Corinthians conceived that they had been reviled by Simonides when he wrote—

' Ilium has no quarrel with Corinth[3].'

25 That is a good, too, which some prudent or good man or woman has preferred,—as Athene chose Odysseus, as Theseus chose Helen, as the goddesses chose Paris, as Homer chose
26 Achilles. And, universally, the objects of deliberate choice are goods. Men choose to do the things above-named, and such things as are bad for their enemies, and good for their
27 friends, and possible. Things are possible in two senses—as having been done, and as being easy to do. Easy things are things done without pain or in a short time; for difficulty is
28 measured either by pain or by length of time. Again, men choose to do a thing, if they can do it as they wish; and they wish either for no evil or for an evil smaller than the good ; but this will be so, if the penalty is either unfelt or trifling. Again, men choose to do those acts which are peculiar to them, or which no one else has done, or which are signal; for so there is more honour. Also, such acts as suit them ; and such are those which befit them in respect to their birth and their power, or in regard to which they think that they are deficient (however small the deficiency may be—for not the
29 less will they choose to do these acts). Also men choose to do things easy of achievement (these, as being easy, are possible):—and things easy of achievement are those in which

---

[1] [καὶ οἱ φαῦλοι]. Bekker and Spengel rightly bracket these words. φαῦλοι here could only mean ' malevolent,' whereas, just below, it has its ordinary meaning as a softened κακοί, and, here, οἱ κακῶς πεπονθότες suits οἱ ἐχθροί only (R. C. J.).

[2] Spengel prints: ὥσπερ καὶ φαῦλοι [οὓς οἱ φίλοι ψέγουσι καὶ ἀγαθοί] οὓς οἱ ἐχθροὶ μὴ ψέγουσι. The text proposed by Jebb is : ὥσπερ καὶ φαῦλοι οὓς οἱ φίλοι ψέγουσι καὶ οὓς οἱ ἐχθροὶ μὴ ψέγουσι. The same text is independently proposed by Roemer.

[3] Simonides, fragm. 50 Bergk, ed. 4.

all men or most, or those like themselves, or their inferiors have succeeded.   Men choose actions, too, by which they will please their friends or incur the hatred of their enemies ; and all such actions as are chosen by men whom they admire. Those actions, too, they choose, in reference to which they are clever and experienced (for they think to succeed more easily); or those which no worthless man chooses ; for such things are more praiseworthy.   And the things which men actually desire ; for such a thing appears, not only pleasant, but also better.   And each class of men chooses especially 30 those things with reference to which they are such or such. 1363 b Thus lovers of victory rejoice in the prospect of victory, lovers of honour in the prospect of honour, lovers of money in the prospect of money, and so on.

vii.   In regard, then, to Good and to the Expedient, our
The topic   proofs must be taken from these premises.
of degree.   Since, however, men often admit that each of
two things is expedient, but dispute which is the more expedient, we must next speak of the Greater Good and the More Expedient.

Let, then, that which excels be defined as a certain 2 quantity and something more; that which is excelled being the original quantity.   The terms ' greater ' and ' more ' always have respect to something else : the terms ' great,' ' small,' ' much,' ' little,' have respect to average magnitude : the 'great' is something which excels; the deficient is 'small'; and so with the terms ' much ' and ' little.'   Now we describe 3 Good as that which is desirable for its own sake, and not on account of something else ; or as that at which all things aim, and which, could they acquire intelligence and prudence, they would choose ; also, as that which tends to produce or pre-serve such things, or on which such things attend ; further, that for which things are done is the end, and an end is that for which all else is done, and that is a good for the individual, which in respect to him has these attributes. Hence the greater number of goods constitute a greater good than one or a smaller number, supposing that one or that

smaller number to be reckoned in with them[1]; for the larger
4 number excels, the original quantity is excelled. And if the
largest specimen of one class excels the largest specimen of
another, the one class excels the other; and if one class
excels the other, the largest specimen of the one excels the
largest specimen of the other. For instance, if the largest
man is larger than the largest woman, men generally are
larger than women, and conversely: for the ratio of
superiority between class and class is the ratio of superiority
5 between their largest specimens. Again, when B attends on
A, but A does not attend on B, A is the greater good: (one
thing may go with another as a concomitant, or as a
consequence, or potentially:)—for the use of the attendant
thing is included in that of the other. Thus life attends as a
concomitant on health, but not health on life: knowledge
attends as a consequence upon learning: cheating attends
potentially on sacrilege, since a man who has robbed a temple
6 is capable of cheating too. Again, that which excels a
given thing by a greater quantity is greater; for it must
7 needs excel the greater also[2]. And those things which
produce the greater good are greater goods: for this was
involved in the assumption that they produce something
greater. Similarly, that which is produced by a greater good
is greater; thus, if the wholesome is preferable to the
8 pleasant, health is a greater good than pleasure. Again, that
1364 a which is desirable for its own sake, is a greater good than
that which is not so; thus strength is better than a wholesome thing; for the latter is not chosen for its own sake, but
9 the former is; and this was our definition of good. Again, if

---

[1] That is to say: 'Virtue, health, wealth, strength, are better than virtue
alone; but this one, *virtue*, must be included in the list; since virtue alone may
outweigh all the *rest* put together' (Schrader's explanation, accepted by Cope,
Introd., 178, and by Jebb).

[2] Let $A=8$, $B=6$, $C=2$. A exceeds C by 6; B exceeds C by 4; $\therefore A$ is
greater than B, which is itself τὸ μεῖζον in respect of C. Here μείζονι means 'by a
greater quantity.' Spengel, however, makes μείζονι depend on τοῦ αὐτοῦ, 'something identical with the greater': *quae superant quod idem est cum maiore, ipsa
maiora sunt.* That which exceeds *something identical with the greater*, is greater
still; for it must also be greater than the greater thing itself, as well as greater
than the equivalent of that greater thing.

one thing is an end, and another is not, the former is the greater good ; for the latter is chosen for the sake of something else,—the former for its own ; as exercise is chosen for the sake of a good state of body. That is the greater good 10 which has the less need of the other or others ; for it is more independent : and *that* has less need, which needs fewer or easier things. And when B cannot come to pass without A, 11 but A can come to pass without B, A is the greater good ; since that which lacks nothing is more independent, and appears a greater good. Again, that which is a first principle 12 is a greater good than that which is not ; and, for the same reason, that which is a cause is a greater good than that which is not ; for, without cause or first principle, it is impossible to be or to become. That, again, which comes from the greater of two first principles or two causes is the greater : and conversely, of two principles, or two causes, the greater is that of which the consequence is greater. It is 13 plain, then, from what has been said, that a thing may be greater in either of two ways. If it is a first principle, and something else is not, it will seem greater ; and also, if it is not a first principle, and the other is ; for the end is greater, and is not a first principle. Thus Leodamas accusing Kallistratos, said that the plotter was a worse offender than the doer ; for, if he had not planned the thing, it would not have been done. Again, accusing Chabrias, he said that the doer was worse than the plotter ; for the thing would not have come to pass, if there had been no one to do it : men plot only in order that they may execute[1].

---

[1] In 366 Oropos was seized by Oropian exiles favourable to Thebes, and occupied by a Theban garrison. An Athenian army was sent against it under Chares ; but *Chabrias* and *Kallistratos* effected a compromise, by which Oropos was left in the hands of the Thebans till the claim should be settled. The Thebans afterwards refused to give it up. Thereupon both *Kallistratos* and *Chabrias* were prosecuted by Leodamas, who attacked *Kallistratos* for devising the compromise, and *Chabrias* for bringing it to practical effect. In the result Chabrias (who was defended by Lykoleon, *Rhet.* iii 10) was acquitted, while Kallistratos was sent into exile in 361, and died in 355. Their prosecutor, Leodamas, is described by Aeschines (*in Ktes.* § 138) as even excelling Demosthenes.

14   Then, what is rarer is a greater good than what is abundant ; as gold, though less useful, is more precious than iron ; for the acquisition, through being harder, is a greater object. (In another way, however, what is abundant is a greater good than what is rare, since there is more of it ; for ' often ' has the advantage of ' seldom '—whence the saying

'Water is best.'[1]

15 In general, the harder thing is a greater good than the easier, as being rarer ; though, in another way, the easier thing is a greater good than the harder, for it is as we wish.

16 That, again, is greater, of which the opposite is greater, or of which the loss is more important. Virtue is greater than *no* virtue, and vice than *no* vice ; for the one set of things are

17 ends, the others are not. Also those things, of which the products are nobler or more shameful, are themselves greater. Those things, again, of which the virtues or vices are greater, have the greatest products ; since, as the causes and the first

18 principles, so are the results ; and *vice versa.* Again, those things are greater goods, of which the excellence is more desirable or honourable : thus, keen sight is more desirable than a keen sense of smell, sight being more important than

1364 b smell ; and, as to be fond of one's friends is more honourable than to be fond of money, attachment to friends is better than love of money. Conversely, the highest degrees of the better and more honourable things are better and more honourable.

19 Again, those things are more honourable and better, the desire of which is so ; for the greater longings have the greater objects ; again, the desire of more honourable and better things is for the same reason more honourable and

20 better. The practice of those things is more honourable and estimable, of which the science is so ; for, as is the science, so is the actuality,—each science enjoining that which belongs to it. Accordingly, and for this reason, the science of the more estimable and honourable things is the more estimable

21 and honourable. Again, that which would be judged, or which has been judged, a greater good by the prudent or by

---

[1] Pindar, *Ol.* i 1.

all men or by the many or by most or by the best, must be so ; either absolutely, or in so far as this judgment was made in accordance with practical wisdom. This, indeed, applies to all other things, no less than to goods ; for the nature, the magnitude, the quality of a given thing are those which science and practical wisdom would assign. We have made the remark, however, only in reference to Goods—Good having been defined as that which things would severally choose if they were indued with practical wisdom[1]. Plainly, then, that is a greater good which practical wisdom announces to be so. That, too, is a greater good which belongs to the 22 better men, either absolutely, or in virtue of their superiority; as Courage is better than Strength. And *that* is the greater good, which the better man would choose, either absolutely, or in virtue of his being such; thus, to suffer a wrong is better than to do one, since the former would be the choice of the just man. The pleasanter thing is a greater good than the 23 less pleasant ; for all things pursue pleasure, desiring it for the sake of the experience itself ; and these are the criteria of the Good and of the End. The greater pleasure is the less troubled and the more enduring one. The more honourable 24 thing, again, is a greater good than the less honourable ; for the honourable is either the pleasant, or that which is desirable for its own sake. All things, too, are greater goods, 25 of which men desire more strongly to be the authors, for themselves or for their friends ; while those things which they least desire to cause, are greater evils. Again, the more 26 enduring goods are greater than the more short-lived, and the more secure than the less secure ; for the use of the more lasting things has the advantage in respect to time, the use of the secure things in respect to our wish ; for it is the use of the secure thing which is the more available at our wish. And so the other relations follow; as they might be inferred 27 from coordinate terms or from inflexions of the same stem[2].

---

[1] § 3 *supra.*

[2] σύστοιχα are coordinate *logical notions*, as δίκαιος, δίκαιον, δικαίως, with δικαιοσύνη. πτώσεις, or 'inflexions,' are these same coordinates in their *grammatical* aspect ; they are not confined to the cases, but include adverbs, and also inflexions of verbs. Cp. *Topica*, ii 9 (Cope's *Comm.* i 138).

Thus, if to act courageously is more honourable and desirable than to act temperately, courage is more desirable than temperance, and to be courageous is more desirable than to

28 be temperate. Again, what all men choose is a greater good than what is *not* chosen by all ; and what the greater number choose, than what is chosen by the smaller; for that which all

1365 a desire is (we agreed) a good ; and so, that is the greater good which excites the more desire. Again, that is a greater good which is declared so by disputants or by enemies or by umpires or by those whom they choose ; since this is equivalent, in the one case, to a general consent, in the other,

29 to an authoritative and intelligent verdict. Sometimes, that in which all share, is the greater good, since not to share in it is a dishonour : sometimes, however, that in which there are few

30 or no sharers, since it is rarer. Again, the more laudable things are greater goods, for they are more honourable. And so those things of which the prices are greater, price being a sort of worth[1]. Those things, too, are greater for which the

31 penalties are greater. Also, those things which are greater than things admittedly or apparently great. Again, the same things seem greater when divided into their parts (than when taken collectively) ; for they seem to excel a greater number of things. Hence, the poet says that (Cleopatra) persuaded Meleager to arise by reminding him[2]

'How many ills come to men whose town is taken. The folk perish and fire consumes the city and strangers lead the children away.'[3]

The same effect is wrought by combining and accumulating in the fashion of Epicharmos[4]—and for the same reason as in the case of the distributive process—because the combination

[1] Or, 'And things may be regarded as greater, of which the *honours and rewards* are greater; because honours and rewards are as it were a kind of *valuation*' (Cope, *Comm.* i 140 f).

[2] ὁ ποιητής φησι πεῖσαι λέγουσαν τὸν Μελέαγρον ἀναστῆναι κτλ. (λέγουσαν is omitted in the Paris MS and is bracketed by Buhle and Spengel, and by Roemer, who holds that the subject of πεῖσαι is the language of the poet).

[3] *Il.* ix 592, κήδε᾿ ὅσ᾿ ἀνθρώποισι πέλει τῶν ἄστυ ἀλώῃ· ἄνδρας μὲν κτείνουσι κτλ.

[4] Arist. *De Gen. An.* i 18, 34, ὡς Ἐπίχαρμος ποιεῖ τὴν ἐποικοδόμησιν, ἐκ τῆς διαβολῆς ἡ λοιδορία, ἐκ δὲ ταύτης ἡ μάχη κ.τ.λ. It is the figure called *climax* by the Greek and *gradatio* by the Latin rhetoricians (Cope, *Comm.* i 142).

makes the excellence striking, and because the thing seems to
be the beginning and cause of great effects.   And since that 32
which is harder and rarer is greater, seasons and ages and
places and times and faculties make things great.   Thus, if a
person has done anything beyond his natural power or beyond
his years or beyond the wont of his fellows, or in a given
way, at a given place or time, this will involve greatness in
honourable acts, good acts, just acts, or their opposites ;
whence the epigram on the Olympic victor—

> 'Of yore, with a rough yoke on my shoulders,
> I used to carry fish from Argos to Tegea.'[1]

Thus Iphicrates extolled himself by saying 'from what
beginnings' his fortunes had grown[2].   Again, the natural is 33
better than the acquired ; for it is more difficult.   Whence
the poet—

> 'Self-taught am I.'[3]

Also a conspicuous good is that which is the greatest part of 34
a great whole.   Thus Pericles, in his Funeral Oration, said
that the loss of the youth to the city was as if the spring
were taken out of the year[4].   Those are greater goods which 35
are useful at greater need, as in old age or sickness.   Of two
things, that is the greater good which is so, both for the
individual and absolutely.   And a possible good is better
than an impossible ; for the former is a good for the
individual, but the latter is not.   Also, goods at the end of
life are greater goods ; for those things are more ends which
are close to the ends.   And things chosen in reference to 36
their reality are greater goods than things chosen with a view **1365 b**
to reputation ; the definition of a thing chosen for reputation
being 'a thing which a man would not choose, if he was not
going to attract notice.'   Therefore, to receive benefits would
seem to be more desirable than to confer them ; for a man
will choose the former, even if he is not to attract notice ; but

---

[1] Simonides, fragm. 163, Bergk, ed. 4.
[2] c. ix 31 *infra*, ἐξ οἵων εἰς οἷα.   The father of Iphicrates was a shoemaker.
[3] *Od.* xxii 347.
[4] III x 7 *infra*.   This simile is not found in the Funeral Oration ascribed to
Pericles by Thucydides.

seems unlikely to decide on conferring a benefit which will
37 not be noticed. Those things, again, are better which men
wish to be, rather than to seem ; for they are chosen more
with respect to reality. Hence people say that justice is a
small thing, because it is more desirable to seem, than to *be*
38 just ; whereas it is not so in the case of health. That is a
greater good which is more useful for many purposes ; as that
which tends to life, and to living well, and to pleasure and to
honourable actions. Hence wealth and health are thought
39 the greatest goods ; for they contain all these things. That
is a greater good which is the more free from pain, being
combined with pleasure ; for there is more than one element ;
and so both the pleasure and the freedom from pain are
goods. Of two goods, that is the greater which, being added
40 to the same, makes the whole greater. And those goods, of
which the presence is perceived, are greater than those of
which the presence is unnoticed ; for the former tend to be
more real. Hence to be rich would appear to be a greater
41 good than to be thought rich[1]. That is a greater good which
is a man's cherished joy, or which is his all, while his
neighbours have it along with other things[2]. Thus, to put
out the eye of a one-eyed man is a greater injury than to put
out one of another man's two eyes : for the former has been
robbed of what he specially prized[3].

---

[1] διὸ τὸ πλουτεῖν φανείη ἂν μεῖζον ἀγαθὸν τοῦ δοκεῖν. 'Those goods of which
the presence is perceived are greater than those of which the presence is not
perceived.' How does the example illustrate this ? (R. C. J.). Cope has similarly
noticed that the text, as it stands, does not exemplify the preceding rule ; he
accordingly accepts Munro's suggestion, τῷ δοκεῖν, 'the value of wealth by this
rule may be considered to be augmented *by the addition of the prominent and
conspicuous display of it*' (*Comm.* i 150). τῷ δοκεῖν is also accepted by
Roemer.

[2] τὸ ἀγαπητόν, καὶ τοῖς μὲν μόνον τοῖς δὲ μετ' ἄλλων, 'that which is dearly prized,
and in some cases the only one, but in others in company with other things.' The
latter clause prevents us from rendering ἀγαπητὸν by 'unique' in the present
passage.

[3] 'Has been robbed of *his little all*' was Jebb's first translation, altered in pencil
into '*what barely sufficed him.*' The former makes ἀγαπητὸν equivalent to μόνον ;
the latter, equivalent to one of the uses of ἀναγκαῖον. The rendering here sub-
stituted for both is supported by the previous context, in which ἀγαπητὸν is
translated as 'a man's cherished joy.'

viii. The premisses, then, from which we must draw our proofs in exhorting or dissuading, may be taken as stated. But the greatest and most effectual of all helps to the faculty of persuading, and giving good counsel, is to have ascertained all the forms of government and to have discriminated the customs, institutions and interests peculiar to each. For all men obey their interest ; 2 and their interest is that which preserves the commonweal. Again, authority resides in the edict[1] of the authoritative body ; and this is different for each form of government ; for the several authorities are the same in number as the several forms of government. The forms of government 3 are four :—democracy, oligarchy, aristocracy, monarchy : hence the governing and arbitrating power is always a part or the whole of these. Democracy is 4 a form of government under which the magistracies are assigned by lot ; oligarchy one in which property[2] governs ; aristocracy, one in which power goes by discipline. I mean by 'discipline' that laid down by the law ; for, under an aristocracy, the rulers are they who have been loyal to the institutions. And such men must needs appear the best ; whence that polity has been called 'the Rule of the Best.' Monarchy, as its name denotes, is a form of government 1366 a under which one man is master of all ; but of monarchies the regulated form is called a kingdom, the unrestricted a tyranny. The end, then, of each form of government must 5 not escape us ; for men choose the means to their end. Now the end of democracy is freedom ; of oligarchy, wealth ; of aristocracy, the maintenance of discipline and the institutions ;...[3] of tyranny, police. It is clear then that we must distinguish those customs, institutions and utilities which conduce to the end of each, since men choose by that standard. And since 6 proofs are wrought, not only by demonstration, but also by

Marginal notes:

Forms of government.

Democracy
Oligarchy
Aristocracy
Monarchy.

---

[1] Reading ἀπόφανσις with the inferior MSS instead of ἀπόφασις. ' Aristoteli ἀπόφασις contrarium est καταφάσει, unde cum deterioribus libris ἀπόφανσις scribendum est ' (Spengel).

[2] [οἱ] ἀπὸ τιμημάτων, Camot, Spengel, Roemer.

[3] The 'end' of monarchy has been accidentally omitted, as observed by Spengel.

moral suasion (since we believe because the speaker appears such or such a sort of man), and there is moral suasion, if he appear good or well-disposed or both, it will be needful for us to know the moral character peculiar to each form of government ; since, for each, its own character must needs be most persuasive.   These characters will be ascertained by the same means ; for character is manifest in moral choice ; and this has reference to the end.

7   The objects, then, future or present, which we should have in view in exhorting ;—the premisses, from which our proofs must be taken in regard to the Expedient ;—further, the means and the method, by which we shall become well instructed as to the characters and institutions proper to the several forms of government ;—have now been explained, so far as suits the present occasion ; they have been accurately examined in the *Politics*[1].

ix.   Let us next speak of Virtue and Vice and of the Noble
The laudatory branch of Rhetoric.   and the Shameful (these being the objects of praise or blame) ; for, in speaking of these, we shall incidentally show the means of producing such or such an impression about our own characters (and this, we saw[2], is the second kind of proof); since the same means will enable us to make either another person or
2   ourselves trustworthy in respect to virtue.   And since it happens that people often praise, in jest or in earnest, not only a human being or a god, but this or that of the lower animals, as well as inanimate things, we must, in the same way as before, get our propositions about these.   Let us, then, go on to speak of these matters, so far as is needful by way of illustration.

3   That, then, is Morally Beautiful or Noble, which, being desirable for its own sake, is also laudable ; or
The popular conception of Virtue and Vice.   which, being good, is pleasant because good. And if this is the Noble, it follows that Virtue is noble : for Virtue is at once a good and a laudable
4   thing.   Now Virtue seems to be a faculty of providing and

---

[1] III vii–xviii, IV *init.*   [2] ii 4.

preserving 'goods'; and a faculty of doing many and great
benefits to all men in all cases. The parts of Virtue are 5
Justice, Courage, Temperance, Magnificence, Magnanimity, 1366 b
Liberality, Gentleness, Prudence, Wisdom. And the great 6
virtues must be those which are most useful to others, if
virtue is a faculty of beneficence. For this reason men most
honour the just and the brave; for Courage is useful to others
in war, and justice in peace also. Next comes Liberality;
for liberal men are open-handed and do not contend about
money—the chief object of other people's desire. Now Justice 7
is a virtue, through which everybody has his own according
to the law; Injustice is a vice, through which a man has,
against the law, what is *not* his own. Courage is a virtue, 8
through which men tend to do noble deeds in perils and as
the law commands, and to support the law; Cowardice is the
opposite. Temperance is a virtue, through which men are 9
disposed as the law enjoins towards the pleasures of the body;
Intemperance is the opposite. Liberality is a virtue tending 10
to confer pecuniary benefits; Illiberality is the opposite.
Magnanimity is a virtue tending to confer great benefits; 11
[Meanness of spirit is the opposite[1]]. Magnificence is a virtue 12
productive of greatness in expenditure; Meanness of spirit
and Shabbiness are the opposites. Prudence is a virtue of 13
the intelligence, in respect to which men are able to consult
for their own happiness about the goods and evils above-
mentioned...[2]

Virtue and Vice, then, universally and in their parts, have 14
been examined sufficiently for our immediate purpose; the
Noble and the Shameful are not hard to discern. For mani-
festly those things which produce Virtue must be noble, since
they tend to Virtue; and also those things which come from
it; these being its signs and its works. And since these 15
signs, and such deeds or sufferings as belong to the good man,
are noble, it follows that all deeds or signs of courage, and
all deeds courageously done, must be noble; likewise, just

[1] Bracketed by Spengel as redundant in view of § 12 ad fin.
[2] The definitions of the opposite of φρόνησις, and those of σοφία and its opposite, are here wanting. Roemer.

deeds and deeds done in a just way; (not, however, just
sufferings; it is distinctive of this virtue that to suffer justly
is not always noble,—as in the case of punishment it is more
shameful to suffer it justly than unjustly ;)—and so in regard
16 to the other virtues.   Also those deeds are noble, for which
the prize is honour, or honour in a greater degree than money;
and all desirable things which a man does, not in his own
17 interest; also absolute goods,—such as the deeds which a
man does for his country, regardless of his private interest;
and natural goods; and goods which are not such for the
individual, since things good for the individual are sought
18 selfishly.   Also those goods which may exist for one after
1367 a death rather than in life; since goods to be enjoyed in life
19 supply a stronger selfish motive.   Also all things which are
done on account of others, since here there is less selfishness.
And all successes which benefit others and not oneself :—and
good deeds done to one's benefactors, for this is just; and
20 benefits generally—for they have no selfish bearing.   Also
the opposites of those things of which men are ashamed; for
men are ashamed when they say, do, or mean to do shameful
things; as Sappho has written, in answer to the words of
Alcæus :

> ' Something I would say, but shame hinders me '[1]:—

> ' If thy desire were for good things or noble, and thy tongue were not labour-
> ing to utter something base, shame would not have covered thy eyes, but thou
> wouldest speak about thy rightful wish.'[2]

21   Those things are noble, too, about which men feel trepidation, without feeling fear; for it is by those goods which tend
22 to fame that they are thus affected.   The naturally better
persons or things have the nobler excellences and works,—
23 as those of a man are nobler than those of a woman.   Also
those excellences are nobler which give enjoyment to others
rather than to their possessors : whence justice and the just
24 are noble.   Again, it is noble to be avenged on one's enemies
and not to make up the quarrel; for requital is just; and the
just is noble; and it is the part of a courageous man not to

---

[1] Alcæus, fragm. 55, Bergk, ed. 4.
[2] Sappho, fragm. 28, *ib.*

be worsted. Victory, too, and honour are among noble 25
things; for they are desirable though sterile; and they show
a superior excellence. Memorable things are noble, and the
more memorable, the nobler. So it is with those goods which
do not wait on the living, and with those on which honour
attends, and with signal things. Again, unique possessions
are the nobler, since they are more memorable. So are pos- 26
sessions which yield no fruit; for they are more worthy of a
free man. Those things, too, are noble which the special
usage of a people makes so, and which are symbols of things
which that people counts praiseworthy; thus in Lacedæmon
it is noble to have long hair, for it is a sign of a free man;
since it is not easy for a man with long hair to do any menial
work. Again, it is noble not to ply any sordid trade; for it is 27
the part of a free man not to live in dependence upon others.
Then those qualities which border on a man's actual qualities 28
must be assumed to be identical with them, for the purpose
either of praise or of blame; thus, the cautious man may be
called cold and designing; the foolish man may be called
goodnatured, or the callous man, mild. And so each char- 29
acter may be interpreted by the character which ranges beside
it—always in the better sense: for instance, the passionate
and violent man may be called straightforward,—the arrogant
man, majestic and dignified. Men who represent the extremes **1367 b**
must be taken as representing the virtues; thus, the rash man
must be called courageous; the prodigal, liberal; for it will
seem so to most people, and at the same time a fallacy may
be derived from the man's motive. Thus, if he runs risks
where there is no need, much more (it will be thought) would
he brave danger where honour required; or if he is lavish to
the crowd, much more will he be generous to his friends: for
it is an excess of virtue to do good to all. But one must 30
consider too, to whom[1] the praise is addressed, for as Socrates
said, it is not hard to praise Athenians to Athenians[2]. One
must represent, as existing, that which is honoured by each

---

[1] *i.e.* 'the audience to whom.'
[2] *i.e.* 'before an audience of Athenians.' Plato, *Menexenus,* 235 D.

set of people—as by Scythians, or Lacedæmonians, or philosophers. And, generally, one must draw the honourable into the sphere of the noble,—as, indeed, they seem to be neighbours. And all things may be treated as noble which befit the doers—deeds, for instance, worthy of their ancestors and their antecedents; for it is happy and noble to acquire fresh honour. Again a thing is noble, if done, beyond mere fitness, with a better and nobler tendency; for instance, if a man is moderate in prosperity, but magnanimous in adversity; or better and more conciliatory, the greater he becomes. An instance of this is the saying of Iphicrates about his origin as compared with his fortunes[1]; and the epigram on the Olympic victor:

> ' Of yore I had a rough yoke on my shoulders,' &c.[2]

also the verses of Simonides:

> ' She whose father, husband, and brothers were princes,' &c.[3]

32 Now, since praise is founded upon actions, and it is distinctive of the good man to act according to moral choice, we must try to show that our man acts by moral choice. It is a help towards this that he should be seen to have done the thing often. Therefore coincidences and accidents should be treated as results of moral choice; for, if many similar instances are brought forward, 33 these will appear to show virtue and moral choice. Now praise is language which brings out the greatness of a virtue. We must make it evident, therefore, that the actions are of such or such a character. But encomium is concerned with achievements; the external circumstances, such as good birth and education, being used merely to increase the credibility; since it is likely that good men should come of good men, and that a man brought up in a given way should be of a given character. Hence we give encomium to men who *have done* something. The results achieved, however, are mere indica-

Episode on ἔπαινος, which expresses moral approbation; and ἐγκώμιον, which is given to ἔργα, as such.

---

[1] I vii 32 *supra*.   [2] *ib.*

[3] παίδων τ', οὐκ ἤρθη νοῦν ἐς ἀτασθαλίην, Simonides, fragm. 111 Bergk ed. 4; Thuc. vi 59. Archedikê, daughter of Hippias, married Aeantides, son of Hippoklês, tyrant of Lampsakos. Her tomb was at Lampsakos.

tions of the moral habit; for we should *praise* a man, even if
he had not done the thing, if we were sure that he was of such
or such a character. Felicitation and gratulation are synony- 34
mous terms, but not the same things as praise and encomium ;
rather, as happiness includes virtue, gratulation includes the
rest.

Laudatory and Deliberative Speaking have a topic in 35
common ; since those things which, in debate,
Relation of
Laudatory to one would suggest, become, when differently
Deliberative
Rhetoric. expressed, encomia. Given, then, the right 36
actions and the right character, these, when **1368 a**
we use them for admonition, must be expressed in an altered
and inverted form. Thus 'A man should be proud, not of
fortune's gifts, but of what he owes to himself.' So when you
wish to praise, think what you would advise ; and, when you
wish to advise, think what you would praise. The modes of 37
expression will necessarily be opposite, when the prohibitive
and the non-prohibitive clauses are interchanged.

One must use, too, many means of amplification. Suppose, 38
for instance, that a man is the only one, or the first, or one of
a few who has done something, or that he has done it in the
highest degree ; all these things are noble. The conditions
of time and occasion may also be used ; these serving to
show that the deed was more than could have been expected.
Note, too, if he has succeeded often in the same things, for
this is great, and can seem no accident, but due to himself ;
or, if the incentives and prizes of achievement were first
devised and established on his account. Such is the case of
a man like Hippolochus[1] on whom the first encomium was
written ; or of Harmodius and Aristogeiton, on whose
account the first statues were set up in the market-place[2].
And so with facts of the opposite kind. If you lack topics

---

[1] 'Of Hippolochus nothing is known' (Cope, *Comm.*).

[2] Demosthenes, *Lept.* p. 478 § 70, χαλκῆν εἰκόνα (of Konon), ὥσπερ Ἁρμοδίου καὶ
Ἀριστογείτονος, ἔστησαν πρῶτου. The first portrait-statues of the tyrannicides
were the work of Antênor, and were carried off by Xerxes. Their place was
taken by the work of Critios and Nêsiôtês, which was standing in the market-
place at the time when Aristotle wrote the *Rhetoric*. The earlier statues were
recovered at a later date.

of absolute praise, you must praise by comparison, as Isokrates used to do from the habit of pleading law-suits[1]; and your comparison must be with eminent men; for this amplifies and
39 is noble, if one is better than men of consideration. Amplification naturally falls in the province of Praise,

Of all the topics, that of amplification is most useful in Laudatory branch of Rhetoric, while examples are most useful to the
40 *Deliberative and Enthymemes to the Forensic branch.*

—for it represents an excellence, and excellence belongs to noble things. Therefore, even if you do not compare your man with the eminent, at least you should compare him with the world in general, since excellence is held to reveal virtue. And, universally, of those topics which are common to all speeches, Amplification is most suitable to the Epideictic,—since the actions are taken for granted, so that it remains only to invest them with grandeur and beauty; Illustration is most suitable to Deliberative Speaking, for we judge the future by divination from the past;—Enthymemes are most suitable for Forensic Speaking; since the past, through its obscurity, gives the largest scope to explanation and demonstration.

41   These, then, are the premisses, from which, in almost every case, praise or blame is drawn; the objects, with a view to which we must praise or blame; and the sources of encomia and of reproaches. These ascertained, their opposites are manifest; blame being derived from the opposite things.

1368 b   x. We must next state the number and the nature of the

Forensic Rhetoric. Accusation
2 *and Defence being the elements, and*

premisses from which syllogisms are to be derived in reference to Accusation and Defence. Three things, then, have to be ascertained; the nature and the number of the motives from

---

[1] διὰ τὴν συνήθειαν τοῦ δικολογεῖν, the reading of the inferior MSS, was preferred by Jebb (1) for the reasons given by Vater, (2) because Cicero, *Brutus*, 48, describes Isokrates as having been in the habit of composing forensic orations for the use of others, and because six of these orations are still extant, (3) because Dionysius of Halicarnassus, *Isokr.* c. 18, refers to his forensic orations. Isokrates nowhere *denies* having written for the courts. On the other hand Spengel, Cope, and Roemer prefer accepting the reading of the Paris MS, διὰ τὴν ἀσυνήθειαν. ' Isocrates cultivated the habit of comparing his hero with others in consequence of his want of *actual* practice in the law-courts ' (Cope, *Comm.* i 185).

*the end,
justice or
injustice, we
must begin
by analysing
injustice, and
inquiring
what are the
motives and
aims of wrong-
doing.*

which men do wrong; the states of mind in
which they do wrong; the characters and situations of those whom they wrong. We will first 3
define wrong-doing and then proceed.

Let wrong-doing, then, be defined as doing
harm wilfully against the law. Law is either
special or general. By special law I mean that
written law, under which each community lives; by general
laws, those unwritten ordinances, which seem to be acknowledged on all hands. Men do wilfully such things as they do
knowingly, but not under compulsion. Not all

*Actions are
[1] Voluntary,
from habit,
reason, anger,
or lust;
[2] Involun-
tary, from
chance,
nature, or
force.*

wilful acts are done by moral choice, but all acts
done by moral choice are wilful; since no man
is ignorant of what he deliberately chooses.
The causes, through which men elect to do harm 4
and to do worthless acts contrary to the law, are
Vice and Intemperance; for if people have a
bad quality or bad qualities, in respect to this or these they
are unjust, as well as bad; thus the illiberal man is unjust in
respect to money, the intemperate man is unjust in respect to
the pleasures of the body, the luxurious man in respect to the
means of ease, the coward in respect to dangers; for cowards
leave the comrades of their peril in the lurch through fear; as
an ambitious man will betray for the sake of honour, a passionate man through anger, a lover of victory for the sake of
victory, a bitter man for revenge, a foolish man because he is
deceived about right or wrong, a shameless man through disregard for reputation. And so each of the rest will do wrong
in respect to the subject-matter of his vice.

All this, however, is clear—partly from what has been 5
said about the Virtues[1], partly from what will presently be
said about the Affections[2]. It remains to say wherefore, and
under what circumstances, men do wrong, and to whom.
First, then, let us determine what things men want to get, or 6
to shun, when they set about doing wrong; for it is plain
that the accuser has to consider what and how many of those

[1] I ix *supra*.   [2] II i-xi *infra*.

objects, with which all men rob their neighbours, exist for his adversary; the defendant has to consider what, and how
7 many of them, do *not* exist. Now, all men do all things, either of themselves, or not of themselves. Of those things, which they do *not* of themselves, some are done by chance, some of necessity. And necessary acts are done either perforce or by nature; so that all things, which men do, *not* of
1369 a themselves, are done either by chance or by nature or perforce. Actions which men do of themselves, and of which they are themselves the causes, are done either from habit or
8 from appetite, rational or irrational. Now *wish* is an appetite of good; for no one wishes, unless he thinks the thing good: the irrational appetites are anger and lust. So that every act of men must have one of seven causes—chance, nature,
9 force, habit, reason, passion, lust. It is superfluous further to discriminate men's acts according to their ages, or their moral states; for, if it is incidental to youth to be passionate or lustful, yet youths do corresponding acts, not through their youth, but through anger or lust. Wealth, again, and poverty are not causes; rather it is incidental to the position of poor men that they desire money because they lack it, and to the position of rich men that they desire needless pleasures, because they command them: but these men, too, will act accordingly, not through wealth or poverty, but through desire. Likewise the just and the unjust and the rest, who are said to act in accordance with moral states, will act through the above-named causes; either from reason or from some affection; some, however, from good dispositions and affections, some
10 from the opposite. It is incidental, however, to this or that kind of moral state to be attended by this or that kind of impulse; for, no sooner is a man temperate than, because he is so, he is presumably prone to good opinions and desires in regard to pleasant things; and the intemperate man, to their
11 opposites. Such distinctions, then, may be left alone; we need only consider on what sort of conditions given results usually depend. For instance, no one of the results noticed above is regularly dependent on a man being fair or dark or tall or short; but, whether he is young or old, or just or

unjust—*this* makes a difference. And generally all those accidents are important, which make a difference in men's characters ; for instance, it will make a difference in a man whether he thinks himself rich or poor, prosperous or unfortunate. These points, then, shall be discussed by and by[1] : let us first finish the matter in hand.

Those things happen by chance, of which the cause is 12 indefinite and which do not happen on account of anything, or always, or usually, or regularly : the definition of chance, however, will make all this clear. Things happen naturally, 13 of which the cause is in themselves, and regular ; for they 1369 b have the same issue, either always or usually. As to things contrary to nature, there is no need to enquire minutely whether they happen according to *some* nature or other cause ; chance, however, would seem to be the cause of these also. Acts are done perforce, which are done contrary to desire, or 14 to calculation, by the agents themselves. Acts are done from 15 habit, which men do because they have often done them. Acts are done by calculation when, being in the number of 16 the above-mentioned goods, and seeming expedient as ends or means, they are done because they are expedient ; since intemperate men, also, do some expedient things, — not, however, because they are expedient, but because they are pleasant. The acts done through passion and anger are acts 17 of retribution. There is a difference between retribution and chastisement ; chastisement being inflicted for the sake of the patient, retribution for the satisfaction of the agent. As to 18 the nature of Anger, that will appear from what we say on the Affections[2] ; the acts done through desire, are such as seem pleasant. A habit, whether unconsciously or painfully acquired, is among pleasant things ; for there are many things which are not naturally pleasant, which people do with pleasure, when accustomed to them. Thus, to put it shortly, all things which men do of themselves are good or apparently good, pleasant or apparently pleasant : for I reckon among goods riddance from evils or apparent evils, and the

---

[1] II xii–xvii *infra.*   [2] II ii *infra.*

exchange of a greater evil for a less, since these things are in their way desirable; and, similarly, I count among pleasures riddance from a pain or apparent pain, and the exchange of a greater pain for a less. We must ascertain, then, the number 19 and nature of things Expedient and Pleasant. The Expedient has already been discussed under the head of Deliberative Rhetoric[1]: let us now speak of the Pleasant. Our definition is to be considered adequate in each case if, without being exact, it is clear.

xi.   Let us assume, then, that Pleasure is a kind of motion of the soul, and a settling, sudden and sensible,

The analysis of Forensic
2 *Rhetoric continued.*
1370 a *Popular definition and analysis of Pleasure and 'the pleasant.'*

into our proper nature; and pain the contrary. If pleasure is this kind of thing, plainly the pleasant is that which tends to produce the condition described; while that which tends to destroy it, or to produce the opposite, is pain-

3 ful.   It must be pleasant, then, as a rule, to conform with nature, particularly when the things done according to the general law have their special natures satisfied. Habits, too, must be pleasant; for an acquired habit comes to be as a natural instinct,—habit having a certain likeness to nature; for 'often' and 'always' are neighbours, and nature is concerned with the invariable, as habit 4 with the frequent.   That is pleasant, too, which is not done perforce; for force is against nature; wherefore the compulsory is painful, and it has been rightly said,

'Every compulsory thing is grievous.'[2]

Acts of attention, earnest or intense efforts, must be painful, for they involve compulsion and force, unless one is accustomed to them; and then the habit becomes a sort of pleasure. Again, the opposites of these are pleasant; so opportunities of ease, moments of respite from toil or attention, sports, seasons of repose and sleep are among pleasant things; for none of 5 these is compulsory. Everything, too, is pleasant of which the desire exists in one; for desire is appetite of the pleasant.

[1] I vi *supra.*
[2] Euenus, fragm. 8, Bergk, ed. 4.

Desires are either irrational or rational.   By irrational desires
I mean those, which men form on no definite theory ; such
being those which are called natural, as the bodily desires,—
for instance, the desire of nourishment, namely, hunger and
thirst, and so in each kind, with reference to taste, touch,
smell, hearing, sight.   Rational desires are those which men
form on conviction ; for men desire to see and possess many
things, because they have heard of them and have been convinced.   And since to be pleased is to experience a certain   6
feeling, and imagination is a kind of weak perception[1], the
man who remembers or hopes must always be haunted by a
certain image of that which he remembers or hopes.   If this
is so, it is clear that there are pleasures, since there is perception, both for those who remember and for those who
hope.   So it follows that all pleasures consist either in per-   7
ceiving things present, or in remembering things past, or in
hoping things future ; for men perceive the present, remember
the past, hope the future.   Now remembered things are pleasant,   8
not only in those cases in which they were pleasant at the   1370 b
time, but sometimes, though they were unpleasant ; provided
that their sequel be noble and good : whence the saying

<blockquote>' Sweet it is from safety to look back on toil.'[2]</blockquote>
And
<blockquote>' A man takes joy afterwards even in griefs, when he looks back upon much
suffered and done.'[3]</blockquote>

The reason of this is, that mere exemption from evil is   9
pleasant.   Things are hoped for as pleasant, which, when
present, appear to bestow great joys or advantages.   And,
generally, all things which, when present, give joy, also supply,
as a rule, pleasures of memory or hope.   Hence it is pleasant
to be angry ;—as Homer said of passion that it is

<blockquote>' Sweeter far than dripping honey'[4] ;</blockquote>

---

[1] See Cope's *Comm.* i 205.   In the sense of ' creative imagination,' φαντασία is
not found until five centuries later, in Philostratus (Sandys, *History of Classical
Scholarship*, i 72, ed. 1906).

[2] Euripides, *Andromeda*, fragm. 133 Nauck, ed. 2.

[3] *Od.* xv 400 f, where the second line runs differently,—ὅστις δὴ μάλα πολλὰ
πάθῃ καὶ πόλλ᾽ ἐπαληθῇ.

[4] *Il.* xviii 108.

for no one is angry with a person, who seems beyond the reach of vengeance, or who is greatly above himself in power;
10 or, if angry at all, he is less angry. And so most of the desires are attended by a certain pleasure; since either the memory or the hope of attainment gladdens people with a pleasurable feeling; as men in the thirst of fever rejoice both
11 in the memory and in the hope of drinking; and lovers delight in talking, writing, or in some way busying themselves about the beloved. Indeed, this is the beginning of love with all men, when they rejoice, not only in the presence, but in the recollection of the beloved, and absence is attended with
12 pain. Similarly, a certain pleasure follows on mourning and lamentation; for, as the pain consists in the loss, so there is a pleasure in remembering the lost, and, in a manner, seeing him as he lived and moved; so that there is truth in the verse

'Thus spake he; and in all of them moved the longing for lament.'[1]

13 Also revenge is pleasant; since what is painful to miss is pleasant to get; and angry men are pained above measure
14 by the loss, as they are rejoiced by the hope, of revenge. To conquer is pleasant, not only to lovers of victory, but to all men; for it becomes an image of superiority[2],—a thing which
15 everybody desires more or less. And since to conquer is
371 a pleasant, it follows that sportive fights and contests are so, as offering many opportunities of victory; also games with the knuckle-bones; games at ball, dice and draughts. So likewise the graver sports; some of them being pleasant, when one is used to them, others from the first, as hunting and every kind of field-sport: for, where there is rivalry, there may be victory. Hence litigation and disputation, too, are pleasant
16 to people with the habit and the faculty. Honour, again, and reputation are among the pleasantest things; since each man comes to imagine that he is such, as the estimable man should be,—especially when people, whom he thinks truthful, say so: and such are the near rather than the distant;—associates

---

[1] *Il.* xxiii 108; *Od.* iv 183.
[2] 'It gives rise to an impression (fancy or notion) of superiority' (Cope, *Comm.* i 210).

and fellow-citizens rather than foreigners; contemporaries
rather than a later generation; prudent men rather than
foolish; many rather than a few: since these, rather than
those, are likely to speak the truth. Thus, no one cares for
honour or reputation (for its own sake, at least) with those,
on whom he decidedly looks down, such as children or beasts;
if he does care, it is for some other reason. Again, a friend is 17
among pleasant things; since to love is pleasant (no one
loving wine, who does not find joy in it), and to be loved is
pleasant; for here, too, one has the imagination[1] of possessing
a goodness, which all, who perceive it, desire. To be loved 18
is to be dear to another for one's own sake. Again, to be
admired is pleasant, simply because one is honoured. Flattery, too, and a flatterer are pleasant things;—the flatterer
being an apparent admirer and friend. And to do the same 19
things often is pleasant; for habit, as we saw[2], is pleasant.
To change is pleasant; for to change is to follow nature; 20
since what is always the same creates an excess of the established state: whence the saying,

'Change of all things is sweet.'[3]

For this reason, too, occasional visitors or things are
pleasant; for it is a change from the present, and, besides,
the occasional has variety. To learn and to admire are 21
pleasant, as a rule; for admiring implies desiring to learn,
so that the object of admiration is an object of desire; and
learning implies coming into the track of nature. Again, the 22
doing and the receiving of benefits are among pleasant things;
for to receive a benefit is to get what one desires; while bene- **1371 b**
ficence implies having enough and to spare;—both which
things are objects of men's ambition. And since the Pleasant
is that which benefits, it is pleasant to men to set their neighbours right, and to complete imperfect things. Again, since 23
learning and admiring are pleasant, it follows that pleasure is
given by acts of imitation, such as painting, sculpture, poetry,
and by every skilful copy, even though the original be un-

---

[1] 'Impression' or 'fancy' (Cope, i 214).   [2] x 18.
[3] Euripides, *Orestes*, 234.

pleasant : for one's joy is not in the thing itself; rather, there is a syllogism—' *This is that* '; and so it comes that one learns

24 something[1]. Sudden reverses and narrow escapes are pleasant,

25 being all in the nature of marvels. Then, since that which is according to nature is pleasant, and kindred things are natural to each other, all things akin to one and like one are pleasant to one, as a rule ;—as man to man, horse to horse, youth to youth ; whence the proverbs, ' mate delights mate,' ' like to like,'[2] ' a beast knows his fellow,' ' jackdaw to jackdaw,' and

26 so forth. And, since everything like and kindred to oneself is pleasant, and a man is like nothing so much as himself, it follows that everybody is more or less selfish, self being the very standard of all such resemblances. And, since everyone is selfish, it follows that all find pleasure in their own things, —for instance, in their deeds and words ; whence people are fond, as a rule, of their flatterers, of their lovers, of honour, of their children ; for their children are their own work. So, to complete imperfect things is pleasant; for at this point the

27 work becomes one's own. And, since to rule is most pleasant, to seem wise is also pleasant ; for intelligence befits a ruler ; and wisdom is the knowledge of many admirable things. Further, since people are, for the most part, ambitious, it follows that it is pleasant to censure one's neighbours, as well

28 as to rule. It is pleasant also to spend one's time in the occupation in which one seems to be at one's best: as the poet says

' Towards this he spurs, giving the greatest part of each day to it,—to the work which shows him at his best.'[3]

29   In like manner, too, since sport and all relaxation are among pleasant things, it follows that causes of laughter must

1372 a be pleasant, whether people, or words, or deeds ;—the subject

---

[1] With the whole of § 23, cp. *Poët.* c. 4 §§ 2–5.

[2] *Od.* xvii 218, ὡς αἰεὶ τὸν ὁμοῖον ἄγει θεὸς ὡς τὸν ὁμοῖον.

[3] Euripides, fragm. 183, Nauck, ed. 2. The whole of this fragment is rendered thus in Cope's *Translation of the Gorgias*, 484 E :—

' Each shines in that, to that end presses forward,
Devotes to that the better part o' the day,
Wherein he chances to surpass himself.'

of the Laughable, however, has been discussed separately in the *Treatise on Poetry*[1].

This account, then, of pleasant things may suffice; the painful things are manifest in[2] the opposites of these.

xii. These, then, are the motives of wrong-doing; let us now consider in what frames of mind men do wrong, and to whom. The agents are ready, when they think that the thing is possible, and possible for them; next, if[3] they think that they can escape detection; or that, if detected, they will not be punished; or that, though they be punished, the punishment is less than the gain for themselves, or for those for whom they care. What things appear possible, and what 2 impossible, will be said by and by[4],—for the subject is common to all kinds of speaking. Those who think that they, personally, can do wrong with the greatest impunity, are those who can speak or act, or who have had experience of many trials, or who have many friends, or are rich. They think 3 themselves most able to do wrong, if they themselves are in the circumstances just named; failing that, if they have friends, assistants, or associates, so situated; for thereby they are enabled to act and to escape detection or to avoid punishment. Or, if they are friends of the persons wronged or of 4 the judges; since friends are not on their guard against wrong, and, besides, make up the quarrel before prosecuting; while judges favour their friends, and either acquit them altogether or inflict light penalties. Men are likely to escape 5 detection, when there is a contrast between the accused and the accusation; as when a weak man is charged with assault and battery, and a poor and ugly[5] man with adultery. Or when the acts are done with great publicity; for such are not guarded against, because they are inconceivable. Or if the 6

The characters which dispose men to do wrong; and which expose men to suffer wrong.

---

[1] Not preserved in the extant *Treatise*.
[2] Literally, ' from,' *i.e.* ' from a consideration of.'
[3] εἶτ' ἐὰν Spengel: the manuscript reading, εἴτε ἂν, is retained by Roemer.
[4] II xix *infra*.
[5] ὁ πένης καὶ [ὁ] αἰσχρός, Spengel, Roemer.

wrongs are so great, or of such a sort, that no one would do them; for against these, again, there is no watch; since it is only against customary wrongs (as against customary maladies) that all men are on their guard;—no one being on his guard against a malady which no one has ever had.

7 Or if the wrong-doer has no enemy or many enemies; as, in the one case, he thinks to escape detection through not being watched, while, in the other, he escapes detection because it seems impossible that he should have attacked vigilant foes,

8 and because he can allege this impossibility in defence. Or if the wrong-doer has means of concealment, or other facilities of disposal.

Again, men do wrong when, if they do not escape detection, they can stave off the trial, or get delay, or corrupt the judges. Or if, supposing a fine to be inflicted, they can stave off payment, or delay it for a long time. Or if[1], through

9 poverty, they have nothing to lose. Or if the gains are manifest, great, or immediate, while the penalties are small,

1372 b uncertain or distant. If, again, there can be no retribution equivalent to the advantage—as seems to be the case with a

10 despotism. And if the wrong deeds are gains, while the penalties are merely disgraces. Or, conversely, if the wrong deeds are in a way praiseworthy (as, if it happened to the wrong-doer at the same time to avenge father or mother, as it did to Zeno[2]), while the penalty consists in a fine, in exile, or the like. Men do wrong for both these reasons, and in both these moods; not the same men, however, but those of opposite

11 characters. Again, people do wrong, if they have often escaped detection or punishment, or have often failed in the attempt; for in crime, as in war, there are men prone to try the issue

12 afresh. Or if the pleasure is immediate and the pain subsequent, or the gain immediate and the loss subsequent; as is the case with intemperate men; and there is intemperance in

13 regard to all the objects of men's appetite. Or if, conversely, the pain or loss is immediate, while the pleasure or advantage is subsequent and more distant;—such conditions being sought

---

[1] ἤ <εἰ> conjectured by Spengel, and accepted by Bekker, ed. 3.
[2] 'Of Zeno's case, nothing is known' (Cope).

by the temperate and the prudent.   Or if there is a possibility   14
of being thought to have done wrong by chance, of necessity,
by nature or through habit,—in short, to have made a mistake,
instead of being guilty of a wrong.   Or if the wrong-doer is   15
sure of equitable consideration.   Or if he is needy,—'needy'
meaning two things,—in need of something necessary, as poor
men are, or in need of a superfluity, as rich men may be.
Wrong is done, again, both by the very respectable and by   16
the very disreputable; by the former because they will not
be suspected, by the latter because they have no character to
lose.

The doers of wrong, then, set to work in these moods; and   17
they do wrong to those persons, or to the possessors of those
things, of which they themselves stand in need,—in reference
either to necessaries or to superfluities or to enjoyment,
whether such persons are distant or near; in the latter case,   18
the gain is speedy, in the former, the retribution is slow,—as
it is for plunderers of the Carthaginians[1].   They, too, are   19
objects of injury who are not cautious or vigilant, but trust-
ful; for it is always easy to elude their notice.   And easy-
going people; for it is the keen man who prosecutes.   And
shy people; for they are not apt to fight about gain.   And   20
those who have been wronged by many without prosecuting,
—these seeming, as the proverb has it, 'Mysian spoil.'[2]   And   21
those who have never, or who have often, been wronged;
both being off their guard,—the former, as being secure, the
latter, as being now exempt.   And those against whom people   22
are, or may easily be, prejudiced; for such people neither
choose to appeal to judges whom they fear[3], nor have the
power to persuade; among whom are the hated or disliked.

---

[1] The Latin transl. has *Calcedonios*; Gaisford conjectured Χαλκηδονίους;
Spengel τοὺς Καλχηδονίους ἢ Καρχηδονίους, the former being near at hand, the
latter far off.

[2] Plato, *Gorgias*, 521 B; Dem. *De Corona*, § 72.   The proverb refers either to
the helplessness of the Mysians at some given time, or to their national character
for cowardice (Cope, *Comm.* i 235 f).

[3] The text is improved by Vahlen's proposal οὔτε προαιροῦνται <ἐπεξιέναι>,
φοβούμενοι τοὺς κριτάς, 'such people have neither the will *to prosecute*, from fear of
the judges.'   This is accepted by Roemer.

23 And those against whom the wrong-doer has a pretext, relat-
1373 a ing to their ancestors, themselves, or their friends, for actual
or pretended injury to the wrong-doer, his ancestors, or those
for whom he cares; since, as the proverb says, 'Vice wants
24 only a pretext.'[1]   And enemies and friends; for it is easy to
wrong friends, and pleasant to wrong enemies.   And people
who have no friends.   And people who are not able to speak
or act; since they either do not attempt to prosecute, or make
25 it up, or effect nothing.   And those whom it does not profit
to spend time in waiting for a trial or a payment, as foreigners
or husbandmen; since they compromise the matter at a cheap
26 rate, and are easily induced to desist.   And those who have
done many wrongs, or wrongs of the kind done to them; for
it seems next to no wrong, when a man is injured in the way
in which he had been wont to injure others: I mean, for
instance, if one was to assault a man accustomed to commit
27 outrage.   And those who have done evil to one, or who have
wished to do; for the requital is both pleasant and honourable,
28 and appears next to no wrong.   And those, by wronging
whom one will gratify one's friends or admirers or lovers or
masters or, generally, those in dependence on whom one lives.
And those whose adversary is sure of equitable consideration.
29 And those against whom one has a grievance and with whom
one has already quarrelled; as Kallippos did in the affair of
30 Dion[2]: for such things seem next to no wrong.   And those
who will be wronged by others, if not by oneself,—since here
there seems to be no alternative; thus, Ænesidêmos is said
to have sent the prize of *Kottabos* to Gelon on the latter
enslaving a town, because he had outstripped the giver in his
31 own game[3].   And those, by wronging whom the injurer will

---

[1] 'Any pretext will serve a knave' (Cope, *Comm.* i 237).
[2] Kallippos, the Athenian friend of Dion and the partner of his expedition to
Sicily, ingratiated himself with Dion's mercenaries, whom he incited to murder
their general and thereby made himself master of Syracuse.   Dion, who had been
informed of the plot, took no precautions for his own safety, and accordingly lost
his life.   Aristotle says that Kallippos justified his act by arguing that, as Dion
had obtained knowledge of his designs, and his own life was in danger, this
anticipation of the other was a mere measure of precaution and not a crime
(Cope, *Comm.* i 241 f).
[3] Gelon, the tyrant of Syracuse (485–478), had anticipated Ænesidêmos, the

be able to do many just acts ; the supposition being that the wrong can easily be healed.   Thus, Jason the Thessalian said that one ought to do some wrongs, in order to have the power of doing much right[1].

Again, men do those wrong things, which all or many 32 are wont to do ; for they think to find forgiveness.   And they 33 take things which are easy to hide ; such, for instance, being those which are quickly made away with, as eatables.   Or 34 things which admit of speedy alteration in form, colour, or combination, or which it is easy to put out of sight in many places ; such being portable things, and those which can be stored in small places.   Or a man steals things which are 35 indistinguishable from many things of the same kind already in his possession.   Or he does wrongs, of which the wronged are ashamed to speak,—such as outrages on the women of their household, on themselves, or on their sons.   And wrongs for which it would be thought litigious to prosecute—that is, petty or excusable wrongs.

xiii.   These, then, may be said to be the moods in which 1373 b
Classification of just and unjust actions (*a*) in reference to law, either special or universal, (*b*) as wrongs done to the individual or the community.
men do wrong,—the nature of the wrongs and the wronged,—and the motives.   Let us now discriminate the various kinds of wrong deeds and just deeds, starting from this point.   Justice and Injustice have been defined as being relative to the laws, and to the persons affected ; and this in a twofold way.   I mean that a law is either 2 particular or universal ; the particular law being that which each community defines in respect to itself (a law partly written, partly unwritten) ;—the universal law being that of nature.   For there is a certain natural and universal

tyrant of Leontini, in enslaving some State that was the neighbour of both. Ænesidêmos accordingly sends Gelon a present of eggs, cakes and sweetmeats, the ordinary prize in the game of *Kottabos*, in acknowledgment of his superior dexterity.   The game of *Kottabos* was a Sicilian invention, and success in this game depended mainly on manual dexterity (Cope, *Comm.* i 242 f).

[1] This saying of Jason of Pheræ has its parallel in Robin Hood's plea, that he robbed the rich to give to the poor.   Cp. *Merchant of Venice*, 'To do a great right, do a little wrong' (Cope, i 243).

right and wrong, which all men divine, even if they have no intercourse or covenant with each other ; as, in Sophokles, Antigone is found saying that, in spite of the interdict, it is right to bury Polyneikes, this being naturally right.

'For the life of these laws is not of to-day or yesterday, but from all time, and no man knows when they were first put forth.'[1]

Such, too, is the precept of Empedokles against killing a living creature ; for this is not unjust merely for one community, and just for another ;

'But a universal law, stretching without break through the wide domain of the sky and through the vast earth too.'[2]

Such, again, is the saying of Alkidamas in his *Messeniakos*[3]....

3   Then, as to the object of the wrong, it must be one of two ; as things right or wrong to do are such in respect either of the community, or of an individual member of the community. Therefore wrong deeds and right deeds may have that quality in either of two respects,—in respect to a definite individual or in respect to the community ; thus the adulterer or striker wrongs a definite individual ; the defaulter in military service wrongs the State.

4   All wrongs, then, having been divided into two classes, according as they have respect to the community or to a person or persons, let us, before going further, repeat our
5 definition of being wronged[4].   To be wronged is to be unjustly treated by a voluntary agent ; since wrong-doing
6 has already been defined as a voluntary act.   The person

[1] Sophokles, *Antigone* 456,
    'Not of to-day nor yet of yesterday
    Is this, but everlasting is its life,
    And none doth know what time it came to light' (Cope).
[2] Empedokles, 380, ed. Stürz,
    'Law universal of no human birth
    Pervades the sovereign sky and boundless earth' (Cope).
[3] A declamation justifying the Messenians in their revolt from Sparta. The declamation on the other side is the *Archidâmus* of Isokrates. The scholiast supplies the missing quotation thus : 'God has given freedom to all men ; Nature has made no man a slave' (Spengel and Cope). These words may be regarded as appropriate to the context, in so far as they insist on the *universal law* of Liberty. Alkidamas, a contemporary of Plato, was a popular rhetorician of the school of Gorgias, cp. III iii 3 *infra*.
[4] I x 3.

wronged must be harmed and wilfully harmed; and the
nature of the various harms is clear from what has gone
before. A separate list of goods and of evils has already
been given[1]. As to voluntary acts, they have been seen to be
those which men do knowingly[2]. So it follows that all accu- 7
sations have respect to a public or a private interest, and to
acts either unconscious and involuntary, or voluntary and
conscious; the latter being results either of moral choice or of
emotion. Passion will be discussed when we speak of the 8
Emotions[3]; the objects of moral choice, and the moods in
which it is made, have already been stated[4]. And since people, 9
while admitting an act, often repudiate the accuser's descrip- 1374 a

The definition of an offence often raises a legal issue. It is needful, then, to define and distinguish the principal crimes.

tion of it, or deny the point which the description
assumes;—admitting, for instance, that they have
taken something, but denying that they have
stolen,—admitting that they have struck a blow,
but denying that they have committed outrage,
—admitting intercourse, but denying adultery,
or admitting a theft, but not a sacrilege (since
the property was not consecrated),—admitting that they have
encroached in tilling land, but denying that the land belongs
to the State,—admitting that they have had parley with the
enemy, but denying treason,—it would seem necessary to
define also what is a theft, outrage, adultery; in order that,
when we wish to show the existence or the non-existence of
the offence, we may be able to make our case clear. Now, in 10
all such instances, the question is whether a man is unjust and
bad, or just; for vice and wrong-doing depend on the moral
purpose, and such terms as outrage and theft denote, besides
the fact, the moral purpose; since it does not necessarily
follow that, because one has struck a blow, one has committed
outrage, but only if the blow was struck with a certain motive,
—as for the dishonour of the person struck or the pleasure of
the striker. Nor does it follow that, because a person has
taken something privily, he has stolen, unless he took the

---

[1] I vi.
[2] I x 3.
[3] II ii *infra.*
[4] I xi and xii.

thing to another's detriment[1] and in order to make it his own.
And, as in these instances, so it is in all others.

11   We saw that there are two kinds of rules about right and
wrong, the written and the unwritten. The things about
which laws are express have been stated. The unwritten
12 rules are of two kinds. One kind refers to excess of virtue
or vice,—to acts which merit disgrace or praise,

Distinction between equity and justice.

dishonour or honour, and public distinctions,—
such as gratitude to a benefactor, requital of a
benefit, readiness to help friends, and the like.
The other kind is supplementary of a particular written law.
13 For the equitable seems to be just, and equity is a kind of
justice, but goes beyond the written law. This margin is left
by legislators, sometimes voluntarily, sometimes involuntarily;
involuntarily, when the point escapes their notice; voluntarily,
when they are unable to frame a definition, and it is necessary
to lay down an absolute rule, but not really possible to lay
down more than a general rule; also in cases which inex-
perience makes it hard to define,—such as the case of wounding
with iron of a given size and kind; for life would be too short
14 for a person who tried to enumerate the cases. If, then, it is
impossible to be definite, yet necessary to legislate, one must
speak generally; and so, if even the wearer of a ring lift his
hand against another or strike him, he is guilty of a wrong
1374 b under the written law, but not in reality; and here equity
15 comes in. Now, if the equitable is such as it has been
described, it is clear what sorts of things and persons are
16 equitable or inequitable. Those acts are equitable, which
are to be excused. It is equitable not to take the same
account of mistakes, of wrongs, and of misfortunes: misfortunes being things which could not be reckoned upon,
and which do not result from vice; mistakes, things which

---

[1] All the MSS here have ἀλλ' εἰ ἐπὶ βλάβῃ ἔκλεψε. ἔκλεψε, which is wrongly
inserted instead of ἔλαβε, has been omitted by Bekker. The Latin translation,
in nocumentum eius, a quo accepit, has since enabled Dittmeyer to restore the true
text, ἀλλ' εἰ ἐπὶ βλάβῃ <τούτου, ἀφ' οὗ ἔλαβε> καὶ σφετερισμῷ ἑαυτοῦ. This is
accepted by Roemer. The clause must have dropped out owing to the similarity
between βλάβῃ and ἔλαβε, and, when once the clause had been omitted, its place
was wrongly supplied by the insertion of ἔκλεψε.

might have been reckoned upon, but which do not result from
vice ; wrongs, things which were reckoned upon, and which
resulted from vice.   It is equitable to excuse human failings.   17
Also, to consider the legislator and his meaning, rather than the
law and its letter ; the moral purpose, rather than the action ;   18
the whole, rather than the part ; the past character, invariable
or usual, of a man, rather than his character at this moment.
It is equitable to remember benefits rather than injuries, and
benefits received rather than benefits done.   It is equitable to
be patient under wrong ; to be willing that a judicial sentence
should be nominal rather than real ;—to desire an appeal to   19
arbitration rather than to a law-court,—for the arbitrator looks
to equity, the jury-man to justice,—the arbitrator having been
invented expressly to enforce the claim of equity.

xiv.   In regard then to the cases for equity, this general account may suffice. The greater wrong is that which
comes from greater injustice ; whence the smallest
things may be the greatest wrongs,—like that
with which Kallistratos charged Melanôpos[1]—
viz., having defrauded the curators of the temples[2] of three
consecrated half-obols ; and, conversely, in regard to justice.
This results from a great wrong being potentially included in
the small one; since the stealer of three sacred half-obols
would be capable of any wrong.   Sometimes, then, the greater
wrong is measured thus; sometimes, by the damage done.
That is a greater wrong, for which there can be no equal
retribution, every punishment falling short of it ; or for which   2
there is no remedy ; for this is hard, and indeed impossible,
to punish adequately[3] ; or for which the person wronged cannot get satisfaction,—since such a wrong is irremediable, the

*The topic of
degree,
applied to
injustice.*

---

[1] Kallistratos and Melanôpos, as stated in Xen. *Hell.* vi 3, 2 f, were both
present at the congress at Sparta in 371 B.C.   In Plutarch's *Life of Demosthenes,*
c. 13, they are mentioned as political rivals and opponents, but nothing is known
as to the charge mentioned in the text.   Kallistratos is also named in 1 vii 13.

[2] The ναοποιοί are the ἱερῶν ἐπισκευασταί of Aristotle's *Resp. Ath.* 50 ; neither
term is found elsewhere.

[3] χαλεπὸν γὰρ καὶ ἀδύνατον.   F. Portus proposed χαλεπὸν γὰρ τὸ ἀδύνατον,
Thurot χαλεπὸν γὰρ καὶ <τὸ> ἀδύνατον, and Muretus, approved by Vahlen, χαλεπὸν γὰρ πᾶν ἀνίατον.

3 judge's verdict and the punishment being a remedy. A wrong is the greater, if the person aggrieved by it inflicted heavy chastisement on himself; for the wrong-doer deserves to be chastised still more severely. Thus Sophokles[1], pleading for Euktêmon, when the latter had cut his throat on account of

1375 a the outrage done to him, said that he would not ask for a smaller penalty than the sufferer had awarded to himself.

4 That is a greater wrong, which no one else has done, or of which one has been the first doer, or one of a few. It is a great offence, too, to commit the same mistake many times. That is a great offence, on account of which the means of prevention or punishment were sought and devised. Thus, at Argos a man is punished, if he has been the cause of legislation. Another instance is that of the persons on whose

5 account the prison was built. The more brutal wrong, again, is the greater; and that which was more deliberate; or that which persons who hear of it dread more than they pity. The rhetorical topics of amplification are of this sort;—that a man has abolished or transgressed many restraints, as oaths, plighted faith, pledges, ties of affinity; for here there is an

6 excess of wrong-doing; or that he has done the wrong in the very place where wrong-doers are punished,—as false witnesses do; for, where will not a man do wrong, if he does it even in a law-court? Those, again, are the greater offences, which carry the greater shame. It is a greater offence to wrong one's benefactor; for one does more than one wrong,—first,

7 in injuring, next, in not benefiting. That is a greater wrong, which transgresses the unwritten rules of right; for it is a mark of the better man to be just without compulsion; now, the written laws are compulsory, but the unwritten are not. In another way, that is the greater wrong, which is against the written law; since one, who does wrong where there *is* a danger and a penalty, will also do wrong where there is no penalty.

[1] Not the poet, but a statesman and orator advanced in life at the close of the Peloponnesian war. He was one of the ten πρόβουλοι appointed after the Sicilian disaster in 413 B.C., to devise measures for the public safety, Thuc. VIII 1, *Rhet.* III xviii 6; xv 3 (Cope, *Comm.* i 263).

xv. We have now said what makes a wrong deed greater
or less. Next we must take a rapid survey of the
so-called inartificial proofs, these being proper to
forensic rhetoric. They are of five sorts :—Laws, 2
Witnesses, Covenants, Torture, Oaths.

Analysis of the inartificial proofs.

First, then, let us speak of the Laws, and of the way to use 3
them in accusation or defence. Now it is mani- 4
fest that, if the written law is adverse to the case,
we must rely on the universal law, and on the principles of a
higher equity or justice. Plainly, too, the clause—' I will 5
use my best discretion '—means that one will not absolutely
obey the written laws. Again, it may be urged that equity 6
and the universal law are eternal and immutable, for they are
according to nature ; whereas the written law often changes.
Hence the doctrine in the *Antigone* of Sophokles ;—Antigone
pleads that she buried her brother against the State-law, but
not against the unwritten law :

Laws.

'For these ordinances are not of to-day or yesterday, but for all time...*These*, **1375 b**
then, I was not going to transgress for any man.'[1]

Or it may be argued that justice is true and expedient, 7
but the semblance of justice is not so, and therefore neither is
the written law ; since it does not do the work of a law. Or
that the judge is like an assayer of money, whose part is to
discern spurious from real justice. Or that constant obedience 8
to the unwritten law is the mark of a better man than constant obedience to the written law. It may be noticed, too, 9
if this written law happens to conflict with another approved
law or with itself. Thus, it may happen that one law enjoins
the validity of all compacts, while another forbids the making
of illegal compacts. Again, the ambiguity of the law may be 10
used for the purpose of turning it round and seeing which
construction will fit justice or expediency, and then adopting
that construction[2]. Or if the circumstances for which the law 11
was made have ceased to exist, while the law survives, one

[1] Sophokles, *Antigone*, 456, 458, where the text of Soph. has τούτων ἐγὼ, and
that of Aristotle ταῦτ' οὖν ἐγώ.

[2] καὶ εἰ ἀμφίβολος (ὁ νόμος, χρηστέον αὐτῷ), ὥστε στρέφειν (αὐτὸν) καὶ ὁρᾶν
κτλ. (Cope, *Comm.* i 273).

should try to show this, and in this way to combat the law.

12   Again, if the written law favours the case, one should say that the clause, 'I will use my best discretion,' is not meant to encourage verdicts contravening the law, but to save the judge from perjury, if he does not know what the law means ; that one chooses, not the absolute good, but what is good for one-self ;—that, if a law is not used, it might as well not have been made ;—that it is no gain in any other art to outmanœuvre the doctor, since the expert's mistake does less mischief than the habit of disobeying authority ;—and that the attempt to be wiser than the laws is just what the most approved laws forbid.

13   In regard to laws, these rules will suffice. As to witnesses,
Witnesses.   they are of two kinds, the ancient and the recent ;
          the recent being either concerned or not con-
cerned in the issue. By ancient witnesses I mean the poets and other celebrities whose judgments stand on record. Thus the Athenians used Homer as a witness about Salamis[1], and the people of Tenedos lately made Periander of Corinth a witness against the people of Sigeum[2]. Kleophon[3], too, used against Kritias the verses of Solon, and argued that the house must have been unruly from of old, else Solon would not have written—

          ' Prithee bid Kritias with the yellow locks to obey his father.'[4]

14   Such as these, then, are witnesses for the past. In regard
1376 a to the future, soothsayers are also witnesses : thus Themis-tokles urged naval warfare by referring to the wooden wall[5].

---

[1] *Il.* II 557 f,

Αἴας δ' ἐκ Σαλαμῖνος ἄγεν δυοκαίδεκα νῆας,

στῆσε δ' ἄγων, ἵν' Ἀθηναίων ἵσταντο φάλαγγες.

These lines were quoted by Solon as an 'authority' in favour of the Athenian claim to the possession of Salamis. Line 2 is said by Diogenes Laërtius, *Vit. Sol.* 48, to have been interpolated by him for this purpose. Cp. Quintilian, V 11, 40 (Cope, *Comm.* i 275).

[2] Of this event nothing more is known.

[3] The demagogue tried and condemned in 405 B.C. Kritias was the well-known leader of the oligarchical party opposed to Kleophon.

[4] Solon, fragm. 22 Bergk, ed. 4, εἰπέμεναι Κριτίῃ ξανθότριχι πατρὸς ἀκούειν. The father of this earlier Kritias was Solon's brother, Dropides (Cope).

[5] Herodotus, vii 141, 143.

Proverbs, again, are in the nature of evidence. Thus, if one advises another not to make a friend of an old man, he is supported by the proverb

'Never do a good turn to an old man.'[1]

Again, the principle of killing the sons when one kills the fathers is supported by the proverb

'He is a fool who slays the father and leaves the children behind.'[2]

Recent witnesses are any well-known persons who have decided a point; as their discussions are useful to those who are contending about the same questions. Thus Eubulos[3] used in the law-courts against Chares[4] what Plato said in reply to Archibios[5], that the habit of confessing to vice had gained ground at Athens[6]. Those, too, are contemporary witnesses who, in case they are suspected of perjury, share the risk of the trial. These last testify only to the fact of a thing having been done or not done, being so or not being so; they cannot testify to the quality of an act, as for instance to its being just or unjust, expedient or inexpedient; but contemporary witnesses *not* concerned in the case, are very trustworthy about such qualities also. The most trustworthy of all are the ancient witnesses, since they cannot be corrupted.

The arguments in regard to testimony are these. If one has no witnesses, he may argue that the decision should rest upon probabilities, and that this is the meaning of the juror's oath 'to use his best discretion'; that probabilities cannot be bribed to deceive; that probabilities are never convinced of perjury. If *you* have witnesses, and the adversary has not,

---

[1] Diogenianus, vi 61, iii 89 (Spengel).

[2] 'Foolish is he that slayeth the sire but spareth the children.' Stasinus, *Cypria*, fragm. 22 in Kinkel's *Epicorum Gr. Fragmenta*, i 3.

[3] Eubulos, the orator and political opponent of Demosthenes, cp. *Fals. Leg.* §§ 290–293, and *De Cor.* § 29.

[4] An Athenian general, who succeeded Chabrias in the command of the Athenian fleet in 356 B.C. He was also in command in the Olynthian war (349), and was one of the Athenian generals at the battle of Chaeronea (338).

[5] Otherwise unknown; 'Αρχῖνον was suggested by Meineke.

[6] Meineke assumes that Plato is the Comic Poet of that name, but he makes no attempt to restore the quotation. Possibly it was a trochaic tetrameter, as follows: ὁμολογεῖν εἶναι πονηροὺς ἐπιδέδωκ' ἐν τῇ πόλει. Spengel assumes that Plato is the philosopher; if so, it would be unnecessary to turn the prose into verse.

you may argue that probabilities are irresponsible things, and
that the evidence of witnesses would not have been wanted, if
it had been enough to take a theoretical view of a case.

18   The evidence of witnesses may refer either to ourselves or
to our antagonist, and either to fact or to character.   Plainly,
then, one can never be at a loss for serviceable testimony ;
for, if we have no evidence of fact agreeable to our own story,
or against that of the adversary, at all events we can get
evidence of character, tending to show our own respectability
19   or our adversary's worthlessness.   Particular points about a
witness—as whether he is friendly, hostile, or impartial,—of
good, bad, or indifferent character,—and such-like distinctions
must be argued from commonplaces of the same sort as those
from which we take our rhetorical syllogisms.

20   In regard to Contracts, the resources of rhetoric may serve
to exalt or depreciate their value, to confirm or
Contracts,
1376 b **or other**   to discredit them.   If we have contracts on
documents.
our own side, we will support their credit and
authority ; if they make for the adversary, we will do the
21 opposite.   The method of establishing or destroying the
credit of contracts is just the same as the method of dealing
with witnesses ; since the credit of contracts varies as the
character of the subscribers or custodians.   The existence of
the contract being admitted, we must, if it is on our side,
make much of it ; for the contract is a private and particular
law, and it is not the contract that gives validity to the law,
but the law to a legal contract.   And, universally, the law
itself is a kind of contract ; so that anyone who disobeys or
22 annuls a contract, annuls the law.   Besides, most of the
dealings between man and man—indeed, all voluntary
dealings—are matters of contract ; so that, if contracts are
invalidated, the intercourse of men is abolished.   The other
23 appropriate arguments are obvious.   If the contract is against
us and on the side of the adversary, we may, in the first place,
use those weapons which one would use against an adverse
law—arguing that it would be strange, if we were forced to
comply with all contracts, while we repudiate the duty of

complying with ill-framed and faulty laws. Or, we may argue 24
that the umpire of justice is the judge ; and that, therefore,
he must not look to the contract, but to the higher justice :—
adding that absolute justice cannot be changed by fraud or
force, since it is natural ; whereas contracts may be made
under a delusion, or under compulsion. Further, we ought to 25
see whether the contract is against any law, written or universal ; and, if against a written law, whether against one of
our own or of a foreign country ; next, whether it is contrary
to any other contract, later or earlier ;—arguing, as may suit
us, either that the later contract is valid, or that the earlier
contract is right and the later fraudulent. Then, we should
look to expediency, and see whether the contract may not be
against the interest of the judges ; and so on, with other
topics of the same kind, no less obvious than in the former
case.

Torture is a kind of evidence, and is thought to be trust- 26
Torture.
worthy, because it is attended by a sort of
compulsion. Here, too, it is easy to point out
the available arguments. If the testimony extorted is in our
favour, we must magnify its worth, and say that this is the
only kind of evidence which is absolutely true. If the testi- 1377 a
mony is against us and for the opponent, we may quash it by
saying what is the truth about torture generally,—namely,
that, under compulsion, men are as likely to lie as to tell the
truth, whether they persevere in refusing to tell the truth,
or lightly make a false charge in hope of a speedier release ;
and one should be prepared to refer to cases in point, which
are known to the judges.

[It may also be argued that extorted testimony is not true, since there are
many thick-witted men—men with thick skins, too, and resolute souls—who
endure tortures gallantly ; whereas cowardly and timid men are scornfully bold,
until they have seen the ordeal of the others : so that torture is utterly untrustworthy[1].]

[1] The above sentence, though preserved in the best manuscript, is un-
Aristotelian in language. It is omitted in the old Latin version, and is already
implied in the previous context. It is therefore rejected by Victorius and Bekker,
and by Spengel, who suggests that the copyist may have quoted it from some other
rhetorical treatise (Cope, *Introd.* 201 note).

27   In regard to oaths, four cases may be distinguished. A
person may either tender and accept the oath;
or he may do neither, or one without the other,
—that is he may tender the oath (to his opponent) without
accepting (*i.e.* taking) it himself, or he may take the oath
himself, without tendering it to his opponent.   In addition to
these, there is the case of an oath having been previously
taken by either of the parties.

28   The arguments for *not* tendering the oath are—that men
lightly perjure themselves ;—that the adversary, if he takes the
oath, is sure not to make restitution, whereas, if he does not
take the oath, you think that the judges will condemn him ;
—or again, that you prefer to put your stake upon the honour
of the judges, for you trust *them* and do not trust *him*.

29   If you refuse the oath, you may say—that it represents so
much money :—that, if you had been a knave, you would have
taken it at once—for it were better to be a knave for something than for nothing : 'so, by taking the oath, I should win
at once—by refusing, I risk it ; and so my refusal must come
from a high motive, not from mere fear of perjury.'   And the
saying of Xenophanes[1] is in point—that

'No equal challenge can come from a godless to a god-fearing man'.[2]

It is as if a strong man were to challenge a weak man to strike
30 or to be beaten. If you accept the oath, it is because you
have confidence in yourself, but not in the other.   Then you
may reverse the saying of Xenophanes and argue that the
fair way is not for the godless man to tender the oath and the
god-fearing man to take it ; and that it would be monstrous,
if *you* were not willing to swear to facts, which you ask the
31 judges to affirm under oath by their verdict. If you tender
the oath, you may say that it is religious to leave the decision
to the gods, and that your adversary ought not to require
others to judge for him, as you commit the judgment to him-
32 self.   And you may say that it is absurd for him to refuse an

Oaths.

---

[1] Of Kolophon, founder of the Eleatic school of philosophy.

[2] Xenophanes, fragm. 25, Mullach, οὐκ ἴση πρόκλησις αὕτη ἀσεβεῖ πρὸς εὐσεβῆ,
a trochaic tetrameter, with *hiatus* after αὕτη, and the first syllable of ἀσεβεῖ
lengthened (Cope, i 288).

oath about matters which he expects others to decide under oath.

As it is now clear how we ought to argue in the simple cases, it is also clear how we are to argue when these cases are combined; as, for instance, (1) when you are willing to take the oath but not to tender it, or (2) to tender but not to take it, or (3) to accept and to tender it, or (4) to do neither. Such cases are necessarily combinations of those above-mentioned, and so the arguments, too, must be framed by combination. 1377 b

Suppose that you have already made an oath contrary to your present oath—you must argue that it is no perjury; for wrong-doing must be voluntary, and perjury is wrong-doing; but things done under constraint or delusion are involuntary. And here you should argue that perjury, in particular, depends 33 on the intention, not on the utterance. If, on the other hand, it is your adversary who has sworn conflicting oaths, say that he is subverting all things by breaking his first oath; is it not because oaths are sacred that justice is administered under an oath? 'They expect *you* to observe the oath, under which you sit in judgment, while they do not observe it themselves.' And so on, with the other arguments for exalting the majesty of an oath.

[This, then, may suffice as an account of the inartificial proofs.]

BOOK II[1]

i. THIS, then, is an account of the premisses to be used in exhorting or dissuading, praising or blaming, accusing or defending, and of the popular notions and propositions available for producing belief in each case; since the enthymemes concern these and come from these, if we take each branch of

2 Rhetoric by itself. And since Rhetoric has a view to judgment, for, both in debates and in lawsuits, there is judging, the speaker must not only see that the speech shall prove its point, or persuade, but must also develope a certain character

3 *The speaker may produce a good impression of his character by means of his speech.* in himself and in the judge, as it matters much for persuasiveness,—most of all in debate, but secondarily in lawsuits too—that the speaker should appear a certain sort of person, and that the judges should conceive him to be disposed towards them in a certain way;—further, that the judges them-

4 selves should be in a certain mood. The apparent character of the speaker tells more in debate, the mood of the hearer in lawsuits. Men have not the same views when they are friendly and when they hate, when they are angry or placid, but views

1378 a either wholly different or different in a large measure. The friendly man regards the object of his judgment as either no wrong-doer or a doer of small wrong: the hater takes the opposite view. The man who desires and is hopeful (supposing the thing in prospect to be pleasant), thinks that it will be, and that it will be good; the man who is indifferent, or who feels a difficulty, thinks the opposite.

---

[1] The arrangement of Book II is singular. In Book I the λογικὴ πίστις,—the third of the ἔντεχνοι πίστεις, was partly analysed. Chapter 20 of Book II returns to this subject, and completes it. But the first eighteen chapters deal with the other two ἔντεχνοι πίστεις,—the ἠθική and the παθητική (R. C. J.).

The speakers themselves are made trustworthy by three 5
things ; for there are three things, besides demon-

He should
make his
audience
feel that he
possesses
intelligence,
virtue, and
good-will.

strations, which make us believe. These are,
intelligence, virtue and good-will. Men are false
in their statements, and their counsels, from all
or one of the following causes. Either through 6
folly, they have not right opinions ; or having
right opinions, they say through knavery what they do not
think ; or they are sensible and honest, but not well-disposed ;
whence they may happen not to advise the best course, although
they see it. Besides these cases there is no other. It follows
that the man who is thought to have all the three qualities
must win the belief of the hearers. Now the means of appear- 7
ing intelligent and good are to be got from the

In this pur-
pose we must
analyse (a) the
virtues and
(b) the moral
affections.

analysis of the virtues[1] ; for the same means will
enable one to give such a character either to
another person or to himself. Good-will and
friendliness have now to be discussed under the
head of the Affections.[2] The Affections are those things, being 8
attended by pleasure or pain, by which men are altered in
regard to their judgments ;—as anger, pity, fear, and the like,
with their opposites. In respect to each, three 9

In regard to
each of the
affections we
have to see
(1) its nature;
(2) its ante-
cedents;
(3) its objects.

points are to be determined ; in respect to anger,
for instance, in what state men are prone to
anger,—with whom they are wont to be angry,
—and at what things : for, supposing we knew
one or two, but not all, of these things, it would
be impossible to excite anger ; and so in the other cases. As
then, in the former part of the subject, we sketched the available propositions, so we propose to do here also, applying an
analysis of the same kind.

ii. Anger, then, may be defined as an appetite, attended
with pain, for revenge, on account of an apparent

Analysis of
the affections.
Anger and
mildness.

slighting of things which concern one, or of
oneself, or of one's friends, when such slighting
is unmeet. If, then, this is anger, it follows that 2

[1] I ix *supra.*   [2] iv *infra.*

the angry person is always angry with an individual (as with
1378 b Kleon, not with the genus 'man'), and because that individual
has done something, or intended something, against the angry
person or his friends : it follows, too, that all anger is attended
by a certain pleasure which comes from the hope of revenge ;
for it is pleasant to think that one will attain one's aim ; and
no one aims at things impossible for him—the angry man
aims at things distinctly possible for him. So it has been
well said of anger that

> 'It swells in men's breasts far sweeter than honey dripping from the rock.'[1]

A certain pleasure attends on it, not only for this reason,
but also because men dwell in thought on the act of the
revenge. So the image, which then arises, excites pleasure,
like the imagery of dreams.

3   Now, slighting is an active form of opinion about something thought worthless. We think both bad things and good
things worthy of earnestness—and the things which tend to
them. But things which tend to them not at all, or very
little, we deem worthless. There are three species of slighting
4 —disdain, spite, and insolence. The man who disdains,
slights ; for people disdain all things which they fancy worthless ; and what is worthless, they slight. Again, the man
who spites appears to disdain ; for spiting is a thwarting of
wishes, not for the spiter's gain, but for the other's loss.

A man slights, then, not for his own gain. Clearly he
supposes that the other can do him no harm (or he would
fear instead of slighting) ; and also that he is not likely to do
him any good worth mentioning (or he would give heed to be
5 his friend). The man who insults, again, slights ; for insolence is to do and say things which shame the sufferer ; not
in order that anything may accrue to the insulter, or because
anything has been done to him, but in order that he may have
6 joy. Requiters do not insult ; they avenge. The source of
pleasure to the insulters is this,—they fancy that, by ill-
treating the other people, they are showing the greater
superiority.

---

[1] *Il.* xviii 109, quoted in I xi 9, *supra*.

Hence young men and rich men are insolent; they fancy
that, by insulting, they are superior.   Dishonouring is a part
of insolence; and the man who dishonours, slights.   For what
is worth nothing has no honour,—no *price* either as good or
evil.   So Achilles says in his wrath—

> 'He dishonoured me : for he hath taken the prize himself,'[1]

and

> 'Like some dishonoured vagabond,'[2]

—as if it was these things that made him angry.   Men think 7
that they ought to be made much of by their inferiors (1) in
birth, (2) in power, (3) in goodness; and generally, a man
expects honour for that in which he decidedly excels[3],—as, in **1379 a**
respect to money, the rich man excels the poor,—in speaking,
the man of rhetorical faculty excels the man of none ; as the
ruler excels the ruled, and the man, who thinks himself worthy
to rule, excels the man who deserves to be ruled.   Whence
the saying

> 'Great is the anger of Zeus-nurtured kings'[4]

and

> 'Yet afterwards he bears a grudge.'[5]

It is their superiority which makes them feel indignant.
Again, (a man resents a slight) from those to whom good has 8
been done, is meant or was meant, by himself, or by some one
else at his instance, or by one of his friends.

It is now plain, therefore, from what has been said, in what 9
moods men are angry, and with what persons, and at what
things.   Men are angry when they are pained ; for the man
who is pained is aiming at something.   Whether, then, he is
thwarted directly in anything—as, if a thirsty man were
thwarted about drinking—or indirectly, the offence appears
the same ; whether one acts against him, or fails to act with
him, or in any other way annoys him, while in this state of
desire, he is alike angry.   Hence people who are ill, who are 10
in poverty, (who are at war,)[6] who are in love, who are thirsty,

---

[1] *Il.* i 356.   [2] *Il.* ix 648.
[3] The translator here accepts ἐν ᾧ ἄν τις ὑπερέχῃ πολύ,—Spengel's conjecture
for ἐν ᾧ ἂν ταὐτῷ ὑπερέχῃ πολύ.   The Paris MS has ταῦτα ὑπερέχει, and Roemer
ταῦτα ὑπερέχῃ.
[4] *Il.* ii 196.   [5] *Il.* i 82.
[6] πολεμοῦντες added by Bekker, ed. 3.

—generally, who have some ungratified desire—are irascible or easily incensed, chiefly against those who slight their present need. Thus, a sick man is enraged by want of sympathy with his illness,—a poor man, by indifference to his poverty, the wager of a war by indifference to his war, the lover by indifference to his love, and so in the other cases ; ...[1] each person being predisposed by his actual plight to his

11 particular anger. Again, a man is made angry by a result contrary to that which he expects ; for a great surprise is a greater pain, just as, when the desired thing happens, it is a greater joy. Hence it is plain what times and seasons, what circumstances, what periods of life, are favourable to the exciting of anger ; and the more people are under these conditions, the more easily they can be excited.

12   These, then, are the moods in which men are prone to anger ; the persons with whom they are angry are those who laugh at them and jeer them and mock them ; for these insult ;—and those who do them such harms as are signs of insolence. Such are necessarily those which are neither retributive nor of advantage to the doers ; for it seems to

13 remain that the motive is insolence. Men are angry, too, with those who disparage and despise them in regard to the things about which they are most in earnest ; as those who pride themselves on their philosophy are made angry by disparagement of their philosophy, those who are proud of their appearance by disparagement of their appearance, and so

14 forth ; and they feel this much more strongly, if they suspect that the thing in question does not belong to them, or belongs

1379 b to them insecurely, or is not recognised ; for, as soon as they are quite sure that they possess the things about which they

15 are mocked, they do not care. And the anger is felt against friends more than against those who are not such ; for men think that from their friends they deserve good treatment

16 rather than bad. A man is angry, too, with those who are wont to show him honour or regard, if they alter this be-

---

[1] < εἰ δὲ μή, κἂν ὁτιοῦν ἄλλο ὀλιγωρῇ τις > is inserted in the text by Susemihl, followed by Roemer. The old Latin transl. has *si autem non, et quodcunque aliud parvipendat quis.* εἰ δὲ μὴ corresponds to μάλιστα μὲν, four lines earlier.

haviour; for he thinks that he is despised by these persons; else they would go on doing as before. He is angry, too, 17 with those who do not requite his benefits, or who do not make an equal return; and with those who act the contrary way to himself, if they are inferiors; for all such persons seem to despise him,—the latter sort treäting *him* as their inferior, the former sort treating (his benefits as coming) from an inferior.

And men especially resent a slight from men of no account; 18 for the anger caused by a slight is assumed to be directed against those whom it does not become to inflict it, and it does not become inferiors to do so. A man is angry with his 19 friends for failing to speak well of him, and to do him good,— still more for speaking and doing evil; or for failing to perceive his need,—as Antiphon's[1] Plêxippos was angry with Meleager; for the non-perception is a sign of slighting; since things, about which we care, do not escape our notice. Again, 20 we are angry with those who rejoice over our misfortunes, or who, in a general way, are made cheerful by them; since this is the token of an enemy or a contemner. And with those who do not care whether they give pain; hence men are angry with the bearers of bad news. And with those who 21 hear of, or behold, their weaknesses; since these are like contemners or enemies, since friends share one's pain, and all men feel pain in contemplating their own weaknesses. Fur- 22 ther, men are angry with those who slight them before five classes of people—(1) their rivals; (2) those whom they admire; (3) those by whom they wish to be admired; (4) those whom they revere; (5) those by whom they are revered; a slight in the presence of these makes men especially angry. Again, men are made angry by slights 23 directed against objects which they are bound in honour to vindicate—as against their parents, children, wives, subjects. We are angry, too, with those who do not requite a favour;

---

[1] This Antiphon is the tragic poet mentioned in II vi 27. The text here refers to his *Meleager*, two lines of which are quoted in II xxiii 20. Plêxippos was the brother of Meleager's mother, Althea. Cp. Nauck, *Trag. Gr. Fragm.*, p. 792, ed. 2.

24 for the slighting is undue[1]. And with those who meet our
25 earnestness with irony ; for irony implies disdain. And with
those who do good to all others, if they do not do good to us ;
for it is a mark of disdain to rate us below the whole world[2].
26 Forgetfulness, again, tends to produce anger,—forgetfulness
of names, for instance, small as the matter is ; since forgetfulness, too, seems to be a sign of slighting ; for forgetfulness
comes through carelessness, and carelessness is a kind of
slighting.

27   The persons, then, with whom men are angry ; the moods
1380 a in which they are angry, and the causes of their anger, have
been stated together. It is plain that it will be necessary to
bring the judges by our speech into a mood which lends itself
to anger, and to represent our adversaries as guilty of these
things, at which men are angry, and as the sort of people,
with whom they are angry.

iii. And since growing mild is the opposite of growing
angry, and anger of mildness, we must ascertain in what moods
men are mild, and towards whom, and by what means they are
2 made mild. The process of making mild, then, may be de-
3 fined as the allaying and calming of anger. If, then, men are
angry with those who slight them, and slighting is a voluntary
act, plainly men are mild towards those who do nothing of
this kind, or who do it involuntarily, or who seem to be of
4 such a character ;—towards those who meant the opposite of
what they did ;—towards those who treat themselves in the
5 same way,—for no one is supposed to slight himself ;—towards
those who confess their fault and are penitent ;—for we accept
this pain for the offence as satisfaction, and forego our anger.
A case in point is the punishing of servants :—we chastise
more severely those who bandy words with us and deny the
fault, but we cease to be displeased with those who admit the
justice of the punishment. The reason is, that denial of the

---

[1] παρὰ τὸ προσῆκον γὰρ ἡ ὀλιγωρία, 'for the slight is a violation of the *natural*
claim, duty, or obligation' (Cope, *Comm.* ii 30 f).

[2] lit. 'to consider us unworthy to be treated in the same way as every one else'
(Cope, ii 31).

manifest is shamelessness; and shamelessness is a kind of slighting and disdain; at least we feel no shame before those whom we greatly disdain. Again, we are softened towards 6 those who humble themselves before us and do not gainsay us; for they seem to admit their inferiority; inferiors feel dread; and no one slights while he dreads. That anger is disarmed by humility, the very dogs show, when they abstain from biting those who sit down[1]. We are softened, too, towards 7 those who deal earnestly with our earnestness; for this earnestness seems to exclude disdain;—towards those who have laid 8 us under obligations; towards those who entreat and deprecate,—for, so far, they are humble;—towards those who do 9 not insult, jeer or slight anyone, or any good man, or anyone like ourselves. And, generally, the things which make men 10 mild are to be inferred from the things which make them angry. We are not angry with those whom we dread or revere, so long as we have those feelings; for it is impossible to feel fear and anger at the same time. With those, again, 11 who acted through anger, we are not angry, or we are less angry; since they do not appear to have meant a slight:— for no one who is angry slights, as slighting is painless, while anger involves pain. And we are mild towards those who revere us.

Plainly, too, men are mild under the conditions adverse to 12 anger,—as in sport, in laughter, at a festival, in good days, **1380 b** in success, in fulness of content,—and generally, in painlessness, and in pleasure, which is not insolent, and in a worthy hope. Also, if a long time has gone by, and their anger is no 13 longer fresh,—for time cures anger. And an earlier vengeance taken upon one person can cure a stronger anger against another; so that Philokrates[2] was right when some one said —'The people is angry—why do you not defend yourself?'— and he answered, 'No, not yet'; 'When, then?'; 'When I see that some one else has been slandered.' Men become mild when they have spent their anger on some other head—

---

[1] Homer, *Od.* xiv 29–31.

[2] Philokrates, whose name is best known in connexion with the 'Peace of Philokrates' (346 B.C.), was impeached by Hypereides and went into voluntary exile in 343.

as happened in the case of Ergophilos; for, though they were
more irritated against him, than against Kallisthenes, they
acquitted him, because the day before they had doomed
14 Kallisthenes to death[1]. Men are softened, too, if they pity[2],
or if the offender has suffered a greater ill than the angry
persons would have inflicted; for they think that, in a way,
15 they have received satisfaction. Or, if they think that they
themselves are in the wrong and are suffering justly; for
anger does not arise at what is just, since men no longer think
that they are suffering unduly; but anger, we saw, implied
this. Hence it is well to reprove before we punish; for then
16 even slaves resent punishment less. Men relent, too, if they
think that the offender will not perceive that he is punished
on their account, and in return for their sufferings; for anger
is against the individual—as is plain from the definition.
So there is truth in the verse—

> 'Say that it was Odysseus, sacker of cities,'[3]

—as if the Cyclops would not have been punished, unless he
perceived both for whom and for what he was punished.
Hence we are not angry with such as have no consciousness of

---

[1] In 362 B.C. Athens was at war with Perdikkas III, king of Macedonia, and
also with Kotys, king of Thrace. Kallisthenes was in command against Perdikkas,
and, without authority from the people, made terms with him. Ergophilos was
beaten back by Kotys.

Kallisthenes was put to death. From Aeschines, *De falsa legat.* § 30, it appears
that his condemnation was commonly ascribed to his defeat; but that the Athenians
were at least ashamed of this report, since Aeschines takes credit for having denied
it (A. Schaefer, *Dem. und seine Zeit*, ii 14).

[2] (1) καὶ ἐὰν ἐλεῶσι, a reading due to the corrector of the Paris MS, accepted by
Bekker and Spengel. Spengel points out that ἐὰν ἐλεῶσιν must be taken closely
with what follows:—if they pity the offenders, *on the ground that* they have suffered
&c. It would be a truism to say absolutely that 'if they pity' they are appeased :
ἐὰν ἐλεῶσιν [καὶ] is merely a way (Spengel thinks) of prefacing the statement of a
special ground for pity, that is, for clemency. (2) The ordinary text, καὶ ἐὰν
ἕλωσιν means, 'if they have *convicted* him.' Spengel objects that this, if taken of
judicial conviction, clashes with ὥσπερ εἰληφέναι. Why? if there is a full stop at
ἕλωσιν? The real thing, and the image of the thing, will then be kept distinct
(R. C. J.). καὶ ἐὰν ἕλωσιν is retained by Roemer, who defends it by quoting Plato's
Rep. 558 A, ἡ πραότης ἐνίων τῶν δικασθέντων οὐ κομψή; κτλ., which is only parallel
to the present passage (πρᾶοι γίγνονται), if πραότης κτλ. means 'mildness towards
the condemned' (see Adam, *Rep.* vol. ii 312 f).

[3] *Od.* ix 504.

us, nor are we any longer angry with the dead, deeming that
they have paid the last penalty, and can no more have that
conscious pain which the angry man aims at exciting. So
the poet says well, speaking of Hektor, and wishing to cure
Achilles of his anger against the dead—

'Indeed, 'tis the dull earth he vexes in his fury.'[1]

It appears, then, that those who wish to soothe must use 17
these topics, bringing their hearers into the moods described,
and representing those with whom their hearers are angry as
formidable, as worthy of reverence, as having conferred favours,
as unwilling offenders, or as very sorry for what they have
done.

iv. Let us now state the objects and the causes of men's
Friendship friendship and hatred,—after first defining friend-
and hatred. ship and friendliness. Friendship, then, may be 2
defined as wishing for a person those things which one thinks
good,—wishing them for his sake, not for one's own,—and
tending, in so far as one can, to effect these things. A friend 1381 a
is one who likes, and is liked in return ; and men think themselves friends, when they think that they are thus related to
each other. This granted, it follows that a friend is one who 3
rejoices in our good and grieves for our pain, and this purely
on our account. All men rejoice at the occurrence of what
they wish, and grieve at the reverse ; so that the feelings of
pain or pleasure point to the wish. They are friends, then, 4
for whom the same things are good and evil, and who are
friends and enemies of the same people ; for they must needs
have the same wishes ; and so, one who wishes for another
just what he wishes for himself, appears to be that person's
friend. Men like, too, those who have done good to them- 5
selves, or to those for whom they care ;—whether such benefits were great, or zealously done, or done at such or such a
moment, and for the recipient's sake.

We like also those who, we think, wish to do us good.
We like our friends' friends, and those who like the persons 6

[1] *Il.* xxiv 54.

whom we like; and those who are liked by those that are
7 liked by ourselves; and those who are the enemies of our
enemies—who hate the persons whom we hate—who are
hated by the objects of our hatred; for all these consider
the same things to be good as ourselves, so that they must
wish our good,—and this, we saw, is the part of a friend[1].
8 Also, we like those who are apt to benefit us pecuniarily, or
in regard to the protection of life; hence we honour the
9 generous and brave, and the just.   Such we conceive to
be those, who do not live on others; and such are they,
who live by labour,—chief among these, agriculturists, and
10 chief among the agriculturists, the small farmers.   We like
temperate men, too, because they are not unjust; and men
11 who are no meddlers, for the same reason.   We like those
whose friends we wish to be, if they show themselves willing;
and such are the morally good and those held in repute either
by all or by the best or by those whom we ourselves admire,
12 or by those who admire us[2].   Again, we like those who are
pleasant to live with, and to pass one's time with—such being
the good-tempered,—those who do not tend to expose our
mistakes,—those who are not disputatious or quarrelsome;
for all such are combative, and combatants seem to wish
13 against us.   Men are liked, too, who have tact in giving and
taking badinage; for the good-humoured butt, as well as the
14 judicious joker, has the same drift as his neighbour[3].   We
like those who praise the good things which we possess,

---

[1] As defined in § 2.

[2] ἢ ἐν τοῖς θαυμαζομένοις ὑφ' αὐτῶν ἢ ἐν τοῖς θαυμάζουσιν αὐτούς, so Bekker
(and Roemer). If this is right, ἐν ἅπασιν and ἐν τοῖς βελτίστοις must mean
persons, not *things*.   (All the MSS have ἐν οἷς θαυμάζουσιν followed in the
inferior MSS by αὐτούς, and in the Paris MS by αὐτοί.)   Spengel, with the Paris
MS, has ἢ ἐν οἷς θαυμάζουσιν αὐτοί, bracketing the previous clause, which is
identical in meaning; for the clause in brackets he proposes to substitute ἢ ἐν οἷς
θαυμάζονται αὐτοί—but this topic comes below.   What is the objection to Bekker's
text? (R. C. J.).   The only objection is that it departs from the reading of all the
MSS by changing οἷς into τοῖς, and abandons the Paris MS by accepting αὐτούς.
Jebb's note shows that he preferred *Bekker's* text; his translation of *Spengel's* text
('the morally good and *the distinguished—whether in all things or in the best
or in those which we ourselves admire*') has been altered accordingly.

[3] 'The mind of each party is set upon the same thing as his neighbour,' *i.e.*
on mutual amusement (Cope, ii 48).

especially those which we fear we do *not* possess. We like 15
those who are cleanly in their person, their dress, their whole
life. We like those who do not reproach us with our mis- 16
takes, or their benefits; for both tend to put us in the wrong. 1381 b
We like those who do not bear a grudge, who do not hoard 17
their grievances, but are ready to make up a quarrel; for we
think that they will be to ourselves such as we conceive that
they are to the rest of the world. We like those who are not 18
evil-speakers, and who know, not the bad, but the good, in
their neighbours and in us; for this is the part of the good
man. We like those who do not strain against the angry or 19
the eager; for such are combative. We like those who have 20
some earnest feeling towards us, as admiration, a belief that
we are good, or a delight in us; especially when this is felt
about the things, for which we ourselves most wish to be
admired, or to be thought good or pleasant. We like those 21
who resemble us and have the same pursuits, provided that
they do not thwart us, and that our livelihood does not come
from the same source; for then it becomes a case of ' potter
against potter'[1]. We like those who desire the same things, 22
—provided it is possible for us to enjoy them at the same
time: if not, the last case is repeated. We like those to whom 23
we are so related that, while we do not despise them, we do
not feel shame with them as to appearances; and those before 24
whom we *are* ashamed of the things really shameful. We
like those with whom we vie, and those by whom we wish to
be emulated, not envied; to these we are, or wish to be,
friends. We like those, with whom we work for good, sup- 25
posing that we ourselves are not to have greater ills. We are
friends to those who show kindness equally to the absent and
to the present; hence all men like those who are thus true to 26
the dead. And, generally, we like those who are strongly
attached to their friends, and do not leave them in the lurch:
for, of good men, we most like those who are good at liking.
We like those, too, who do not sham to us; and such are they 27
who speak even of their own weaknesses. For, as has been

---

[1] 11 x 6 *infra*; Hesiod, *Op. et D.*, 15,

καὶ κεραμεὺς κεραμεῖ κοτέει καὶ τέκτονι τέκτων,
καὶ πτωχὸς πτωχῷ φθονέει καὶ ἀοιδὸς ἀοιδῷ.

said, we feel no shame with friends about appearances. If, then, one who feels such shame is not a friend, he who does

28 not feel it, resembles a friend. We like those who are not formidable, and with whom we feel confidence[1]; for no one likes

29 him whom he dreads. The several species of friendship are —Companionship, Intimacy, Kinship and the rest. Among the *things* which cause friendship are graciousness—doing a thing unasked—and doing without publishing it; for so it seems to be done simply for our own sake.

30   Enmity and Hatred of course may be illustrated by the
1382 a   opposite considerations. Among things which
    Hatred.
31   cause Enmity are anger—spiting—slander. Now anger arises from things which concern ourselves; but Enmity may exist without this personal concernment; since, if we conceive a person to be such or such, we hate him. Anger is always concerned with particulars, as with Kallias or Sokrates; Hatred is directed also against classes; for everyone hates a thief and an informer. Anger can be cured by time; Hatred is incurable. Anger is an aiming at pain; Hatred, at evil; for the angry man wishes the other to feel; the hater does not care. Now, painful things are all to be felt; but the worst evils are the least to be felt,—Injustice and Folly; for the presence of the vice gives no pain. Anger is attended with pain, hatred is not; for the angry man is pained, but not the hater. The angry man is capable of pity, when much has happened,—the hater, never; for the one wishes the object of his wrath to suffer in return,—the other wishes him not to be.

32   Hence, then, clearly we can prove that people *are* enemies or friends; or, if they are not, make them such; or, if they pretend, refute them; or, if they contend with us through anger or through enmity, bring them into whichever mood we choose[2].

---

[1] οὓς θαρροῦμεν the reading of the Paris MS, supported by the old translation, and accepted by Bonitz, and Spengel, and Roemer; the inferior MSS have οἷς θ., adopted by Bekker; Shilleto conjectured οὓς ('in whose presence'), which proved to be the reading of the best MS.

[2] (1) If they are angry, to greater anger or to friendliness; if hostile, to greater enmity or to mildness; or (2) if angry, to mildness; if hostile, to friendship. (1) seems best. Does the plural favour (1)? (R. C. J.)

v. The objects of fear, whether things or persons, and the moods in which men fear, will be seen from what follows. Fear may be defined as a pain or trouble arising from an image of coming evil, destructive or painful; for men do not fear *all* evils,—as, for instance, the prospect of being unjust or slow; but only such evils as mean great pains or losses, and these, when they seem, not distant, but close and imminent. We do not fear very distant things; thus, all men know that they will die, but because it is not near, they do not care. If, then, fear is this, such things must 2 be fearful as appear to have a great power of destroying, or of doing harms which tend to great pain. Hence the signs, too, of such things are fearful, since the dreaded thing seems near; for this is danger, the approach of something dreaded. Among 3 such things are the enmity and anger of persons who can *do* something: for it is plain that they have the will, and so they are close to the act. Again, injustice armed with power is 4 terrible; for the unjust man is such in virtue of his choice to do wrong. Outraged virtue, when it has power, is terrible; 5 for plainly, when it is outraged, it *wills* to punish, and in this **1382 b** case it is *able*. Again, fear felt by those who can do some- 6 thing is fear-worthy; for such persons, too, must be in the act of making ready. And since most people are more or less 7 bad,—unable to resist lucre, and cowards in danger, it is terrible, as a rule, to be in another man's hand; and so the accomplices of a criminal inspire him with the fear that they will denounce him, or leave him to his fate. Also, those who 8 can wrong are formidable to those who can be wronged; for, as a rule, men do a wrong when they can. Those, too, who have been wronged, are formidable; for they are always biding their time. And those who have done a wrong, if they have power, are terrible, being afraid of requital;—for we saw above[1], that powerful injustice was terrible[2]. We fear, 9 too, those who are our competitors for things which cannot belong at once to them and us;—we are always at war with such persons. And we fear those who ought to be feared by 10

Fear.

---

[1] § 4 *supra.*

[2] ὑπέκειτο γὰρ τὸ τοιοῦτο φοβερόν. τὸ τοιοῦτο—this general character. (R. C. J.)

our betters (since, if they can hurt our betters, rather will they be able to hurt us);—and, for the same reason, those
11 whom our betters actually fear. We fear those, too, who are attacking our inferiors; for they are to be feared, either already, or when they shall have grown. Among our victims, our enemies or antagonists, we fear, not the quick-tempered, and outspoken, but the mild, the ironical, the unscrupulous; for it is uncertain, whether they are close on us, and so it is
12 never plain that they are far off. All formidable things are more so, in which a mistake cannot be repaired,—whether it is absolutely irreparable, or reparable only at the discretion of our enemies, not at our own. Those things are formidable, too, for which there is no help, or no easy help. And, generally speaking, those things are fearful to us, which, when they befall or threaten others, are piteous.

These, then, may be said to be the chief things which deserve or which excite fear. Let us now describe the moods
13 of the fearers. Now, if fear is attended by an expectation of some destructive suffering, it is plain that no one fears unless he thinks that something will happen to him; nor does he fear things, which he does not think will happen, or persons, at whose hand he does not expect them, or at times when he does not expect them. It follows, then, that those who fear are those who expect to suffer something—and this from certain persons and in a certain form and at a certain time.
14 Suffering is not expected by those who are, or seem to be,
1383 a in great prosperity—whence they are insolent, supercilious, and rash, the things which make such characters being wealth, strength, multitude of friends, power—nor by those who fancy that they have already suffered every horror, and are callous to the future, like those who are on the point of being beaten to death. There must be left some hope of deliverance from that, about which they feel trepidation. Here is a token:— fear makes men deliberative; but no one deliberates about
15 hopeless things. We must therefore bring our hearers into this state of mind, when it is better for them to fear, that they are liable to suffering;—arguing that greater people have suffered—showing, too, that persons like them are suffering,

or have suffered, and this from persons at whose hands they did not think to suffer, and in a way, and at a time, which they did not expect.

It being manifest what fear is—what things are fearful— 16 and in what several moods[1] men fear, it is further

Boldness. manifest from this, what it is to be bold, and about what things men are bold, and under what conditions ; for boldness is the opposite of fear, and that which emboldens of that which terrifies ; so that the hope is attended by an image of salutary things as near, and of terrible things as non-existent or far off. We are emboldened both by the distance 17 of danger and by the nearness of comfort. Also, if the means of amendment and succour are many, or great, or both ; or if people have neither suffered nor done a wrong ; and if they are not our adversaries ; or if, having power, they are our friends, and have done us good or received good from us. Men are bold, too, if those who have the same interests with them are the larger party, or the stronger, or both. And 18 when they themselves are in the following circumstances :— when they think that they have succeeded in much and suffered little, or when they have often come into danger and escaped. For men are made indifferent to peril by two things —by want of experience, and by having resources ; as perils at sea are faced boldly by those who have never been in rough weather, and by those whom experience has taught how to meet it. We are bold, too, in regard to anything which is 19 not terrible to those like us, or to our inferiors, or to those whose superiors we think ourselves,—that is, to those whom we have conquered, or whose betters or peers we have con-quered. Or if we think that we possess in superior number 20 or degree, those things, excellence in which makes men terrible— these being riches, bodily strength, wealth of **1383 b** friends or land, or of all or the chief munitions of war. Or 21 if we have done wrong to no one, or to few, or not to those of whom we are in fear. Or generally, if we have the favour of the gods, as shown especially by signs and oracles ; for

---

[1] or circumstances. (R. C. J.)

anger gives boldness[1]; to be a sufferer, not a doer of wrong, excites anger; and heaven is supposed to help the wronged. And we are bold when we think that, by our enterprise, we are likely or certain to take no harm, or to succeed.

vi. These are the things which terrify, or embolden. The
things or persons in regard to which men are
Shame. ashamed or shameless, and the conditions in
2 which they are so, will appear from what follows. Shame,
then, may be defined as a pain or trouble about those ills,
present, past or future, which seem to tend to ignominy;
Shamelessness is a kind of negligence or indifference about
3 these things. Now, if Shame is such as it has been defined,
the evils of which men are ashamed must be those which
they think shameful to themselves, or to those for whom they
care. Such evils are all the acts which come of vice—as
throwing down one's shield, or running away; for it is an act
4 of cowardice. Withholding a deposit or doing a wrong; for
5 these are acts of injustice. Intercourse with improper persons
or in forbidden places or at forbidden times; for it comes of
intemperance. Making gain from petty or base sources, or
from helpless persons, such as the poor or the dead (—whence
the proverb, 'to plunder a corpse,')—for this comes from a
6 love of base gain, and from meanness. Not to help another,
when we can, with money, or to help less than one can; or to
7 accept help from those who are worse off. To borrow when
one will be thought to ask a gift,—to ask a gift when one will
be thought to claim a debt, or *vice versa*;—to praise in order
that one may seem to ask,—and this no less, though one has
8 failed—for all these are signs of meanness. It is shameful,
again, to praise people to their faces—to praise their good
points extravagantly, and gloss over their weak points—to
show exaggerated sympathy with one in pain; and the like;
9 for these are signs of flattery. It is shameful not to endure
1384 a toils, which are borne by older men or the luxurious, or by those
higher in authority, or generally by those less fit to suffer;

---

[1] *i.e.* if the gods are with us (in a strife), we have been wronged; this makes us angry, and anger makes us bold (R. C. J.).

for all this is a sign of effeminacy. To receive benefits, or 10 repeated benefits, and to upbraid another with a benefit done; for all such things show a small and abject soul. To talk at 11 large of oneself, and make large promises; or to claim what belongs to others as one's own: for these things show a braggart. And so the acts which come from each of the other moral vices, with their signs and the things like them; for they are shameful, and tend to make ashamed[1]. More- 12 over, it is shameful to have no part in those honourable things, in which all men or all who are like us, or most of them, share. By those like us I mean people of the same race—fellow-citizens, contemporaries, kinsmen, and generally those who are on the same footing with us; for at this point it becomes shameful to be excluded,—as, for instance, not to be educated up to a certain point,—and so in other things. All these deficiences are the more shameful, if they seem to be our own fault; for then they come to be results of vice rather than anything else, supposing that we ourselves are the authors of such things as have belonged to us, or belong, or are to belong.

The things which men are ashamed of suffering, or having 13 suffered, or being about to suffer, are those which tend to dis-honour and reproach; these are such as have to do with subservience in lust or in base deeds,—among which is the endurance of outrage. In relation to intemperance, the suffering is shameful whether willing or unwilling; in regard to compulsion, when it is unwilling; since the endurance and the failure in self-defence must come from unmanliness or cowardice.

These, then, and such-like are the things of which men are 14 ashamed; and since Shame is the imagining of ignominy,—ignominy considered in itself, and not with a view to its con-sequences—it follows that we feel shame before those of whom we make account. Now we make account of our 15 admirers,—of those whom we admire, of those by whom we wish to be admired, of those with whom we vie,—of those

[1] αἰσχυντικά, Bekker; ἀναίσχυντα, 'shameless,' the Paris MS, followed by Spengel.

16 whose opinion we do not despise. We wish to be admired
by those, and we admire those, who possess some good thing
which is honourable ; or from whom we greatly need some-
17 thing of which they are masters,—as lovers need ; we vie with
those like us ; we respect as truth-speakers the intelligent ;
18 and such are the elderly, and the educated. Greater shame is
felt for things done before all eyes and openly ;—whence the
proverb that ' Shame sits in the eyes.'¹ For this reason men
feel more shame of those who will be always with them, or
who give heed to them ; since, in both cases, eyes are upon
1384 b them. We feel shame before those who are not liable to the
same charges ; for it is plain that they hold the opposite
19 views. And before those who are not indulgent to those who
seem to err ; for what a man does himself, he is said not to
resent in his neighbour ; so it is clear that what he resents is
20 what he does not do. Or before those who are apt to spread
a report widely ; for, if no report is spread, it is all one as if
we were not suspected. Those who tend to spread reports
are they who have been wronged—since they are on the
watch—and evil-speakers ; for, if the latter do not spare the
innocent, much less will they spare the guilty. We feel
shame, too, before those who give their whole minds to their
neighbours' mistakes,—as scoffers and comic poets ; for these
are, in a way, evil-speakers and spreaders of reports. We
feel shame before those who have never seen us break down ;
for we are in the position of people who are admired. Hence
we are ashamed to refuse those who make a first request of
us, because we are as yet blameless in their sight ; and such
are they who are just inclining to be our friends ; for they
have seen our best side, (hence the answer of Euripides to the
Syracusans² is good,)—or, among old acquaintances, those

---

¹ Euripides, *Kresphontês*, fragm. αἰδὼς ἐν ὀφθαλμοῖσι γίγνεται, τέκνον.

² According to the scholiast, Euripides, when he was sent as an ambassador to
Syracuse, on finding the Syracusans unwilling to agree to terms of peace and
friendship, said :—'Men of Syracuse, you ought to respect our homage and
admiration, if for no other reason, yet because we have only just begun to ask
favours of you.' This embassy of Euripides is otherwise unknown ; but he was
a favourite in Sicily, and may have been sent on some negociations shortly after
the Sicilian expedition. Droysen thinks it was not the poet, but a trierarch
mentioned by Dem. Or. LX § 68.

who know nothing bad of us.   Men are ashamed, not merely 21
of the shameful things just mentioned, but of their signs,—as
in the case of sexual intercourse; not merely of doing, but
also of saying, what is shameful.   In the same way, we feel 22
shame not only before the persons above-mentioned, but
before those who will inform them, as their servants or friends.
Universally, we are not ashamed before those whose opinion, 23
in respect to accuracy, we greatly despise; thus no one is
ashamed before children or beasts; nor of the same things
before familiar friends and strangers; but, before familiar
friends, about things which seem really shameful,—before
strangers, about conventionalities.

The personal situations in which men are likely to feel 24
shame are these;—first, if they have any people related to
them in such a way as those before whom, as we said, they
feel shame.   These, we saw[1], are those whom they admire, or
who admire them, or by whom they wish to be admired, or
from whom they crave some boon, which they will not obtain,
if they are discredited.   And these persons inspire shame,
whether they are eye-witnesses—(as Kydias made them in his
speech on the settlement of Samos[2], when he asked the
Athenians to imagine the Greeks standing around them)—or
neighbours—or likely to become aware.   Hence men are
unwilling to be seen in their failures by those who once
emulated them; for emulators are admirers.   And men feel 25
shame when they have achievements and fortunes to disgrace, **1385 a**
—whether these are their own, or their ancestors', or belong
to other persons, with whom they have some tie.   And,
universally, we feel shame *on behalf* of those whom we ourselves respect;—such being the persons enumerated and
our dependents; or those whose teachers or advisers we
have been; or those, with the like of whom, perhaps, we
have a rivalry.   Men do much, and refrain from much, 26
through shame on account of such persons.   And they feel 27

[1] § 15 *supra.*

[2] Not the allotment of 440 B.C. but that of 352, subsequent to the re-conquest
of Samos in 366.   It was against the latter allotment that a protest was raised by
Kydias (Cope).   The text is the only reference to Kydias quoted in Sauppe's
Fragments of the Attic Orators, p. 318.

the more shame when they are destined to live in the sight of those who know their disgrace.   Hence, when Antiphon the poet[1] was about to be beaten to death by order of Diony-sios, and saw those doomed to die with him covering their faces, as they went through the gates, he said—'Why do you cover your faces?   Are you afraid of some of these people seeing you to-morrow?'

Shame-lessness.   So far of Shame; as to Shamelessness, of course, the opposite considerations will supply topics.

vii.   Towards whom men feel *favour*, and for what things, and in what circumstances, will appear when we
2 Favour.   have defined favour.   *A favour*, considered as the expression of *favour felt*, may be defined as a service rendered to a man at need, not in return for anything, and not for the doer's, but for the other's gain; it is great, if rendered at urgent need, or in great and hard things, or at such or such a time; or if this is the only, the first, or the greatest
3 instance of its being rendered.   The appetites are needs,— especially those of them which are attended by pain if dis-appointed; and such are the desires, as love.   Again, there are the needs which spring from bodily injuries and dangers; and, both in danger and in pain, a man desires.   Hence those who stand by us in poverty or exile, even if their services are small, have our favour, because the need is great and critical.   Take the case of a man who gave a mat to another
4 at the Lyceum[2].   The service, then, must have reference either to these things,—or else to equal or greater things; so that, since it is plain by whom, and for what things, and in what circumstances, favour is gained, we must of course take

---

[1] The tragic poet, mentioned in II ii 19.   Dionysius is said to have given orders for his execution, either because the poet ventured to criticise the tyrant's tragedies, or because, in reply to the question which was the best bronze in the world, the poet answered that the best was that of which the statues of the tyrannicides, Harmodius and Aristogeiton, was made (Cope, ii 87).

[2] The circumstances are unknown.   The scholiast invents a story (R. C. J.). The incident, whatever it was, must have exemplified the principle that 'a friend in need is a friend indeed.'

our arguments from these topics,—showing that the persons obliged are or have been in pain or want of this kind, and that the others have rendered or are rendering them this kind of service in this kind of need. We see, too, how it is possible 5 to do away with the sense of favour, and to make men ungrateful; we may argue that the service is or was done for **1385 b** the sake of the doers alone ; but this, we saw[1], is not 'a favour' ; —or that it happened by chance, or that the doer was driven to it, or that it was a repayment, not a gift, whether consciously or unconsciously made; for, in either case, it is a return, so that here, again, there can be no 'favour.' And we 6 must take account of all the categories[2]; for the favour is such, as being this thing—or so much—or of this kind—or done at a certain time, or in a certain place. It is a sign that one has not done a favour, if he has failed to do a smaller favour, or if he has done the same favour, or an equal, or a greater, to our enemies ; since plainly neither has he done this for our sake. Or if the doer knew the thing to be trifling ; for no one admits that he is in need of trifles.

viii. We have spoken of showing favour and of ingratitude ; let us now say what things are piteous, what persons men pity, and under what conditions.

Pity may be defined as a pain for apparent evil, destructive 2 or painful, befalling a person who does not deserve it, when we might expect such evil to befall ourselves or some of our friends, and when, moreover, it seems near. Plainly the man who is to pity must be such as to think himself or his friends liable to suffer some ill, and ill of such a sort as has been defined, or of a like or comparable sort. Hence pity is not felt by the utterly lost ; for they 3 think that they cannot suffer anything further ; they *have* suffered :—nor by those who think themselves supremely prosperous,—rather they are insolent ; for, if they think that

Pity.

---

[1] § 2 *supra.*

[2] In c. 4 of the *Categories*, Aristotle enumerates ten :—essence or substance ; quantity ; quality ; relation ; place ; time ; position ; possession or having ; activity ; and passivity (Grote's *Aristotle*, i 93 f). Five of these appear in the text.

they have all goods, of course they think that they have
4 exemption from suffering ill; this being a good. The belief
that they may possibly suffer is likely to be felt by those who
have already suffered and escaped,—by elderly persons, on
account of their good sense and experience,—by the weak,
and especially by the rather timid;—by the educated, for
5 they are reasonable.   By those, too, who have parents,
children, or wives; for these are their own, and are liable
6 to the sufferings above-named. And by those who are not
possessed by a courageous feeling, such as anger or boldness,
for these feelings take no account of the future,—and by those
who are not in an insolent state of mind,—as such are reckless
of prospective suffering:—pity is felt by those who are in the
intermediate states. And by those, again, who are not in
great fear; for the panic-stricken do not pity, because they are
7 busied with their own feeling. Men pity, too, if they think
that there are some people who may be reckoned good; for
he who thinks no one good will think all worthy of evil.
1386 a And, generally, a man pities when he is in a position to
remember that like things have befallen himself or his friends,
or to expect that they may.
8   These, then, are the circumstances in which men pity.
What things they pity, is plain from the definition. All those
things are pitiable, which, giving pain or anguish, tend to
corrupt or utterly to destroy; and those great evils, of which
9 Chance is the cause.   Things which give anguish and destroy
are—death in all forms, bodily tortures or harms—old age,
10 sicknesses, want of food. Ills of which Chance is the cause
are—friendlessness, dearth of friends; separation, too, from
friends and familiar companions is pitiable—and deformity,
weakness, being maimed. It is piteous that an evil should
befall from a quarter whence good fortune was due: or that
11 this should happen often. It is piteous that some good
should come, when all is over with a man; as when, after
the death of Diopeithes[1], the presents from the Great King

---

[1] Diopeithes, the Athenian general in the Chersonesus (344–341), was arraigned
at Athens by the partisans of Philip, and was defended by Demosthenes in his
speech *On the Chersonesus* (341). The date of his death is unknown. The

came down for him.   It is piteous that no good should ever
have happened to a man, or that, when it did happen, he
should have been unable to enjoy it.

The things, then, which excite pity are these and the like;
the persons whom we pity are, first, our friends, if they are not   12
very near friends ; in the case of near friends, we feel as if we
ourselves were threatened.   Hence Amasis[1] shed no tears, they
say, when his son was led to death, but wept when his friend
begged ; for the latter thing was piteous, the former dreadful ;
now the dreadful is different from the piteous, and tends to
drive out pity, and often serves to rouse its opposite.   Again,   13
men pity[2] when the danger is near themselves.   And they
pity those like them in age, in character, in moral state, in
rank, in birth ; for all these examples make it more probable
that the case may become their own ; since here, again, we
must take it as a general maxim that all things, which we
fear for ourselves, we pity when they happen to others.   And,   14
since it is when they seem near that sufferings are piteous,
(while things which are ten thousand years off in the past or
the future, and to which we look neither forward nor back, are
not pitied at all, or pitied in a less degree), it follows that
those who aid the effect with gesture, voice, dress,—in a word,
who dramatise,—are more piteous; for they cause the evil[3]
to seem near by setting it before the eyes as future or past.
And things just past or soon to be are more piteous.   Hence   15, 16
we are moved by the tokens and by the actions of sufferers,—   **1386 b**
as by garments and such-like memorials of those who have
suffered, and by the words or such-like traits of those who
are suffering,—as, for instance, of men at the point of death.

scholiast invents a story of his having been 'banished' by the Persian king.   The
king was Artaxerxes III (Ochus), 362–339 B.C. (R. C. J.).

[1] 569–525 B.C.   Herodotus (III 14) tells the story of his son, Psammenitos, who
reigned only six months and was conquered by Cambyses in 525.   Some regard
this as a slip of memory ; while Spengel thinks that Aristotle may have written
Ψαμμήνιτος ὁ 'Αμάσιος (R. C. J.).

[2] ἔτι ἐλεοῦσιν : Vahlen, approved by Spengel and followed by Roemer,
proposes <οὐ γὰρ> ἔτι ἐλεοῦσιν.

[3] τὸ κακὸν is bracketed by Roemer, who understands τὰ πάθη from the previous
context, thus retaining at the end of the clause the neuter plural participle of the
Paris MS :—ὡς μέλλοντα ἢ ὡς γεγονότα.

And it is especially piteous when the men, who are in such crises, are good men.   All these things excite pity the more, because the evil seems near us ; since the suffering is undeserved, and is also set before our eyes[1].

ix.   The proper antithesis of Pity is what is called Indig-
Indignation. nation ; since pain at undeserved good fortune corresponds in a way to pain at undeserved bad
2 fortune, and springs from the same character.   Both feelings show a good character ; since it is right to feel sympathy and pity for undeserved misfortune, and indignation at undeserved prosperity, because all that happens to a man contrary to his deserts is unjust, and this is why we ascribe indignation even
3 to the gods.   Envy, too, might seem to be opposed in the same way to Pity, as being nearly related to, or identical with Indignation ; but it is different.   Envy also is, indeed, a disturbing pain, and is directed against prosperity ; not, however, the prosperity of an undeserving person, but that of our like or equal.   The condition, that we feel thus, not because anything untoward is to befall us, but on our neighbour's account only, must be present alike in Indignation and in Envy ; for it will be no longer either one or the other, but Fear, if the cause of the pain and the trouble is that our neighbour's good fortune is to have some bad result for us.   And, plainly, these feelings will be attended by their counterparts ; thus, he who is pained by undeserved misfortune will feel joy, or no pain, at deserved misfortune ;—thus, no good man would be grieved at the punishment of parricides and assassins ; such things are matters of rejoicing, and so is deserved good fortune : for both are just, and cause the good man to rejoice, since he cannot but hope that, what has come to one like him, may
4 come to him.   All these feelings belong to the same character as their opposites to the opposite ; for the man who envies is
1387 a also spiteful, since, when one is pained at a thing happening or existing, one must needs rejoice at its being taken away or

---

[1] The evil seems near us, (1) because innocence has not served to avert it; and (2) because it is graphically represented (R. C. J.).

destroyed.   Hence all these feelings, though different for the 5
reasons just given, tend to check pity; so that all of them
alike may serve to destroy a plea for pity.

First, then, let us inquire as to Indignation—towards 6
what persons, at what things, and under what conditions,
it is felt;—next, we will take the other feelings.   Our first 7
question is clear from what has been said.   If to be indignant
is to be pained at the appearance of undeserved good fortune,
it is plain in the first place that Indignation cannot be felt at
all goods.   Thus, no one will be indignant with another for 8
being just or brave or for acquiring virtue; since neither is
pity felt in the opposite cases.   Indignation is felt at wealth,
power and the like—in a word, at those things which are
deserved by good men and by the possessors of the natural
goods, such as good birth, beauty and the like.   And since 9
'old' seems neighbour to 'natural,' it follows that, of two
persons that have the same good, he who is new in its possession, and prosperous on account of it, is an object of the
greater Indignation; for the newly rich are more vexatious
than the men of old and hereditary riches; and so in regard
to ruling, influence, wealth of friends, happiness in children,
or any like thing.   And, if through such thing some further
good accrues to the possessor, this again causes Indignation:
for in this case there is greater vexation—as the newly-rich,
when through their wealth they rule, are more annoying than
the men of old wealth; and so in all other instances.   The 10
reason is, that the old possessor seems to have what is his
own, but the new what is not; for, what has appeared all
along to be thus or thus, seems true; and so the new men
seem usurpers.   And, since the goods severally are not meet 11
for any chance man (there being a certain proportion and
fitness, as there are arms which suit, not the just, but the
brave man, marriages which suit not the newly-rich but the
well-born), it follows that, if a man, though good, gets what
does not suit him, it is a case for Indignation.   And it is a
matter of Indignation that the worse man should contend
with the better,—first and most, when they are such in the
same thing (whence the verse—

'But he shunned the battle of Ajax, son of Telamon, for Zeus was indignant with him, when he fought with a better man ; '[1]

1387 b or next, when the worse in any sense contends with the better—as the cultivated man with the just man ; for justice is better than culture.

12 The objects and grounds of Indignation are plain, then, from all this : they are these, or of this sort. Men are in the mood for Indignation, when they are worthy of the greatest goods and possess these ; for it is not just that the like things

13 should be bestowed on inferior men. Or, secondly, if they are (simply) good and estimable[2]; for then they judge well and

14 hate unjust things. Or, if they are ambitious, and eager for certain things ; especially, if the objects of their ambition are

15 things which others get without deserving. And universally, those who think that they themselves have deserts which they do not allow in others, tend to feel indignation towards the others and about these things. Hence the slavish, the worthless, the unambitious, do not feel Indignation ; for there is nothing of which they think themselves worthy.

16 It is clear from this, at what cases of misfortune and disaster, or of non-success, we are to rejoice, or feel no pain ; for the things enumerated make their own opposites clear. Hence, if our speech bring the judges into these frames of mind, while it proves that those who claim pity, and the things for which they claim it, deserve no pity, but the reverse, it will be impossible to feel pity.

---

[1] The first line is found in *Il.* xi 542, but the second has only been preserved by Aristotle, from whom others have quoted it.

[2] δεύτερον δ', ἂν ὄντες ἀγαθοὶ καὶ σπουδαῖοι τυγχάνωσιν. οὐ τυγχάνουσιν (meaning μὴ τυγχάνωσιν) is proposed by Muretus, who thinks that the same class of people are meant as in the last clause. These, being 'worthy of the greatest goods,' are, he says, *of course* ἀγαθοὶ and σπουδαῖοι. Spengel seems to admit this, but contends that the meaning sought by Muretus is virtually contained in the text. He thinks that the distinction is between good people who are also prosperous, and good people simply. May not Aristotle be distinguishing (1) those 'worthy of the greatest goods' as persons who possess the greatest goods of fortune *without deserving* them, while (2) the 'good and estimable' are men of special *moral* worth, whether prosperous or not ? Yet Spengel may be right. Aristotle may mean to distinguish (1) the case of moral worth joined to prosperity ; (2) the case of moral worth alone (R. C. J.).

x. It is plain, also, at what things, towards what persons, and under what conditions Envy is felt; if Envy is pain at apparent prosperity in regard to the goods above-mentioned, and, in the case of equals, *not* because the envier wants the thing, but because the other *has* it. Envy will be felt by those who have, or seem to have, equals. By 'equals' I mean equals in birth, by kinship, in age, in 2 moral state, in reputation, in possessions. They will envy, too, who just fall short of having everything. Hence, men of great deeds or fortunes are envious; for they think that all men are robbing them. So are they who are signally 3 honoured for anything—especially for wisdom or prosperity. And the ambitious are more envious than the unambitious. Pretenders to wisdom, again, envy; for they are ambitious about wisdom. And, generally, they who desire reputation for anything are envious about it. Small-minded men are envious, for everything seems great to them. The good 4 things which excite envy have been stated. All those deeds 1388 a or possessions which arouse the love of honour and the craving for fame, and all the gifts of fortune, may be said to be objects of Envy; especially those things for which the envier himself longs, or which he thinks that he ought to have, or in the possession of which he is rather above, or rather below, the average. The persons, too, whom we envy are 5 clear; they have been named at the same time. We envy those who are near us in time, place, age, reputation[1] (whence the saying

'Aye—kinsfolk can be enviers too');[2]

and those with whom we vie; such being the persons just named,—(for no one vies with people who lived 10,000 years ago, or with the unborn or the dead, or with people at the Pillars of Herakles[3]; or with those, whom, in our own judg-

Envy.

---

[1] Roemer inserts <καὶ γένει>, 'and in kinship,' to lead up to the following quotation.

[2] 'Kinship is well acquainted even with envy'; a line ascribed to Aeschylus (Fragm. 305 Nauck, ed. 2) by the scholiast, who was perhaps thinking of *Agam.* 841, ταύροις γὰρ ἀνδρῶν ἐστι συγγενὲς τόδε, | φίλον τὸν εὐτυχοῦντ᾽ ἄνευ φθόνου σέβειν (R. C. J.).

[3] The western limit of the known world, Pindar, *Ol.* iii 79, *Nem.* iii 35, *Isth.* iv 20.

ment, or, as we think, in the judgment of others, we are far below, or much above). In like manner we vie with those
6 engaged in such or such pursuits[1]. And, since men vie with their competitors, with rivals in love, and generally with those who aim at the same things, it follows that they are especially envious of these; whence the saying

'Potter spites potter.'[2]

7 Those who have got a thing with difficulty, or have failed to
8 get it, envy those who have got it quickly[3]. We envy those whose wealth or success is a reproach to us; and these, again, are those near[4], or like us; for it is plain that, in comparison with these[5], we have missed the good thing; and so this,
9 paining us, causes envy. We envy those who have naturally, or by acquisition, things which were once our own attributes
10 or acquisitions. Hence older men envy younger. And those who have spent much, envy those who have spent little on an
11 object. It is plain, too, at what things[6] such men rejoice, and in the case of what persons, and in what circumstances; for the same mood in which they feel pain will cause them to feel joy in the opposite things[7]. So, if the judges are brought into this mood, while those for whom it is claimed, that they should be pitied, or win some good, are such as have been described, it is plain that they will not win pity from the masters of the situation.

---

[1] ὡσαύτως καὶ πρὸς τοὺς περὶ τὰ τοιαῦτα, the Paris MS, followed by Spengel and Roemer. The earlier editions have: ὡσαύτως καὶ πρὸς τούτους καὶ περὶ τὰ τοιαῦτα, which Cope translates :—'and the same is true with regard to similar *things*, as to these *persons*.'

[2] I xi 25; II iv 21 *supra*.

[3] καὶ τοῖς ταχὺ οἱ ἢ μόλις τυχόντες ἢ μὴ τυχόντες φθονοῦσιν, Bekker's text. Spengel follows the Paris MS in placing this clause, in the form καὶ τοῖς ταχὺ οἱ μήπω τυχόντες κτλ, immediately after § 10, where it harmonises with the previous context.

[4] εἰσὶν δὲ καὶ οὗτοι <οἱ> ἐγγύς, Vater, Spengel, Roemer.

[5] παρ' αὐτούς, rather, 'owing to our own fault' (Cope).

[6] ἐφ' οἷς, Spengel, Cope, Roemer; [ἐφ'] οἷς Bekker.

[7] ὡς γὰρ ἔχοντες λυποῦνται, οὕτως ἔχοντες ἐπὶ τοῖς ἐναντίοις ἡσθήσονται. The best MS has ὡς γὰρ οὐκ ἔχοντες, but οὐκ is omitted in the old Latin translation and by Muretus (who is followed by Roemer). Spengel and Cope object that this makes φθόνος and ἐπιχαιρεκακία the same πάθος. But why should not ἔχοντες denote the *general* moral state, out of which both alike arise? Evidently the envious man will also feel a spiteful joy (R. C. J.).

xi. Under what circumstances emulation is felt, and what

Emulation. things or persons excite it, is seen from what follows. Emulation is a pain at the apparent presence, in the case of those like us by nature, of honourable goods possible for ourselves, *not* because our neighbour possesses them, but because *we* do *not* possess them. Hence, Emulation is good and a mark of a good man, as envy is mean and a mark of a mean man, since the former, through his emulation, prepares himself to win the good things, while the latter, through his envy, aims at depriving his neighbour of them. It follows that they are emulous who think themselves worthy of goods which they have not …[1], for no one 1388 b expects things which seem impossible. Hence the young and 2 the magnanimous are emulous. And they who have such goods as befit honoured men ;—these being[2] wealth, abundance of friends, governments, and the like ; for, in the belief that it becomes them to be good men, they desire such goods, since these, we saw, befit those who are good[3]. They, too, are emulous, whom others think deserving. And they, whose 3 ancestors or kinsmen or intimate friends or nation or city are honourable, are emulous in regard to such honours ; for they think that these are their own, and that they deserve them. And, since the honourable goods are the objects of emulation, 4 it follows that the virtues must be such, and all things which are useful and beneficial to others ;—for we honour benefactors and good men ; also, those goods which yield enjoyment to our neighbours, as wealth, and beauty, rather than health. It 5 is plain, too, who the emulated *persons* are ; they are the

---

[1] Muretus (approved by Spengel) would here insert, ἐνδεχόμενον (or rather ἐνδεχομένων) αὐτοῖς λαβεῖν, 'these being possible for them.'

[2] ἔστι δὲ ταῦτα, as conjectured by Thurot and Roemer ; the old Latin translation has *sunt autem talia.* The MSS have ἔστι γὰρ ταῦτα.

[3] (1) ὡς γὰρ προσῆκον αὐτοῖς ἀγαθοῖς εἶναι, ὅτι προσῆκε τοῖς ἀγαθῶς ἔχουσι, ζηλοῦσι τὰ τοιαῦτα τῶν ἀγαθῶν, the manuscript text, retained by Spengel (and Roemer). (2) Bekker, on Vahlen's conjecture, has in the second clause :—ὅτι ἃ **προσῆκε τοῖς ἀγαθοῖς** ἔχουσι, 'because they already have those things which, we saw, benefit the good.' In that case, we require **προσήκει***. (3) Muretus proposed :— ὡς γὰρ προσῆκον αὐτοῖς ἀγαθοῖς εἶναι, ὅτι προσήκει τοῖς ἔχουσι τὰ τοιαῦτα τῶν ἀγαθῶν, ζηλοῦσι. Spengel would prefer ὅτι προσῆκε **τοῖς ἀγαθῶς ἔχουσι** τὰ τοιαῦτα τῶν ἀγαθῶν, ζηλοῦσι. **ἀγαθῶς**, Spengel says, is certain (R. C. J.).

* Actually found in the *scholium* which suggested Vahlen's proposal.

possessors of these things and the like—namely of the things
above-mentioned, such as Bravery, Wisdom, Power ; for much
good can be done to many by men in power,—by generals,
6 speakers, and all who possess such faculties. They, too, are
emulated, whom many wish to be like, or who have many
acquaintances or friends ; or whom many admire, or whom we
admire ourselves ; or who are celebrated with praise or en-
7 comium by poets or chroniclers[1]. We despise the opposite
sort ; for contempt is opposite to Emulation and contemning
to emulating. And those, who are so circumstanced as to
feel, or to excite, emulation, tend to show contempt to or
about those who have the evils contrary to the emulated
goods. Hence we often despise the fortunate, when their
good fortune is not attended by the honourable goods.

This, then, is an account of the topics, by which the
several feelings are excited or destroyed, and from which the
proofs connected with them are furnished[2].

xii. We will next discuss character—in relation to feel-
2 ings, moral states, ages, fortunes. By feelings I
*In appealing
to the feelings,
the speaker
must take
account of the
general
character of*
mean anger, desire and the like, of which we
have spoken before[3] ; by moral states, I mean
virtues and vices, and these, too, have been
discussed before[4],—when we saw what things

---

[1] 'Speech-writers' (*i.e.* especially, writers of panegyrical speeches) is the
translation preferred by Cope. λογογράφοι, in its earlier signification, means
'chroniclers,' *i.e.* the earliest historians and writers of prose ; in its later and more
common sense, it is applied to 'professional writers of speeches.' λογογράφος
may mean either a 'speech-*writer*,' as opposed to ῥήτωρ, or a writer of *prose* as
opposed to poetry (Cope, ii 136 f). In III xii 2 it certainly means a 'speech-
writer.'

[2] δι' ὧν μὲν οὖν τὰ πάθη ἐγγίγνεται καὶ διαλύεται, ἐξ ὧν αἱ πίστεις γίγνονται περὶ
αὐτῶν, εἴρηται · so Bekker and Roemer. (1) Spengel refers ἐξ ὧν to πάθη, and
puts a comma after γίγνονται, remarking that, for αὐτῶν, we should expect τούτων.
(2) Bekker (whose text is followed in the above translation), has no comma after
γίγνονται. Then, Spengel says, ἐξ ὧν and περὶ αὐτῶν must *both* refer to πάθη,—
which cannot be. But why should not ἐξ ὧν refer to δι' ὧν—to the things *by*
which the various feelings are excited, and *from* which the topics about them are to
be drawn ? One MS has καὶ ἐξ ὧν, and the old Latin translation has, '*et ex quibus*'
(R. C. J.).

[3] II i *supra*.

[4] I ix, and in the immediately previous context.

his audience; whether they are young or old, rich or poor, etc.

are objects of moral choice[1] and of action for each sort of men.   The ages are youth, the prime of life, and old age.   By fortune I mean good 1389 a birth, wealth, influence, and their opposites,—in a word, good fortune and bad.

Young men are lustful in character, and apt to do what 3 they lust after.   Of the bodily desires, they are

Character of the young.

most apt to indulge, and to exceed in, the sexual. They are changeable and fickle in their desires, which are 4 violent but soon appeased; for their impulses are rather keen than great[2], like the hunger and thirst of the sick.   They 5 are passionate, quick to anger and apt to obey their impulse; and they are under the dominion of their passion, for, by reason of ambition, they cannot bear to be slighted, and they are indignant, if they think they are wronged.   They are 6 ambitious, or rather contentious[3]; for youth covets pre-eminence, and victory is a form of pre-eminence.   They are both ambitious and contentious rather than avaricious; this they are not at all, because they have not yet experienced want—as goes the saying of Pittakos[4] about Amphiaraos. They think no evil, but believe in goodness, because as yet 7 they have not seen many cases of vice.   They are credulous, because, as yet, they have not often been deceived.   They are 8 sanguine, because they are heated, as with wine, and also because they have not had many disappointments.   They live for the most part by hope; for hope is of the future, as memory of the past, and for young men the future is long and the past short; since, on the first day of a life, there is nothing to remember and everything to hope.   They are easily deceived, for the same reason,—since they hope easily.   They are comparatively courageous; for they are 9 passionate and hopeful, and passion keeps men from being fearful, while hope makes them bold: no one fears while he is angry, and to hope for a good thing is emboldening.   They 10

[1] Cp. I vi 26.

[2] *i.e.* 'strong or enduring' (Cope).

[3] καὶ φιλότιμοι μέν εἰσι, μᾶλλον δὲ φιλόνικοι, 'fond as they are of honour, they are still fonder of victory' (Cope).

[4] Of Mytilene, *fl.* about 612 B.C.   This saying has not survived.

are shy; for, as yet, they have no independent standard of
11 propriety, but have been educated by convention alone. They
are high-minded; for they have not yet been abased by life,
but are untried in its necessities; and to think oneself worthy
of great things is high-mindedness; and this is characteristic
12 of the hopeful man. They choose honourable before expedient actions; for they live by habit rather than by
calculation; and calculation has the expedient for its object,
13 as virtue has the honourable. They are fond of their friends,
their relations, their companions, more than persons of the
1389 b other ages, because they delight in society, and because, as
yet, they judge nothing by the standard of expediency, and
14 so do not apply it to their friends. All their mistakes are on
the side of excess or vehemence—against the maxim of
Chilon[1]; they do everything *too much*; they love too much,
hate too much, and so in all else. They think they know
everything and are positive; this, indeed, is the cause of their
15 overdoing all things. Their wrong deeds are done insolently,
not viciously. They are ready to pity, because they think all
men good, or *rather* good; for they measure their neighbours
by their own innocence, and so conceive that these are suffer-
16 ing wrongfully. And they are lovers of laughter,—hence also
lovers of wit; for wit is educated insolence.

xiii. Such, then, is the character of the young. Elderly

Character
of the old.
men who have passed their prime are characterised, as a rule, by the opposite things. As
they have lived many years, and have been deceived or have
erred more often, and as most things are disappointing, they
are positive about nothing, and do all things much too feebly.
2 They *think*, but are never *sure*; in their uncertainty, they
always add 'maybe,'—'perhaps'; they speak thus on all
3 subjects, and positively about nothing. They think evil; for
evil-thinking is to put the worst construction upon everything. Further, they are suspicious through their incredulity,
4 being incredulous through their experience. For these reasons

---

[1] μηδὲν ἄγαν, *ne quid nimis.*

they neither like nor hate strongly, but, according to the advice
of Bias[1], like, as if they would afterwards hate, and hate, as if
they would afterwards like.   They are mean-souled, through   5
having been abased by life; for they desire nothing great or
extraordinary, but only the appliances of life.   They are   6
illiberal; for property is one of the necessaries; and, at the
same time, they know from their experience, that it is hard
to acquire, but easy to lose.   They are cowardly, and afraid   7
of everything; for they are of the opposite temperament to
youth; they are chilled, while youth is hot; and so old age
has prepared the way to cowardice, since fear is a chill.   They   8
cling to life, and the more on their latest day, since the object
of desire is the absent, and since, too, men most desire that in
which they are deficient.   They are unduly selfish; for this,   9
too, is a meanness of soul.   And, because they are selfish,
they live too much for the expedient, too little for the honourable; the expedient being a relative good, the honourable an   1390 a
absolute good.   They are not shy, but rather shameless; for,   10
as they do not care, in the same degree, for what is honourable,
as for what is expedient, they disregard appearances.   They   11
are slow to hope, owing to their experience,—since most things
which happen are unsatisfactory and turn out for the worse,
—and also from their cowardice.   They live in memory more   12
than in hope; for the remainder of their life is small, and the
past part large—and hope is of the future, as memory of the
past.   This is the reason of their talkativeness;—they are
for ever speaking of the past, since the retrospect gives them
pleasure.   Their fits of passion are sharp, but feeble; hence   13
they are not lustful, nor apt to act after their lusts, but rather
for gain.   Hence men of this age appear temperate; their
desires have become slack, and they are slaves to lucre.   And   14
their life is regulated by calculation rather than by moral
instinct; calculation having expediency for its object, while
moral   instinct   has   virtue.   Their   wrong   deeds   are   done
viciously, not insolently.   Old men, like young, are com-   15

---

[1] Bias, of Priene in Ionia, the last of the 'Seven Wise Men' flourished about
550 B.C.   The saying in the text is often quoted.   See, for example, Sophokles,
Ajax, 678–680, with Jebb's *Appendix*, p. 231 f.

passionate, but not for the same reason as young men ; the
latter are so from benevolence, the former from weakness ;
for they think that every possibility of suffering is near themselves, and this, we saw, was a condition of pitying. Hence
they are given to lamentation, and are not witty or lovers of
mirth ; for the love of lamentation is opposite to the love of
mirth.

16   Such, then, are the characteristics of the young and of the
elderly.   All men give a hearing to those speeches, which are
framed after their own character, and which reflect it.   It is
now plain how we are to manage our speaking, so as to give
this character to ourselves and to our speech.

xiv.   Men in their prime will evidently be of a character
intermediate between these, abating the excess
of each ;—neither excessively bold, for this is
rashness, nor over-timid, but rightly disposed

Character of
men in their
prime.

2   in both respects, neither trusting nor distrusting all things,
but rather judging by the true standard, and living neither
1390 b   for the honourable alone, nor for the expedient alone, but for
both ; inclining neither to frugality nor to extravagance, but
3   to the just mean.   And so, too, in regard to passion and
desire, they will be courageously temperate and temperately
courageous.   Young men and old men share these qualities
between them ; young men are courageous and intemperate,
old men are temperate and cowardly.   To speak generally—
those useful qualities, which youth and age divide between
them, are joined in the prime of life : between their excesses
4   and defects, it has the fitting mean.   The body is in its full
vigour from thirty to five and thirty ; the mind at about
forty-nine[1].

---

[1] Of the numbers here mentioned, 35 and 49 are multiples of seven. The
septenary theory of the stages of human life is found in a fragment ascribed to
Solon, fragm. 27 (3), which is preserved by Philo and Clement of Alexandria.
According to Solon, a man's strength is best in the 4th septenary period (21–28) ;
his intellect is being matured in the 6th (35–42) ; and he is best in νοῦς and γλῶσσα
in the 7th and 8th (42–56). Cp. *Pol.* IV (VII) 16, 1355 *b* 32, where the διανοίας
ἀκμὴ, according to 'the poets,' is placed at about 49 (Cope, ii 160 f).

xv.   This, then, may suffice as an account of the characters proper to youth, old age, and the prime of life.   We will next speak of those goods of fortune by which the characters, too, of men are influenced in a certain way.   It is characteristic of 2

Character of the well-born. good birth that its possessor is the more ambitious ; for all men, when they have got anything, are wont to add to the heap ; and good birth means an honoured ancestry.   The man of good birth tends to look down even on those who are like his own ancestors ; for the same things are more honourable, and form a greater boast, when they are far off than when they are near[1].   ' Well-born ' 3 refers to goodness of stock ; ' generous ' to non-degeneracy ; —a condition not present, as a rule, in the well-born, most of whom are little worth.   In the human stocks, as in the growths of the fields, there is a certain yield ; sometimes, if the stock is good, extraordinary men spring from it for a space, and then it falls back[2].   The clever stocks degenerate into the type of insanity, as in the posterity of Alkibiades and the elder Dionysios ; the sedate stocks degenerate into stupidity and dulness, as in the posterity of Kimon, Perikles, and Sokrates[3].

---

[1] *i.e.* the noble is apt to despise even those who are in the same position as his own ancestors; since (in the case of his own ancestors) this position of dignity is enhanced by antiquity (R. C. J.).

[2] κἄπειτα πάλιν ἀναδίδωσιν.   (1)   Victorius gives two versions ; in the second he understands the verb as *transitive*, and as equivalent to *rursus edit ac gignit*, approved by Spengel, and by Cope, whose rendering is: 'they begin again to produce them.'   (2)   The verb is translated in the text as *intransitive* ; this is in agreement with Rost and Palm, in their Lexicon, *zurückgehen*, and with Bonitz, in the 'Index Aristotelicus,' *deficit*.

[3] Plato, in the *Politicus*, p. 310, says that insanity comes of men of high spirit (ἀνδρεῖοι) *intermarrying* for generations; and stupidity (νωθρότης) of orderly persons (κόσμιοι) doing the same.   In the *Meno*, p. 93 f, he states that the sons of Themistokles, Aristides, Perikles, and Thukydides (the opponent of Perikles), all degenerated from their fathers.   The younger Alkibiades is the speaker of an oration written in his defence by Isokrates:—*Or.* xvi, *De Bigis* (*c.* 397 B.C.), and he is also the speaker in two orations ascribed to Lysias, *Or.* xiv–xv (*c.* 395 B.C.), where he defends himself on a charge of desertion and of failure to serve in the army.   Dionysios II (who succeeded his father Dionysios I in 367) was an abject voluptuary.   Of the posterity of Kimon, nothing is known ; the sons of Sokrates

xvi.   The character which goes with Wealth is on the

surface for all to see.   Rich men are insolent and
overweening, being distempered by their pos-
1391 a session of wealth; for they feel as if they had all goods,—
wealth being a sort of measure of the worth of all else, so
2 that it seems to command all things.   Rich men are luxurious
and swaggerers; luxurious because they *have* luxury, and
display their prosperity; swaggerers and offenders against
good taste, because all the world is wont to busy itself with
what the rich love and admire, and because they think that
all the world is emulous of the same things as themselves.
Nor is it unnatural, either, that they should be thus affected;
for many are they who have need of the wealthy.   Hence the
saying of Simonides[1] about wise men and rich, in answer to
the question of Hiero's wife—'which is best, to be rich or
wise?'   'Rich,' he said; 'for I see that the wise men spend
3 their time at the doors of the rich.'   It is characteristic of the
rich to think themselves worthy to govern; for they think
that they have things which give a claim to govern.   To sum
up,—the character of wealth[2] is that of a prosperous fool.
4 The character of those who have newly acquired wealth differs
from the character of those who have long had it, in that the
newly rich have all the vices, in a stronger and lower form;
for to be newly rich is, as it were, uneducatedness in wealth[3].
The wrongs which they do are not acts of malice, but either
of insolence or of intemperance, as in the case of assault or of
adultery.

are described as 'stupid' (ἀπόπληκτοι) in Plutarch's *Life of the Elder Cato*,
c. 20.

[1] About 477 Simonides of Keos (556–467) left for the court of Hiero I, tyrant
of Syracuse, and remained there for the rest of his life.   We have an allusion to
the above story in Plato's *Rep.* 489 B, without mention of the name of Simonides.
Aristippos, in Diog. Laërt. II 69, assigns the statement of the reason to Dionysios
and not to Simonides.

[2] ἦθος πλούτου, written by the first hand in the Paris MS (Lat. transl. *mores
divitiarum*), corrected by a late hand into ἦθος πλοῦτος.   ἤθους ὁ πλοῦτος, in
Bekker's text, comes from the inferior MSS.

[3] The *nouveau riche* has never had any training in the proper use of wealth.

xvii. In regard to Power, again, its general characteristics
Character of Power. may be said to be manifest. The characteristics of Power are partly the same as those of Wealth, partly better. Men in power are more ambitious and more 2 heroic in character than rich men, because they aim at such deeds as their power enables them to do. They are more 3 earnest because they are administrators[1] and are forced to look to the interests of their power. They are dignified 4 rather than oppressively important; their rank gives them a certain dignity, and so they are moderate, dignity being a tempered and decent oppressiveness. And, if they do wrong, their wrong deeds are not small but great.

Good Fortune in its several departments has the charac- 5
Character of Good Fortune. teristics of the conditions just described,—Good Birth—Wealth—Power—for the forms of Good Fortune, which are thought highest, tend to these; further, it disposes men to be greedy of happiness in children and of **1391 b** the bodily goods. It makes men, indeed, more arrogant and 6 irrational; but one excellent characteristic attends on it; men stand in a definite relation of love to the gods, believing in them on account of the gifts of Fortune.

This, then, is an account of those characters which depend on age[2] and fortune[3]; for the opposites of the characters described appear from the opposite considerations,—as the characters of the poor, the unlucky, and the powerless.

xviii. The use of all persuasive speech has a view to a
Brief retrospect, with introduction to the analysis decision[4]; for there is no further need of speaking about things which we know and have decided. This is no less the case when the speaker aims

---

[1] σπουδαστικώτεροι διὰ τὸ ἐν ἐπιμελείᾳ εἶναι. 'More active and energetic, by reason of the *constant attention* they are obliged to pay in looking to the means of maintaining their power' (Cope). In I xi 4, ἐπιμέλειαι, 'acts of attention,' are coupled with 'earnest and intense efforts,' σπουδαὶ and συντονίαι.

[2] II xii–xiv.   [3] II xv–xvii.

[4] § 1 ἐπεὶ δ' ἡ τῶν πιθανῶν λόγων χρῆσις—τοὺς λόγους ἠθικοὺς ποιητέον. Here the protasis, ἐπεὶ etc., has no apodosis answering to it, either in grammar or in sense. (1) *Grammar.* This difficulty is not insuperable. Aristotle is often careless in the same way: *e.g.* Poët. 9, ἐπεὶ δὲ...ὥστε ἀνάγκη, Analyt. Post. I 25 p. 866, ἔτι εἰ ἀρχὴ...ὥστε βελτίων. (3) *Sense.* '*Since* all rhetorical speech has

of the four 'universal' classes of argument, applicable to all special premisses derived from special branches of knowledge.

at encouraging or dissuading one man only, as those who seek to admonish or to persuade may do. *That one* man is no less a judge; for he, whom we have to persuade, is, speaking generally, a judge. And it is so equally, whether we are speaking against a real adversary or against an imaginary case; since here we have to use our speech for the overthrow of arguments opposed to us, and to these arguments we address ourselves as to a living opponent. The same thing holds good of epideictic speaking : the speech is framed with reference to the spectator considered as a judge. As a rule, however, he alone is a judge in the simple sense, who decides a question in some issue of civil life ; for there is a question of fact both in regard to the matter of a lawsuit and in regard to the subject of a debate. The characters of the several polities have already been treated under the head of Deliberative Rhetoric[1]. We may be considered, then, to have defined the way and the means of making our speech reflect a character.

2   And since each species of Rhetoric has, as we saw, a distinct end[2]; since, in regard to all of these, we have now

a view to a judge—it follows that it has been shown how to make speeches characteristic.' This is a false connexion of protasis and apodosis. The following solutions have been suggested :—(*a*) Cope thinks that a sentence is lost after βουλεύονται, before the last sentence in § 1. '*Since* all rhetoric is addressed to a judge, < I have therefore analysed the ἤθη and πάθη, in order to help the speaker to conciliate these judges ;> the πολιτειῶν ἤθη, too, have been discussed, *and so* (ὥστε) this part of the subject is finished.' (*b*) Spengel thinks that ἐπεὶ δ' ἡ τῶν πιθανῶν λόγων χρῆσις—βουλεύονται is a mere amplification of II i 2 ἐπεὶ δ' ἕνεκα κρίσεως—τὸν κριτὴν κατασκευάζειν. In his *Rhetores Graeci* he brackets it as an interpolation. He thinks that the end of c. 17 and the first half of c. 18 hang together thus :—περὶ μὲν οὖν τῶν καθ' ἡλικίαν—ἀδυνάτου· περὶ δὲ τῶν κατὰ τὰς πολιτείας ἠθῶν—ποιητέον. ἐπεὶ δὲ περὶ ἕκαστον μὲν γένος κτλ. Muretus and Vater think that the apodosis to ἐπεὶ δ' ἡ τῶν πιθανῶν is λοιπὸν ἡμῖν διελθεῖν περὶ τῶν κοινῶν. But the *second* ἐπεὶ δὲ (§ 2) is against this (R. C. J.). Spengel's view has been supported by Vahlen, *Zur Kritik Ar. Schriften* in the Transactions of the Vienna Academy, xxxviii (1861) 121-132; and opposed by Brandis, *Gesch. der gr. Philos.* III 1, 195, and Thurot, *Études* (1861) 228-236. In Roemer's view, § 1 in the present chapter is the original form of the abridged sentence in II i 4, and this original was accidentally inserted in this place owing to the fortuitous fact that it began with ἐπεὶ δὲ, which is also the beginning of § 2 (*praef.* xcviii-ci).

[1] I viii.   [2] I iii.

got those popular principles and premises from which men take their proofs in debate, in display, in forensic argument[1]; since, further, we have defined the available means of making speeches ethical[2];—it remains for us to discuss the *general appliances*[3]. All men are compelled in speaking to apply the 3 topic of Possible and Impossible; and to try to show, either that a thing will be, or that it has been. Further, the topic of 4 Size is common to all speeches; all men use depreciation and amplification in debate, in praising or blaming, in accusing or defending. When these topics have been defined, we must 5 try to say what we have to say of Enthymemes generally, **1392 a** and of Examples, in order that, by the addition of what is still wanting, we may fulfil our original purpose. Of the general commonplaces, that of Amplification is, as has been said[4], most popular to Epideictic speaking; that of the Past to Forensic, for the decision concerns past facts; that of the Possible and Future to Deliberative.

xix. First, then, let us speak of the Possible and Impossible. Now if, of two opposites, one can exist

The topic of the Possible and Impossible.

or come into existence, the other also would seem to be possible. For instance, if a man can be healed, he can also fall sick : for the potentiality of opposites, as such, is one. And, if of two like things one 2 is possible, the other is. And, if the harder is possible, the 3 easier is so. And, if the good and beautiful form of a thing 4 can come into being, the thing generally can come into being ; for it is harder for a fine house, than for a house, to exist. And, if there can be a beginning of anything, there can be an 5 end ; for no impossibility comes or begins to come into existence. Thus it neither happens, nor could begin to happen, that the diagonal of a square is commensurate with its side. And, if the end of a thing is possible, the beginning is so ; for 6 all things come from a beginning. And, if that which is later in existing, or in being born, can arise, that which is earlier

---

[1] I iv–viii.   [2] I ix; x–xv.

[3] κοινῶν, *i.e.* both the κοινοὶ τόποι and the κοιναὶ πίστεις, Enthymeme and Example (R. C. J.).

[4] I ix.

can; for instance, if a man can come into existence, a boy can; for boyhood is the earlier stage—and, if a boy, then a

7 man; for boyhood is the beginning. Those things, too, are possible, of which the love or desire is natural; for no one, as

8 a rule, is enamoured or desirous of impossibilities. Those things, of which there are sciences and arts, can exist and

9 come into existence[1]. Things are possible, again, which have the beginning of birth in things which we can compel or persuade; such being those powers of which we are the superiors

10 or the masters or the friends. When the parts of a thing are possible, the whole is so; and, when the whole is possible, the parts are so—as a rule. Thus, if the various parts of a shoe, the toe-piece, the strap, the side-leather, are possible, shoes are possible; and, if shoes are possible, the toe-piece, the strap,

11 and the side-leather are possible, and, if the genus belongs to

1392 b the number of possibilities, the species does; and *vice versa*; thus, if a sailing vessel can exist, a trireme can, and *vice versa*.

12 If, of two things naturally interdependent, one is possible, the other is so; as, if double is possible, half is so; and *vice versa*.

13 And, if a thing can come to pass without art or preparation, much more can it do so with them; whence Agathon's saying—

> 'Some things we have to effect by art; others come to us by necessity or chance.'[2]

14 If a thing is possible for the worse and weaker and more foolish, it is more so for their opposites; as Isokrates said that it was strange if Euthynos[3] had learned this, and *he*

---

[1] δυνατὸν ταῦτα καὶ εἶναι καὶ γενέσθαι, Bekker, with inferior MSS and the old Latin translation: δυνατὰ ταῦτα καὶ ἔστι καὶ γίγνεται, Spengel and Roemer, with the Paris MS. The former is the text here followed.

[2] Fragm. 8, Nauck, ed. 2,

καὶ μὴν τὰ μέν γε χρὴ τέχνῃ πράσσειν, τὰ δὲ
ἡμῖν ἀνάγκῃ καὶ τύχῃ προσγίγνεται.

In l. 1 all the MSS have τῇ τύχῃ; in l. 2 all have τύχῃ, except Q, E, m, which have τέχνῃ (accepted by Muretus). Camozzi and others transferred τέχνῃ to l. 1, where τῇ τέχνῃ is accepted by Spengel and Roemer, while χρὴ τέχνῃ is proposed by Porson, on *Medea* 1090 (ed. 1826). For πράσσειν the Paris MS has πράσσει (adopted by Roemer).—Agathon follows the Sophists, who made all things happen either φύσει or τύχῃ or τέχνῃ, Plato, *Laws*, x, p. 185.

[3] Euthȳnos, not the Euthȳnous of Or. XXI (R. C. J.). Possibly a quotation from Or. XVIII (*Against Kallimachos*) 15, θαύμαζω δ' εἰ αὐτὸν μὲν ἱκανὸν γνῶναι

should not be able to discover it. The topics for Impos- 15
sibility are of course to be found in the opposites of these.

The question of Past Fact may be treated on these prin- 16
Past and ciples. First, if the less natural thing has
Future. happened, the more natural thing must have
happened too. Again, if the usually later thing has hap- 17
pened, the earlier has happened ; for instance, if he has
forgotten a thing, he also learned it once. If he could and 18
would, he has done the thing : for all men do what they
would and can ; there is nothing in the way. Again, if there 19
was no external hindrance and he was angry; or, if he had
the power and the *desire*, he has done the thing ; for, as a
rule, men do, if they can, the things for which they have an
appetite,—bad men, through intemperance ; good men, because
they desire good things. Or, if he was going to do the thing[1], 20
(you can say that he has done it) ; for it is *probable* that one,
who intended an action, did it. A thing *has* happened, if 21
those things have happened, of which it was the natural
sequel or motive ; thus, if it has lightened, it has thundered ;
—if he attempted the action, he did it. Or, if, again, those
things have happened, to which it was the natural antecedent
or means ; thus, if it has thundered, it has lightened ; or if he
did the act, he made the attempt. In all such cases, the
conclusion may be either necessarily or only generally true.
The topics for the *negation* of Past Fact will obviously be 22
found in the opposites of these.

The way to treat Fact Future appears from the same con- 23
siderations. That *will* be, for which there is the power and **1393 a**
the wish ; or, which desire or anger[2], coupled with power,
prompts. Hence, too, if[3] there is the impulse or the intention

νομίζει...ἐμὲ δ' οὐκ ἂν οἴεται τοῦτ' ἐξευρεῖν, in which case *Euthynos* (for which the
scholiast has *Euthynous*) is a mistake for *Kallimachos* ; cp. Usener, *Rhein. Mus.*
xxv 603.

[1] εἰ ἔμελλε [γίγνεσθαι καὶ] ποιεῖν Spengel, Bekker (ed. 3), and Cope ; the words
bracketed (on the ground that the *things* come below) are defended by Vater, and
by Vahlen on Ar. *Poët.* p. 153, and retained by Roemer.

[2] Most MSS add καὶ λογισμῷ, omitted by one MS, and bracketed by Spengel,
but retained by Bekker and Roemer.

[3] διὰ ταῦτα καὶ εἰ, so Bekker. ταῦτα καὶ (the reading of the Paris MS) is
accepted by Roemer ; Spengel suggests καὶ τὰ (omitting διὰ ταῦτα and εἰ).

to do a thing, it *will* be; for, as a rule, things which are about to happen, come to pass rather than things which are *not* so.

24 A thing *will* be, if its natural antecedents have already come
25 to pass; thus, if it is cloudy, it is likely to rain.   Or, if the means to an end have come into being, the end is likely to be; thus, if there is a foundation-stone, there will be a house.

26   As to the Greatness and Smallness of things, greater and

More and   less, and generally great things and small, all is
Less.   clear from what has been already said by us. Under the Deliberative brand of Rhetoric we have discussed the relative greatness of goods[1], and the abstract greater and less[2]. Now, as in each kind of speaking the proposed end is a good,—namely, the Expedient, the Honourable, or the Just,—it follows that all speakers must derive their topics
27 of amplification from these goods.   It is waste of words to inquire further about *abstract* greatness and pre-eminence; for particulars are more momentous in practice than universals.

Enough, then, of the Possible and Impossible; Fact Past, Fact Future, the negation of these; and further of the Greatness or Smallness of things[3].

xx.   It remains to speak of the Proofs common to all

Proofs com-   Rhetoric, as we have spoken of their particular
mon to all   elements.   The common proofs are generically
Rhetoric.   two—Example and Enthymeme; for the maxim
2 is part of an Enthymeme.   First, then, we will speak of the Example; for the Example is like Induction, and Induction is the primary process.

There are two kinds of Example.   One kind consists in

Examples.   the use of historical parallel, another in the use
        of artificial parallel.   Artificial parallel takes the form either of comparison or of fable, like Æsop's or the

3   Libyan fables.   It would be using historical
Historical.   parallel, if one were to say that we must arm against the Great King and not let him subdue Egypt; for, in a former instance, Darius did not come over till he had
1393 b got Egypt, but, having got it, he came; and Xerxes, again,

[1] I vii.   [2] I vii, I.   [3] On c. xix see *Appendix* to Book II.

did not attack us till he had got it, but, having got it, he came[1]; and so this man[2] too, if he gets it, will come over— therefore he must not be allowed to get it. 'Comparison' 4 means such illustrations as those of Sokrates—saying, for instance, that magistrates ought not to be appointed by lot, for it is like appointing athletes, not by athletic power, but by lot, or as if the appointment of a pilot from among the crew were to go, not by skill, but by lot[3]. In- 5

Artificial.

stances of fables are that of Stesichoros[4] about Phalaris, and that of Æsop on behalf of the demagogue.

When the people of Himera had made Phalaris their military dictator, and were going to give him a body-guard, Stesichoros told them, among other things, a story about a horse, who had a meadow all to himself, until a deer came and began to spoil his pasturage. When the horse, wishing to be avenged on the deer, asked a certain man whether this could be done with his help, 'Yes,' said the man, 'if you are bitted, and I mount you armed with javelins.' The horse agreed, and was mounted ; but, instead of being avenged, he was himself enslaved to the man. 'So in your own case,' said Stesichoros—'take care that, in your desire to chastise your enemies, you do not fare like the horse. You have the bit in your mouths already ; if you give him a guard, and allow him to mount, you will be finally enslaved to Phalaris.'

Æsop, defending at Samos a demagogue who was being 6 tried for his life, said that a fox, trying to cross a river, was once swept into a crevice in the rocks, and, not being able to get out, suffered miseries for a long while, being covered with dog-fleas. A hedgehog in his wanderings, seeing the fox, took pity on her, and asked whether he should remove the

[1] Egypt became a Persian satrapy in 528 B.C., when it was conquered by Kambyses. In 490 Darius sent Datis and Artaphernes against Greece. In 486 Egypt revolted. In 485 Darius died. In 484 Xerxes reconquered Egypt, and in 480 invaded Greece (R. C. J.).

[2] Artaxerxes III (Ochus), 361–338. Ochus apparently made three expeditions against Egypt,—the first at an uncertain date, the second probably in the winter of 351–350 B.C., and the third (in which he reconquered Egypt) probably in 345. This last is the date accepted by A. Schaefer, in ed. 2 of his *Dem. u. s. Zeit* (i 482–4), instead of 340, the date adopted in ed. 1 (p. 437).

[3] Cp. Xen. *Mem.* i ii 9.   [4] Of Himera, *fl.* 610 B.C. ; accession of Phalaris, 570.

fleas. The fox objected ; and, on the hedgehog asking why, said—'These are sated, and draw little blood ; but, if you take them away, others will come with an appetite, and drain what blood is left to me.' 'Now you, too, Samians, will take **1394 a** no more hurt from this man ; for he is rich ; but, if you kill him, others will come poor, and will fritter and waste your public wealth.'

7   Fables suit public speaking, and have this advantage, that, while it is hard to find historical parallels, it is comparatively easy to find fables in point ; in fact, one must contrive them, as one contrives comparisons, if one can discover an analogy, 8 which literary knowledge[1] will make easy. The fabulous parallels are more easy to provide, but the historical parallels are more useful for the purpose of debate ; since, as a rule, the future is like the past.

9   When we have no Enthymemes, Examples must be used as demonstrations (for they are the means of proof) ; when we have, as testimonies ;—using them as epilogue to the Enthymemes : for, when the Examples are put *first*, they seem like an induction, but induction is not appropriate to Rhetoric except in a few cases ; whereas, if they are *subjoined*, they seem like testimonies ; and, in all cases, a witness is persuasive. Hence, if you put the Examples first, you must use many ; if at the end, even one is enough ; for even one witness is useful, if good.

xxi. It has now been explained how many kinds of
Maxims. example there are, and how and when they
should be used. As to the citation of Maxims ; when a maxim has been defined, it will best appear, in regard to what subjects, and at what times, and by whom, maxims 2 may fitly be used in speaking. A maxim is a statement, not about a particular fact, as about the character of Iphikrates, but general ; not about all things, as about 'straight' being the opposite of 'curved,' but about those things which are the objects of action, and which it is desirable or undesirable to

---

[1] φιλοσοφίας, 'literature'; an Isokratic use of the word. Cp. *Rhet. ad Alex.*, c. 1, ἡ τῶν λόγων φιλοσοφία, 'the study of literature' (cp. Cope, *Comm.* ii 256).

do. So, since the Enthymeme is that syllogism which concerns such things, maxims may be said to be the conclusions and the premisses of Enthymemes without the syllogism :— as

'No man of good sense should have his children brought up over-wise':

this is a maxim ; when the cause, the *wherefore*, is added, it is the complete enthymeme, as :—

'for, besides the general charge of sloth, they reap jealous dislike from their fellow citizens.'[1]

Again :—   1394 b

'There is no man who is wholly prosperous':—[2]

and

'There is no man who is free'—

are maxims ; but, when placed beside the sequel, they are enthymemes :

'For he is the slave of money or of chance.'[3]

If, then, a maxim is what has been said, it follows that 3 there are four kinds of maxims. The maxim either will, or will not, have a reason subjoined. Those maxims which need 4 demonstration are such as state something unexpected or disputed ; those which state nothing unexpected, have no reason added. Of the latter class, some will not need the 5 added reason, because they are familiar beforehand ; as—

'It is an excellent thing for a man to be healthy, to *our* thinking'—[4]

for most people think so. Others do not need the added reason, because they are plain at the first glance, as—

' A lover is ever kindly.'[5]

Of the maxims which have a reason added, some are 6 imperfect enthymemes ; as

'No man of good sense,' &c. ;[1]

others are in the nature, but not in the form, of enthymemes ;

---

[1] Euripides, *Medea*, 296 ff.   [2] Euripides, Fragm. 661 Nauck, ed. 2.
[3] Euripides, *Hecuba*, 858.
[4] Ascribed to Simonides or Epicharmus by the scholiast; the latter ascription is accepted by Meineke.
[5] Euripides, *Troades*, 1051.

and these are the most popular. They are those in which the reason for the statement is *implied*; as

'Do not, being a mortal, cherish immortal anger.'[1]

To say that it is not right to cherish anger is a maxim : the added words, 'being a mortal,' are the wherefore. Similarly—

'The mortal should have mortal, not immortal thoughts.'[2]

7 It is clear, then, from what has been said, how many kinds of maxim there are, and in what case each kind is suitable. When the statement is a disputed, or a startling one, the maxim should have its reason added. We may put this reason first, making a maxim of the conclusion:—as—' For my part, as it is not desirable to be envied or to be inactive, I hold that it is better not to be educated.' Or this maxim may be stated first, and the former clause added. When the statement is not startling, but merely not self-evident, the reason ought to be added in as terse a form as possible.

8 Laconic or enigmatic sayings also suit cases of this kind : as
1395 a the saying of Stesichoros to the Locrians, that it is better not to be insolent, lest the grasshoppers[3] should have to sing on
9 the ground[4]. The use of maxims is suitable to elderly men, and in regard to subjects with which one is conversant; for sententiousness, like story-telling, is unbecoming in a younger man ; while, in regard to subjects with which one is not conversant, it is stupid and shows want of culture. It is token enough of this that rustics are the greatest coiners of maxims, and the readiest to set forth their views.

10 Spurious generalization is most convenient in expressing bitter complaint or indignation[5]; and here, either at the out-
11 set, or when the fact has been proved. Even trite and common maxims should be used, if they can serve ; since, just because

---

[1] Nauck, *Fragm. Adespota*, 79, ed. 2 ; cp. Bentley, *Phalaris*, pp. 229, 243, ed. Wagner.

[2] Ascribed by Bentley to Epicharmus.

[3] Or 'cicalas.'

[4] Implying that the trees would be cut down. The cicalas usually sit on trees when they chirp; *Il.* iii 151 (of τέττιγες), δένδρῳ ἐφεζόμενοι, and Ar. *Hist. An.* v 30, οὐ γίγνονται δὲ τέττιγες ὅπου δένδρα μή ἐστι.

[5] σχετλιασμῷ καὶ δεινώσει. In the former the sense of cruelty is uppermost ; in the latter, the sense of injustice (R. C. J.).

they are common, they seem right, on the supposition that all
the world is agreed about them. Thus, one who calls his men
into danger before they have sacrificed, may quote—

'The one best omen is to fight for one's country';[1]

or, if he calls on them to face danger when they are the
weaker—

'The war-god is for both sides.'[2]

Or, if he is urging them to destroy their enemies' children,
though these are doing no wrong—

'He is a fool, who slays the father, and leaves the children.'[3]

Some proverbs, again, are also maxims;—as the proverb 12
'an Attic neighbour.'[4] Our maxims ought sometimes to con- 13
trovert sayings which have become public property (as 'know
thyself,'—'Do nothing excessively '[5]), if thus our character will
appear better, or if our maxim expresses passion. It would
express passion if, for instance, an angry speaker were to say
—'The saying that it is well to "know thyself," is a lie. If
this man had known himself, he would never have presumed
to be general.' This would make our character more attrac-
tive—'We ought not, as some say, to love in the expectation
of hating—rather we should hate in the expectation of loving.'
One should make one's moral predilections plain by the very 14
statement of the maxim; or, failing this, one should add one's
reason[6],—as by saying—'We ought to love, not, as some say,
but in the expectation of loving always ; for the other sort of
love is insidious.' Else thus :—'But I do not like the saying ;
for the genuine friend ought to love in the expectation of
loving always.' 'Nor do I like the saying, Do nothing excessively. Bad men should be hated excessively.'

One great help, which maxims lend in speaking, arises 15
from the vulgarity[7] of the hearers. They are delighted when 1395 b

---

[1] *Il.* xii 243.   [2] *Il.* xviii 309.   [3] I xv 14 *supra.*
[4] Quoted by Zenobios II 28. The Corinthian envoy in Thucydides (I 70)
describes it as the national character of the Athenians 'neither to remain in peace
themselves, nor to suffer others to do so.'
[5] The maxims of Solon and Chilon, respectively.
[6] *i.e.* you must add the reason *why you disapprove of the received maxim*; xiii 4.
[7] *i.e.* their love of the commonplace.

a general statement of the speaker hits those opinions which they hold in a particular case. My meaning will be clearer when put as follows—and at the same time we shall be set on the track of the best maxims. A maxim is, as has been said, a general statement, and men are pleased when a sentiment, which they already entertain on special grounds, is stated in general terms. Thus, if a man is afflicted with bad neighbours or bad children, he will give ear to the statement, that nothing is so trying as neighbourhood[1], nothing so foolish as begetting children. Hence, we must guess what sort of prepossessions they have, and how they came by them ; then we must express, in general terms, these views on these subjects.

16 This, then, is one of the advantages of using maxims. It has another still greater :—it gives a moral character to our speech. Speeches have a moral character, when they show a moral purpose. All maxims do effect this, since the man who uses a maxim makes a general declaration of his moral predilections ; so that, if the maxims are good, they give the appearance of a good character to him who uses them.

In regard to maxims, then—their nature, their kinds, the way to use them and the advantages they yield—this account may suffice.

xxii. Let us now speak of Enthymemes—first, generally, of the way to look for them—then, of their topics ; for these two parts of the subject are distinct.

2 It has been said already[2] that the enthymeme is a syllogism, and in what sense it is a syllogism, and

The Enthymeme. General precepts.

3 how it differs from the dialectical syllogism[3]. We must not draw conclusions from far back, and we must not take everything in. If we do the former, the length of the chain causes perplexity ; if the latter, our statement of what is obvious is mere garrulity. This is the reason why the uneducated are more persuasive than the educated for popular audiences,—as the poets say of the uneducated, that 'they have a finer charm for the ear of

---

[1] Demosthenes, Or. 55 § 1, χαλεπώτερον οὐδὲν γείτονος πονηροῦ.
[2] I ii §§ 8, 13.   [3] I ii § 11.

the crowd.'[1] Educated men state general principles and draw
general conclusions ; uneducated men draw conclusions, which
lie close at hand, from facts within their own experience. We
must not argue, then, from all opinions, but from those of the
sort defined,—as from those of the judges, or those of persons
in whom they believe ; it must be clear, too, that these opinions   **1396 a**
are universally or generally entertained. And we must reason,
not exclusively from necessary premisses, but also from merely
probable premisses.

Now, first of all, we must grasp the necessity of knowing 4
all or some of the special facts belonging to the subject on
which we are to speak and reason,—whether the subject of
the reasoning be political or of any other kind ; for, if you
know none of these facts, you will have no premisses. How, 5
for instance, could we advise the Athenians on the question of
going to war, unless we knew the nature of their power,—
whether it is a naval force or a land force, or both,—and its
amount ; then, what their revenues are, and who are their
friends or enemies; further, what wars they have waged, and
how ; and so forth. How could we praise them, if we were 6
not prepared with the seafight at Salamis, or the battle of
Marathon, or the services rendered to the Herakleidæ, and
such things ;—since all men found their praise on the glories,
real or seeming, of its object ? Similarly, they rest their 7
censure on the opposite things, considering what dishonour
attaches or seems to attach to the censured—as that they
brought the Greeks under the yoke, or enslaved those who
had bravely fought with them against the barbarians—the
men of Ægina[2] and Potidæa[3]—and so on ; or, if there has
been any like mistake on their part. In the same way,
accusers and defenders have in their view the special conditions of the case. It makes no difference whether our 8
subject is the Athenians or the Lacedæmonians, or a man
or a god. Suppose we are advising Achilles, praising or
blaming, accusing or defending him ; we must take those
things which are, or seem, peculiar to him, in order that our

---

[1] Euripides, *Hippolytus*, 989.   [2] Thuc. II 27 ; IV 57.
[3] Thuc. II 70.

praise or blame may set out from his particular honours or
dishonours, our accusation or defence from his injustice or
9 justice, our advice from his interests or dangers. And so in
regard to any subject whatever. Thus, the question whether
Justice is or is not a good[1] must be argued from the attributes
of Justice and of the Good.

10   So, since we always effect our proof by these means,
whether our reasoning process is comparatively strict, or
1396 b rather lax; since, that is, we do not take our premises from
things in general, but from things peculiar to our special
subject—and it is plain that the properly logical proof can
be wrought in no other way—it is plainly necessary, as we
showed in the *Topics*[2], to have (first of all) a selection of
premises about the possible and the most convenient sub-
11 jects; secondly, to deal with sudden contingencies on the
same plan—that is, by referring, not to indefinite generalities,
but to the special subject-matter of our speech,—bringing into
the sphere of our argument as many facts as possible, which
have the closest bearing on the subject; for, the larger our
knowledge of its particular conditions, the easier will be the
proof; and, the closer we keep to the subject, the more appro-
12 priate and the less general will be our topics. By 'general'
topics I mean, for instance, praising Achilles for being a man
and a hero and having gone against Troy—these things being
true of many other persons, so that such a speaker praises
Achilles no more than he praises Diomede. By 'special'
topics I mean things which are attributes of Achilles and of
no one else—as having slain Hektor, bravest of the Trojans,
and Kyknos[3], the invulnerable, who hindered all the Greeks
from landing—or because he was the youngest man of the
expedition, and bound by no oath—and so forth.

13   This, then, is one principle, and the first, on which our
Enthymemes, enthymemes are to be chosen—in reference to
(1) demonstra- their special materials. Now let us speak of
tive,
(2) refutative. their elementary forms. By the 'elementary

---

[1] ἢ μὴ ἀγαθόν, omitted in the Paris MS and the Latin transl., and bracketed
by Gaisford, is retained by Spengel, who regards it as a reference to the
argument in Plato's *Republic*.   [2] I 14.
[3] Pindar, *Ol.* II 82 (of Achilles) ὃς Ἕκτορ' ἔσφαλε...Κύκνον τε θανάτῳ πόρεν.

form' of an enthymeme I mean the *place* (or class) to which
it belongs.   There are two kinds of enthymemes.   One kind 14
is Demonstrative (affirmatively or negatively); the other kind
is Refutative :—the distinction being the same as in Dialectic
between Refutation and Syllogism.   The Demonstrative 15
Syllogism consists in drawing a conclusion from consistent propositions ; the Refutative, in drawing a conclusion from conflicting propositions.   Now it may be said that we are in possession 16
of our topics in regard to the several special subjects, which
are useful or necessary.   We have chosen our propositions in
regard to each; so that we have already ascertained the topics
from which enthymemes are to be drawn about Good or Evil,
Honourable or Shameful, Just or Unjust[1]; likewise about characters, feelings, moral states[2].   But further, and from another 17
point of view, let us get commonplaces for enthymemes in **1397 a**
general.   We will point out, side by side[3], the Refutative and
the Demonstrative topics; and the topics of what appear to
be enthymemes, but are not so, since they are not syllogisms.
When these matters have been explained, we will determine
the several modes of destroying[4] or attacking[5] enthymemes.

xxiii.   1. One topic of Demonstrative Enthymemes is from
**An enumera-
tion of heads
of argument,
from which
Enthymemes
can be con-
structed.** opposites.   We must see whether the opposite
holds good of the opposite, for the purpose of
refutation, if the argument is not on our side;—
or, for the purpose of establishing the point, if it
is so.   Thus 'It is good to be temperate; for it is
harmful to be intemperate.'   Or, to take the instance in the
Messēniakos[6]—'If war is the cause of the present evils, we
must correct them by means of peace.'[7]

'If it is not just to wax wroth with unwitting wrong-doers, neither are thanks
due to him who does a good deed because he must.'[8]

[1] i iv 7–xiv.
[2] The virtues and vices (II xii 1) ; see, in general, II i–xviii.
[3] παρασημαινόμενοι, 'pointing out, side by side' (as if in parallel columns).
This seems better than the sense given in the Berlin Index, *praeterea adnotare* and
in Liddell and Scott, 'note in passing.'   [4] c. xxv *infra.*
[5] ἐνστάσεων, *instantiarum*, 'objections to one of the premisses.'
[6] Of Alkidamas, cp. I xiii 2, *supra.*   [7] Fragm. 2, Sauppe.
[8] Nauck, *Fragm. Adesp.* 80 ed. 2 ; ascribed to Agathon or Theodektes.

'But, if there is such a thing in the world as specious lying, thou mayest be sure of the opposite—that there is much truth, which does not win men's trust.'[1]

2　　2. Another topic is supplied by the various inflexions of the stem. What can or cannot be said of one form, can or cannot be said of another. Thus—'The just is not always good; else *justly* would be always *well*; but the fact is that it is not desirable to be put to death justly.'[2]

3　　3. Another topic is from Relative Terms. If it can be said of the one person that he *acted* well or justly, it can be said of the other that he has *suffered* well or justly; or, if the command was right, the execution of the command has been right. Thus Diomedon, the farmer of taxes[3], said of the taxes—'If it is no shame for you to sell, it is no shame for us to buy.' And, if 'well' or 'justly' can be predicated of the sufferer, it can be predicated of the doer. This argument, however, may be used fallaciously: for, granting that the man has deserved his fate, it does not follow that he deserved it from you. Hence we ought to 1397 b consider separately the fitness of the suffering for the sufferer, and the fitness of the deed for the doer, and then turn the argument in whichever way is convenient;—for sometimes there is a discrepancy, and (the justice of the suffering) does not hinder (the deed from being wrong). Thus, in the *Alkmœon* of Theodektes[4]:

'But did no one in the world hate thy mother?'

Alkmæon answers—

'Nay, one should take the question in two parts.'

And when Alphesibœa asks 'how?', he rejoins—

'They doomed her to death, but spared my life.'

Take, again, the lawsuit about Demosthenes and the slayers of Nikânor[5]:—since they were judged to have slain him justly, he was held to have deserved his death. Or the case of the

---

[1] Euripides, *Thyestes*, Fragm. 396 Nauck.
[2] I ix 15.
[3] Nothing more is known of him.
[4] 376–335 B.C., pupil of Isokrates; Fragm. 2, Nauck ed. 2. Alkmæon murdered his mother Eriphyle, for betraying Amphiaraos. Alphesibœa was the wife of Alkmæon.
[5] This lawsuit is unknown.

man who was killed at Thebes[1]—in which the accused asks that it may be decided whether that man deserved to die,—meaning that it cannot be wrong to have slain a man who deserved death.

4. Another topic is that of Degree; as—'If the very gods 4 are not all-knowing, men are not likely to be so'; for this means that, if a condition is not present, where it would be *more* natural, of course it is not present, where it would be *less* so. The inference that a man strikes his neighbours, seeing that he strikes his father, comes from this argument—that, if the rarer thing exists, the more frequent thing exists also; for people strike their fathers more rarely than they strike their neighbours. The argument, then, may stand thus. Or it may be argued that, if a thing does not exist, where it is more frequent, it does not exist where it is rarer; or that, if it exists where it is rarer, it exists where it is more frequent —according as it may be needful to prove that it does or that it does not exist[2]. Again, this topic may be used in a case of 5 parity:—hence the lines—

'Thy father is to be pitied for having lost his children ; and is not Œneus to be pitied for having lost his famous son?'[3]

So it may be argued that, if Theseus did no wrong, neither did Paris; or that, if the Tyndaridæ did none, neither did Paris; or that, if Hektor killed Patroklos, Paris killed Achilles[4]; or that, if other artists are not contemptible, neither are philosophers[5]; or that, if generals are not contemptible, because in

---

[1] Euphron, tyrant of Sikyon till about 364 B.C. When an oligarchy was reestablished, he fled. With the aid of Athens, he afterwards regained the city ; but, finding it necessary to gain the support of Thebes, he went thither to obtain it. He was followed by some of his enemies, who murdered him in the *Kadmeia*, Xen. *Hellen.* VII 3 (R. C. J.).

[2] 'The inference'—' does not exist.' A translation of the longer form of this passage, preserved in the Paris MS, and adopted by Spengel and Roemer.

[3] *Fragm. Adesp.* 81 Nauck, from the *Meleager* of Euripides or of Antiphon. The scholiast suggests that Œneus may be speaking to Althæa—Althæa's brother having been killed by Meleager.

[4] Polykrates, Sauppe, *Fragm. Or. Att.* IX. 7. Theseus, with the aid of Peirithoüs, carried off Helen from Sparta, while she was a young girl, and placed her at Aphidnæ in Attica, under the care of Æthra, mother of Theseus. While Theseus was absent in Hades, the Dioskuri made an expedition into Attica,—took Athens, delivered Helen, and brought Æthra a slave to Sparta (R. C. J.).

[5] Isokrates, *Antid.* §§ 209—214.

many cases they are put to death[1], neither are sophists; or, 'if a private person ought to respect the opinion of Athens, Athens ought to respect that of Greece.'[2]

6   5. Another topic is from considerations of time. Thus Iphikrates said in his speech against Harmodios[3]—'If, before doing the deed, I had claimed the statue on condition of doing it, you would have given it: now that I have done the deed, will you not give it? You are ready to promise rewards, when you expect a benefit;—do not withdraw them, when you have reaped it.' Again, the argument about the Thebans

1398 a allowing Philip to pass through into Attica:—'If he had asked this before he came to the help of Phocis, they would have promised it. It is absurd, then, if they are to refuse him a passage because he waived the point and trusted them.'[4]

7   6. Another topic is taken from things said (by the adversary), applied to our own case[5] as compared with his. The ways of doing this are various[6]—as in the *Teucer*[7]. Iphikrates used this against Aristophon,—asking whether Aristophon would betray the ships for money?—and, when he said 'No,' rejoining—'So you, being Aristophon, would not betray them; would I, being Iphikrates?'[8] It is necessary that the adversary should be more liable to the suspicion of crime; else, the effect will be ludicrous—as if one were to say this in answer to the accusations of Aristeides. The argument is

---

[1] θανατοῦνται Paris MS, Spengel: vulgo ἡττῶνται.

[2] Lysias, Or. XVIII, Fragm. 1 Sauppe.

[3] Dionysios, *De Lysia*, c. 12, mentions the Speech *on the Statue of Iphikrates* as probably spurious on grounds of style and chronology (R. C. J.).

[4] Shortly before Chæronea, 338 B.C., Philip and his allies demanded that the Thebans should either join them in invading Attica, or give them a passage through Bœotia, Dem. *De Cor.* § 213. Spengel thinks this is quoted from the representations made by Philip's envoys (R. C. J.).

[5] καθ᾽ αὐτούς vulgo; καθ᾽ αὐτοῦ, 'against myself,' is conjectured by Bywater, and accepted by Roemer.

[6] διαφέρει δ᾽ ὁ τρόπος, 'the character of the speaker is important,' 'it is the character that here makes the difference' (Spengel); 'this method excels all others' (Gaisford). τρόπος is interpreted as τόπος by Victorius and Muretus.

[7] Of Sophokles; cp. III xv 9. Teucer is here defending himself against Odysseus.

[8] Lysias, Or. LXV, Fragm. 1. In 355, Aristophon, the Azenian, and Chares prosecuted Iphikrates for his failure in the last campaign of the Social War. Iphikrates was acquitted; cp. III x 7 (R. C. J.).

meant to create distrust of the accusers; for, as a rule, the accuser is by way of being better than the defendant: this assumption, then, should always be confuted. Generally speaking, a man is absurd when he upbraids others with what he himself does, or would do; or when he exhorts others to do what he himself does not, or is incapable of doing.

7. Another topic is from Definition. Thus—'What is the 8 supernatural? Is it a god or the work of a god? He, however, who thinks that there is the work of a god, must needs think that there are gods.'[1] Or, take the saying of Iphikrates[2], that the best man is the noblest, for Harmodios and Aristogeiton had nothing noble about them, until they had done a noble deed;—and that he himself is more nearly akin to them:—'At all events my deeds are more nearly akin than yours to the deeds of Harmodios and Aristogeiton.'[3] Another example is the remark in the *Alexandros*[4]:—'all will allow that men of unruly life are not contented with the enjoyment of one love.' Or the reason which Sokrates gives for not going to Archelaos:—'It is an insolence not to be able to make an equal return for benefits, just as it is to requite them with evil'[5]. In all these cases the speaker defines and ascertains the meaning of a term with a view to reasoning on his subject.

8. Another commonplace is from the various senses of a 9 word—of which 'rightly' was our example in the *Topics*[6].

9. Another is from Division: as 'All men do wrong from 10 one of three motives—on account of *this*, or *this*, or *this*; here two of the motives are out of the question, and the accusers themselves do not impute the third.'

10. Another topic is from Induction: as, from the case of 11 the woman of Peparêthos[7], it might be argued that women

---

[1] Cp. Plato, *Apol. Socr.* 27 C–E.

[2] In the ἀπολογία against Harmodios, 371 B.C. ; § 6 *supra* (cp. Cope, *Comm.* ii 256).

[3] Lysias, Or. XVIII, Fragm. 2.

[4] Polykrates, *Alexandros*, ix fragm. 2, p. 223 Sauppe.

[5] Xenophon, *Apol. Socr.* 17 ; Diog. Laërt. *Vit. Socr.* II 5, 25.

[6] I 15. The word ὀρθῶς, however, is not used there as an example. Muretus omits the clause ; Robortelli and Riccoboni propose περὶ τούτου ὀρθῶς εἴρηται.

[7] A small island off the coast of Thessaly, east of Halonnêsos. This passage

always discern the truth about their own children. Thus in
1398 b an instance at Athens, when the orator Mantias was at law with
his son, the mother settled the point for him[1]; in another instance at Thebes, the woman of Dodona declared Ismênias to
be father of the son whom Stilbôn was disputing with him, and
on this ground the Thebans held Thettaliskos to be the son of
Ismênias[2]. Take, again, the example in the *Law* of Theodektês[3]:
'If men do not entrust their own horses to those who have taken
bad care of other people's, neither will they entrust their own
ships to those who have upset the ships of others. If it is so,
then, in all cases, we ought not to use for our own protection
those who have ill-guarded the safety of others.'   Or, take the
saying of Alkidamas[4], that 'all men honour the wise:—at least
the Parians have paid honour to Archilochos, though he was a
reviler; the Chians to Homer, though he was not their fellow-
citizen; the Mytileneans to Sappho, though a woman,—the
Lacedæmonians even raised Cheilon to their Senate, though
they are anything but fond of letters; the Italiots honoured
Pythagoras; the Lampsakenes gave burial, and still pay
honours, to Anaxagoras, though an alien...<They who use
the laws of philosophers always prosper> for the Athenians
prospered by the use of Solon's laws, and the Lacedæmonians
by using those of Lykurgos; and, at Thebes, no sooner did

is paraphrased by Eustath. on *Od.* i 215, 'A woman of Peparethos, by her
deposition that a boy was her own son, solved the contention about him,' *i.e.* the
mother, who had not seen her son for a long time, was able, by memory or
insight, to bring some evidence which settled the point (R. C. J.).

[1] The general statement, that mothers always know their sons, is here confirmed
by two instances:—Mantias had one legitimate, and two illegitimate sons. The
legitimate son, Mantitheos, brings an action against the elder of the illegitimate
sons, who claimed the name of Mantitheos, but who ought to bear the name of
Bœôtos (Dem. Or. xxxix πρὸς Βοιωτὸν περὶ τοῦ ὀνόματος). The illegitimate
Mantitheos had previously brought an action against Mantias; and his mother
Plangôn had sworn to his being the son of Mantias and to his brother being so
(Dem. *l. c.* § 4). Again in Or. xl (πρὸς B. περὶ προικὸς) § 4, she is spoken of as
ἐξαπατήσασα ὅρκῳ (R. C. J.).

[2] Ismênias and Stilbôn disputed the fathership of Thettaliskos. The story
seems to be unknown (R. C. J.).

[3] § 17 *infra*. A declamation on the legal regulation of the position of
mercenaries at Athens; Sauppe, *Or. Att.* III 247 *a*.

[4] *Fragm.* 5, from the Μουσεῖον, Sauppe, 155 *a*.

philosophers[1] become the leading men, than the State prospered.'

11. Another topic is taken from a decision on the same 12 point, or on a like point, or on the opposite point—especially if it has been the decision of all men at all times; or else of a majority of mankind,—or of wise or good men, most or all,— or of our own judges, or of them to whom they listen; or of those whose decision, being that of the masters of the situation, it is impossible to reverse, or discreditable to reverse, as that of the gods, or our father or our teachers,—as Autoklês[2] said of Mixidêmidês, that it was strange, if trial before the Areiopagos was good enough for the 'Awful Goddesses, but not good enough for Mixidêmidês[3]. Or, take Sappho's saying that death is an evil—for the gods have so judged, or they would die. Or the remark of Aristippos, in answer to a saying of Plato's, which he thought rather compromising—'Well, at least our friend' (meaning Sokrates) 'said nothing of the kind.'[4] Again, Agêsipolis[5] asked the god at Delphi (after first consulting the oracle at Olympia), whether *he* took the same view as his father—implying that it would be indecent to 1399 a contradict his father. And thus Isokrates represented Helen as good, since Theseus chose her[6]; Paris as good, seeing that the goddesses preferred him[7]; Evagoras, again, he says, is good, inasmuch as Konon after his misfortune[8] passed by all others and came to Evagoras[9].

12. Another topic consists in taking separately the parts 13 of a subject[10]: as in the *Topics*[11]—what sort of motion is the

---

[1] Epameinôndas and Pelopidas.

[2] Autoklês, son of Strombichidês, one of the Athenian envoys at the congress of Sparta in 371 B.C.; Xen. *Hellen.* VI 3 § 2.

[3] Sauppe, p. 220.

[4] Cp. Grote's *Plato*, iii 471, and Cope's *Comm.* ii 265 f.

[5] Muretus and Bekker, ed. 3; cp. Xen. *Hellen.* IV 7 § 2, first quoted by Victorius. The MSS have Ἡγήσιππος retained by Roemer; Spengel points out that Ἡγησίπολις is the normal Ionic equivalent for Ἀγησίπολις.

[6] Isokrates, *Helen*, 18-38.   [7] *Helen*, 41-48.

[8] In 405, after Ægospotami; Xen. *Hellen.* II 1 § 20.

[9] Isokrates, *Evagoras*, 51 f.

[10] No. 12 and no. 8 are hard to distinguish. Here, the idea of *dealing separately with the parts* is uppermost; there, the idea of showing what parts are comprised in the whole (R. C. J.).   [11] ii 4; iv 2, 6.

soul? It must be *this* kind or *this* kind. The *Sokrates* of
Theodektes affords an example—'Against what temple has he
sinned? What gods, acknowledged by the city, has he failed
to honour?'[1]

14   13. Since it happens, in most cases, that the same thing
has the same result, good or bad, another topic consists in
arguing from the Consequence,—whether in exhorting or dissuading, accusing or defending, praising or blaming. Thus:—
'Culture has the bad consequence of exciting envy, and the
good consequence of making one wise.'[2] Therefore 'we ought
not to cultivate ourselves, for it is not well to be envied.' Or
rather—'we *ought* to cultivate ourselves, for it is well to be
wise.' The Art of Kallippos[3] is simply this topic, with the
addition of the topic of Possibility and the rest, as described
above (c. xix).

15   14. It is another topic, when we have either to exhort or
dissuade in reference to two opposite things, and have to use
the method just stated in regard to both. There is this
difference that, in the former case, any two things are contrasted; here, the things contrasted are opposites. For
instance, the priestess urged her son *not* to speak in public;
'for,' she said, 'if you speak justly, you will be hated by men;
if unjustly, by the gods.' Or, '*No*—you *ought* to speak in
public; for if you speak justly, the gods will love you; if unjustly, men.' This is the same thing as the saying about
buying the salt along with the marsh[4]; and in this consists the
'retortion'[5] of the dilemma—when each of two opposite things
has both a good and a bad consequence, opposite respectively
to each other.

16   15. As men do not approve the same things in public
and in their secret thoughts, but in public must approve just

[1] Sauppe, 247 *a*.
[2] Cp. Euripides, *Medea*, 294; II 21 § 2 *supra*.
[3] § 21; one of the early writers on the Art of Rhetoric, possibly the person
described as one of the first pupils of Isokrates in *Antid.* § 93. He is not to be
confounded with the Kallippos mentioned in I xii 29 (Cope, *Comm.* ii 271 f).
[4] *i.e.* 'The unprofitable and unwholesome marsh with the profitable salt
inseparably connected with it' (Cope); a proverb not found elsewhere.
[5] βλαίσωσις from βλαισός, *valgus*, 'with legs bent in,' here used of 'retorting' a
dilemma.

and honourable things, while, from their private point of view, they are apt to prefer their own advantage, another topic consists in trying to infer either of these sentiments from the other. This is the most effective sort of paradox.

16.   Another topic is taken from the symmetry of results. 17 Thus Iphikrates[1], when they were trying to make his son take a public service, because though he was under age, he was a big boy, said that, 'if they count big boys as men, they must enact that little men are boys.'   And Theodektes in his *Law*[2]:   1399 b 'You make citizens of mercenaries, such as Strabax[3] and Charidêmos[4], for their merit; will you not make exiles of those, who have done fatal mischief with the mercenaries?'

17.   Another topic consists in arguing identity of cause 18 from identity of effect.   Thus, Xenophanes[5] said that those who allege the gods to have come into existence are as impious as those who allege that they are dead; for, either way, it results that at one time the gods were not.   And, universally, any given result may be treated as constant:— 'You are about to decide the fate, not of Isokrates, but of the pursuit of Philosophy.'[6]   Or, it may be argued, that ' to give earth and water'[7] means slavery—' to share in the Common Peace'[8] means obeying orders.   (We must take whichever view may serve.)

18.   Another topic is taken from the fact that men do not 19 always make the same choice at a later as at an earlier time, but may reverse it.   This enthymeme gives an example—' It is strange if, when we were in exile, we fought to return, and,

[1] Sauppe, p. 219.

[2] Sauppe, p. 247.

[3] Mentioned by Dem. *Lept.* § 84, as having received *privileges* for the sake of Iphikrates.

[4] Of Ôreos in Eubœa; he first entered the Athenian service as a *mercenary* under Iphikrates about 367.

[5] The Eleatic, *c.* 620–520 B.C. 'The One is God.'   Being is self-existent, and therefore eternal (R. C. J.).   *Fragm. Incert.* 7 Mullach.

[6] Isokr. *Antid.* 173 f, quoted by Spengel in support of his substitution of Ἰσοκράτους (accepted by Roemer) for the manuscript reading Σωκράτους.

[7] Cp. Herodotus, IV 126.

[8] The 'Common Peace' made between the Greeks (except the Lacedæmonians) and Alexander, after Philip's death in 336 B.C.   Pseudo-Demosthenes, Or. XVII 30, τῆς κοινῆς εἰρήνης μετέχειν.

having returned, are to go into exile to avoid fighting[1].   In the one case, they chose to keep their homes at the cost of fighting: —in the other, they chose *not* to fight at the cost of losing their homes.

20   19.   Another topic consists in treating the conceivable as the actual reason for a thing existing or having come to pass. Suppose, for example, that one has given something to another for the purpose of paining him by withdrawing it:—whence the saying—

> ' The god bestows large blessings on many men, not in kindness, but that the troubles which they find may be more signal.'[2]

Or the passage from Antiphon's *Meleager*:—

> ' Not that they may slay the beast, but that they may witness the bravery of Meleager to Greece.'[3]

Or the remark in the *Ajax* of Theodektes, that Diomedes[4] chose Odysseus, not in order to honour him, but in order that his own follower might be a lesser man; for this motive is possible[5].

21   20.   Another topic is common to the lawcourts and to debate—viz. to consider the inducements and drawbacks, the reasons for doing or avoiding an action; for these are the conditions which, according as they are present or absent, make an action desirable or undesirable: the former, if, for example, it is possible, easy, advantageous to the doer or his friends, hurtful and damaging to his enemies,—or if the penalty for the act is comparatively small.   The grounds

1400 a of suasion are these—the grounds of dissuasion are the opposite.   The same motives form grounds of accusation or defence:—the deterring motives, of defence; the inciting motives, of accusation.   This topic represents the whole Art of Pamphilos[6] and of Kallippos.

---

[1] Lysias, Or. XXXIV 11.

[2] *Fragm. Adesp.* 82 Nauck.   Victorius quotes Cæsar, *De B. G.* I 14.

[3] p. 792 Nauck.

[4] *Il.* X 218–254.

[5] p. 801 Nauck.

[6] Pamphilus, like Kallippos (§ 14), 'belonged to the early school of Rhetoricians of the age of Gorgias.' Cicero, *De Or.* III 82 (Cope, *Comm.* ii 285).

21.   Another topic concerns things which appear to have   22
happened, but which are incredible. We may say, that men
would not have fancied them, if they had not been true or
nearly true.   Or we may say, that this makes it *more* certain ;
for the things in which men believe are either facts or probabilities ; if then it be incredible and not probable, it must be
true ; because its probability and plausibility are not the reason.
for this belief about it.   Thus Androkles[1] the Pitthean said in
arraigning the law, when they interrupted his speech—'The
laws need a law to correct them, just as fish need salt—
improbable and surprising as it is that creatures reared in
brine should need salt—just as dried olives need olive-oil—
though it is incredible that olive-oil should be needed by the
sources of its own being.'[2]

22.   Another topic, useful for Refutation, consists in taking   23
account of any inconsistency in the series of dates or acts
or statements, and this in three separate ways.   First, in the
case of the adversary—as :—'He says that he loves you,
but he conspired with the Thirty.'   Secondly, in our own
case ;—'And he says that I am litigious, but cannot prove
that I have ever been engaged in a single lawsuit.'   Thirdly,
in our case, as compared with that of the adversary :—'*He*
has never lent anything, but *I* have ransomed many of you.'

23.   Another topic, useful for persons and causes dis-   24
credited, or seemingly discredited, by a prejudice, is to give
the reason of the paradox; for then there is something which
accounts for the prejudice.   Thus a woman, who had palmed
off her son on another woman, was suspected from embracing
him of being the youth's paramour ; but, when the cause was
stated, the prejudice was dispelled.   Thus, again, in the *Ajax*
of Theodektes[3], Odysseus tells Ajax *why* he is not thought
braver than Ajax, though he is really so.

---

[1] Androkles denounced Alkibiades for the mutilation of the Hermæ, in 415 B.C.;
he was put to death by the oligarchs at the beginning of the reign of terror which
preceded the revolution of the Four Hundred, in 411.   Thuc. VIII 65; Andok.
De Myst. § 27 (R. C. J.).

[2] Sauppe, p. 153.

[3] p. 801 Nauck ; his *Alkmæon* is quoted in § 3.

J.   9

25   24. Another topic consists in arguing, from the presence
or absence of the Cause, the existence or non-existence of the
Effect; for Cause and Effect go together, and nothing is
without a cause.   Thus, when Thrasybulos[1] charged Leôdamas[2]
with having been recorded as infamous[3] on the acropolis, and
having erased the record in the time of the Thirty, Leôdamas
said in his defence—'It is impossible; the Thirty would have
trusted me the more for my enmity with the people being
registered.'[4]

26   25.   There is another topic, when it was or is possible to
devise a better course than the speaker is recommending or
1400 b taking, or has taken.   Clearly, if the course is not this better
course, he has not taken it; for no one willingly and wittingly
chooses the worse.   (This however is a fallacy; for the better
plan often becomes clear after the event, though it was doubtful
before it.)

27   26.   When an intended action is contrary to some former
action, another topic consists in viewing them together.   Thus,
when the people of Elea asked Xenophanes[5] whether they
should sacrifice to Leukothea[6] and wail[7] for her, his advice
was—'If you consider her a goddess, do not wail: if a woman,
do not sacrifice.'

28   27.   Another topic consists in founding accusation or
defence upon mistakes.   Thus, in the *Medea* of Karkinos[8],
the accusers contend that she has slain her children—at any
rate, they are not to be found;—for Medea had made the
mistake of sending her children away.   She says, in her
defence, that she would have slain, *not* the children, but
Jason; for, supposing her capable of the other murder, it

---

[1] Of Steiria, the restorer of the Democracy in 403 B.C.

[2] I vii 13 *supra* (cp. Cope, *Comm.* ii 291).

[3] στηλίτης, cp. Isokr. *De bigis*, § 9, στηλίτην ἀναγράφειν (of 'posting'
Alkibiades as a public traitor), Dem. *Phil.* III 45; Andok. *de Myst.* 51. A
similar argument is used by Lysias on behalf of the men denounced by Agoratos,
Or. XIII 51 (R. C. J.).

[4] Sauppe, *Orat. Att.*, *Fragm.*, p. 216.   [5] § 17 *supra*.

[6] The name of *Ino* after her death, just as Palæmon was the name of
Melikertes.

[7] Probably the ritual represented her sufferings in life (R. C. J.).

[8] Nauck's *Fragm. Tr. Gr.*, p. 798.

would have been a blunder for her not to have done *this*. This special topic of enthymeme constitutes the whole of the Art in use before Theodôros[1].

28. Another topic is from a play on names. Thus 29 Sophokles—

> ' Steel, truly, like the name thou bearest.'[2]

This is commonly used in praises of the gods. Thus, too, Konon punned on the name of Thrasybulos[3]; Hêrodikos[4] on the names of Thrasymachos[5] and Pôlos[6], and said of Draco the lawgiver that his laws are 'not the laws of a man but of a dragon—they are so cruel.' And thus in Euripides, Hecuba says of 'Aphrodite (the Foam-born),'

> ' Well may her name be the beginning of folly.'[7]

And Chærêmôn—

> ' Pentheus, with name prophetic of his doom.'[8]

The Refutative Enthymemes seem more brilliant[9] than 30 the Demonstrative, because the refutative enthymeme is the bringing together of opposites in a small compass; and, when two things are put side by side, they are plainer to the hearer. But, of all syllogisms, whether refutative or demon-

---

[1] ἡ πρότερον Θεοδώρου τέχνη. Spengel remarks that what is known of Korax and Tisias agrees with this. Inferior MSS have ἡ προτέρα, either (1) 'the former Art of Theodôros,' implying that he had written two Arts, or (2) 'the earlier Art of Theodôros,' as compared with Aristotle's own time. On Theodôros cp. III xiii 5, and Plato *Phaedr.* 266 E (R. C. J.).

[2] Frag. 597, Nauck, ed. 2. The line refers to the cruelty of Sidêrô (the wife of Salmôneus) to her step-daughter Tyro. σιδήρῳ, the reading of the best MS, is preferred by Nauck and accepted by Roemer.

[3] § 25 *supra*.

[4] Hêrodikos of Selymbria, besides being a physician (cp. I v 10), was a sophist (πάσσοφος ἀνήρ, Plato, *Protag.* 316 A).

[5] ἀεὶ Θρασύμαχος εἶ, Thrasymachos of Chalkêdon, the second of the technographers, Tisias being the first, Theodôrus the third (Ar. *De Soph. El.*). Cp. Plato, *Phædr.* 361 C. 'Mitioris sophistae obiurgatio est in vehementiorem' (Spengel).

[6] ἀεὶ σὺ πῶλος εἶ, 'Colt by name and colt by nature' (Thompson's Introd. to *Gorgias* p. v, n. 4). *Gorg.* 463 E.

[7] *Troades*, 990. Aphrodite and ἀφροσύνη have the first half of the word in common (Cope).

[8] Fragm. 4, Nauck. Chærêmôn, an Athenian tragedian, later than Aristophanes. Some think he was alive in Aristotle's time, *Poët.* 1 and 24, *Probl.* III 16. This line probably comes from his *Dionysos* (R. C. J.).

[9] εὐδοκιμεῖ. Cp. III ix 17.

strative, those are most applauded, of which we foresee the
conclusion from the beginning—and this, not because they are
superficial ; for we are at the same time pleased with our own
quickness[1]:—or those, with which we can just keep up, as soon
as they are stated.

xxiv.   As there can be both a real and a sham syllogism,
it follows that there can be both a real and a
sham enthymeme,—the enthymeme being a sort
of syllogism[2].

Topics of apparent enthymemes.

2   1.   Among the topics of Apparent Enthymemes is the topic
1401 a   from Diction[3]. (*a*) One department of this topic, as in Dialectic,
consists in making a final statement, as if it were a logical
conclusion, when no reasoning process has been performed.
' *So* it is not thus or thus'; ' *So* it must be thus or thus.'   And,
in the case of enthymemes, a compact and antithetical expression has itself an air of enthymeme[4]; such expression
being the province of enthymeme.   The *figure* of the Diction
seems to be the source of this fallacy.   It is a help towards a
syllogistic style of Diction to state the sum of many syllogisms
—' He saved some—he avenged others—he freed Greece.'[5]
Each of these points has been proved from other things; and,
when they are put together, we have the effect of a fresh
result.

(*b*)   Another department of the topic consists in Equivocation:—as, to say that the mouse is a noble animal, since the
most august of all rites, that of the Mysteries, is derived from

---

[1] We are pleased (not only with the speaker and his enthymeme, but) with
ourselves also (ἅμα) for our sagacity in anticipating the conclusion ; (and therefore
we do not think it superficial).   Cope, *Comm.* ii 300.

[2] I i 11 *supra*

[3] παρὰ τὴν λέξιν.   Here the Fallacies of Diction are classified as (1) παρὰ τὸ
σχῆμα, arising from the fashion or style of the language used (Cope), (*a*) when a
conclusion is drawn, without having been established by reasoning ; (*b*) when
mere smartness of antithesis is made to do duty for an enthymeme ; (2) παρὰ τὴν
ὁμωνυμίαν, depending upon equivocation, or play on words (R. C. J.).   On the
classification in *De Soph. El.* cp. Cope, *Comm.* II 301, 304.

[4] <καὶ ἐν> τοῖς ἐνθυμήμασι τὸ συνεστραμμένον καὶ ἀντικειμένως εἰπεῖν φαίνεται
ἐνθύμημα, Vahlen's proposal, approved by Spengel and Roemer.

[5] Isokrates, *Evagoras*, 65–69.

it[1]. Or, suppose that the encomiast of a dog were to avail himself of the constellation so called, or of Pindar's saying about Pan—

'Blest one, whom the Olympians call the Great Mother's faithful hound, taking all forms by turn.'[2]

Or one might argue :—' As it is a great disgrace that there should be no dog in a house—so it is plain that the dog is honourable.' Or—' Hermes is the most liberal of the gods ; for he is the only one, about whom there is such a proverb as " Shares in the luck of Hermes!"'[3] Or ' The gift of speech[4] (by which we express our *estimates*) is the best of things, since good men are not valued at so much money—they are *esteemed*'; for the same words may mean 'worthy to have the gift of speech' or 'worthy of esteem.'

2. Another topic consists in putting together two separate statements or dividing a composite statement ;—for, since things which are not identical often seem so, one should represent the fact in whichever way will serve best. This is the argument of Euthydêmos; as, about knowing that there is a trireme in the Peiræus: the man knows the two facts *separately*[5]. Or the argument that he who knows the letters knows the word, since the word is the same thing;—or that, if twice anything is noxious, the thing by itself cannot be wholesome; for it is absurd that two good things should make a bad thing. Put thus, the enthymeme is refutative ; thus, demonstrative[6]—' A good thing cannot consist of two bad things.' The whole topic lends itself to false reasonings.

---

[1] Polykrates, Fragm. vi p. 221 f, Sauppe.

[2] Pindar, Fragm. 96 Christ. Pan is the κύων παντοδαπός, 'the faithful guardian, taking all forms by turn,' of the Great Mother, because his statue stood before her temple. Cp. *Fragm.* 95, ὦ Πάν, Ἀρκαδίας μεδέων, καὶ σεμνῶν ἀδύτων φύλαξ, Ματρὸς μεγάλας ὀπαδέ, σεμνᾶν Χαρίτων μέλημα τερπνόν, and *Pyth.* III 77 (R. C. J.).

[3] κοινὸς Ἑρμῆς, Theophrastus, *Char.* xxx (xxvi Jebb).

[4] λόγος is here used in two senses :—(1) speech, *ratio*, (2) thought, or estimate, *oratio* (R. C. J.).

[5] *De Soph. El.* c. 20 p. 177 *b* 12, καὶ ὁ Εὐθυδήμου δὲ λόγος, ἆρ' οἶδας σὺ νῦν οὔσας ἐν Πειραιεῖ τριήρεις ἐν Σικελίᾳ ὤν ; 'Do you, being in Sicily, know that there are triremes now in the Peiræus?' (see Cope's *Comm.* ii 307 f).

[6] ἐλεγκτικόν, it refutes the contention that the thing is good; δεικτικόν, it establishes that contention (R. C. J.).

Take, again, the saying of Polykrates[1] about Thrasybulos, that he put down thirty tyrants[2]—where the speaker uses Composition[3]. Or the passage in the *Orestes* of Theodektes, which illustrates Division:—

‘ ’Tis just that whoso slays her husband ’[4]

1401 b should die: it is just moreover that the son should avenge his father: well, these are the things which have actually been done[5]:—(a fallacy,) for, when put together, they perhaps do not form a just act. (This might, however, be a Fallacy of Defect—as the speaker does not say by *whose* hand the woman should die.)

4   3. Another topic consists in establishing or destroying a statement by indignant assertion[6]. This is when the speaker, without proving the fact, makes much of it; for it is made to appear either that the thing has not been done, when it is the defendant who amplifies, or that it has been done, when it is the accuser who is passionate. This is not, then, an enthymeme: the hearer wrongly concludes that the act was or was not done, though this has not been proved.

5   4. Another topic is from a Sign[7]; for here, again, the reasoning is not strict. Thus suppose one to say—‘Lovers are serviceable to States; for the love of Harmodios and Aristogeiton overthrew the tyrant Hipparchos.’[8] Or suppose one to say ‘Dionysios[9] is a thief, for he is a bad man.’ This, of course, is inconclusive,—for a bad man is not always a thief, though a thief is always a bad man.

6   5. Another fallacy is from the Accident—as in the saying

---

[1] Quint. III vi 26; Sauppe's *Or. Att., Fragm.*, p. 221 *b*.

[2] Sauppe, p. 221 *b*.

[3] συντίθησι γάρ. It is true, in regard to each of thirty men individually, that he was a member of a government put down by Thrasybulos. But the speaker joins each of those thirty to his 29 colleagues, and makes him represent a *separate* tyranny (R. C. J.).

[4] Fragm. 5 Nauck.

[5] οὐκοῦν [καὶ] ταῦτα πέπρακται, Spengel, Roemer.   [6] δεινώσει, xxi 10.

[7] *De Soph. El.* c. 5 refers this to the next topic but one,—where the fallacy is due to ‘the Consequence.’

[8] Thuc. VI 54 f; Plato, *Symposium*, 182 C.

[9] Dionysios, like Sokrates and Koriskos, elsewhere, here means ‘anybody’ (Cope).

of Polykrates[1] about the mice, that they did good service by gnawing through the bow-strings[2].   Or one might argue that an invitation to dinner was a great honour, for it was on account of not being invited that Achilles was wroth with the Greeks at Tenedos[3]: he was wroth on the ground that he was slighted, and the slight consisted in the absence of the invitation.

6.   Another fallacy is from the Consequence.   Thus, in 7 the *Encomium on Paris*[4], he is said to be high-minded; for, scorning the converse of the crowd, he lived alone on Ida.   As high-minded men are of this character, Paris also might be deemed high-minded.   Again—because he is finely dressed and goes about at night, he is an adulterer; for these are their ways.   A like argument is that poor men sing and dance in temples, and that exiles can live where they please.   These are attributes of men reputed prosperous; and so people might be thought prosperous for having these attributes.   It is the 'how' that makes the difference; hence this fallacy comes also into the topic of Defect.

7.   Another topic is to treat as cause that which is no 8 cause—on the ground (for example) that one thing has happened along with another, or just after it,—the sequel being assumed to be the effect.   This is a favourite topic with men in public life: thus Dêmadês said that the policy of Demosthenes had been the cause of all the mischief; for after it came the war[5].

---

[1] Sauppe, p. 221 *b*.   [2] Herodotus, II 141.

[3] Sophokles, Ἀχαιῶν σύλλογος, p. 161 Nauck.

[4] Polykrates, p. 223, Sauppe; quoted in c. 23 §§ 3, 8, 12.

[5] Fragm. 2, p. 318 Sauppe.   Spengel asks, Why should Aristotle quote this charge against Demosthenes from *Dêmadês*, when the same charge is made by a more illustrious speaker, Aeschines, in the Speech against Ktêsiphôn, § 134 (330 B.C.)?   He answers :—(1) probably the words μετ' ἐκείνην γὰρ συνέβη ὁ πόλεμος are the actual words of Dêmadês; (2) probably the *Rhetoric* was written before 330.   The passage of Philip through Phocis (338 B.C.) is mentioned in II xxiii 1 ; and the 'Common Peace' of 336 is noticed, *ib.* § 18.   Spengel would put the *Rhetoric* between 336 and 330.   He makes a needless difficulty in assuming that the words μετ' ἐκείνην κτλ, as applied by Aristotle, imply that Demosthenes' public activity did not continue after the war.   They only imply that it had begun before the war (R. C. J.).

9   8. Another topic is from the Defect[1] of 'when' and 'how': as in the argument[2] that Paris had a right to take Helen; for the choice was given to her by her father[3]. Not, it may be supposed, for ever, but only in the first instance. After the first choice, the father's authority ceases. Or, one
1402 a might argue that to beat free men was outrage. It is not so in every case, but only for him who strikes the first blow.

10   9. Again, an apparent syllogism may be derived, as in Eristic, from the interchange of the absolute with what is not absolute, but only particular:—as, in Dialectic, it may be argued that the non-existent *is*, for the non-existent *is* non-existent; and that the unknowable can be known, for we can know about the unknowable that it is unknowable. Thus, in Rhetoric also, an apparent enthymeme may be derived from the confusion of *particular* with *absolute* probability. A probability is *not* universal—as[4] Agathon says

'Perhaps one might call this very thing a probability—that many improbable things should happen to men.'[5]

For that which is against probability (sometimes) happens, and so that too which is against probability is probable. And if this is so, the improbable will be probable. In fact, however, probability is *not* absolute. Just as in Eristic, it is the omission to add *in what respect*, and *in reference to what*, and *in what way*, which makes the trap; so here it comes from the prob-
11 ability not being absolute but particular. The rhetorical art of Korax[6] is made up of this topic. If a man is *not* liable to

---

[1] παρὰ τὴν ἔλλειψιν. He has said, above, that a case of διαίρεσις belonging to Topic (2) might be referred to this; so, again, of Topic (6). In *De Soph. El.* c. 5, he refers Topic (4) to no. 6, and also says that the Topic παρὰ τὴν ἔλλειψιν *might* be treated as παρὰ λέξιν. This illustrates the crudity of the whole classification (R. C. J.).

[2] Polykrates, p. 223 Sauppe.   [3] Eur. *Iph. Aul.* 66.

[4] Does ὥσπερ refer to καθόλου or to οὐ καθόλου? Probably the latter. τάχ' ἂν λέγοι implies the poet's dissent, which the context perhaps explained (R. C. J.).

[5] Fragm. 9 Nauck.

[6] ἡ Κόρακος τέχνη. Plato, *Phædr.* p. 273 A, quotes this very abuse of εἰκός from the τέχνη of Tisias, with the illustration of the brave man tried for beating a coward (Thompson, p. 131). There is probably an allusion *there* to Korax—Τισίας ἢ ἄλλος ὅστις δήποτ' ὢν τυγχάνει καὶ ὁπόθεν χαίρει ὀνομαζόμενος. Cp. Spengel's συναγωγὴ τεχνῶν, p. 33 (R. C. J.).

a charge—(if, for instance, a weak man is charged with assault and battery,) you say—'It is not probable.' If, again, he *is* liable to the charge (as, by being strong), you say—'It is not probable; for it was sure to seem probable.' And so in all other cases. A man must be either liable or not liable to the charge. In either case there is an apparent probability; but, in the one case, it is an (abstract) probability[1]; in the other, it is not abstract, but, as has been said[2], particular. This, again, is what is meant by 'making the worse seem the better cause,'[3] and for this reason men justly disapproved[4] of the undertaking of Protagoras[5]. It is a fallacy—not a real, only an apparent probability—and has a place in no art except Rhetoric and Eristic.

xxv. An account has now been given of Enthymemes,
Methods of refutation. real and apparent[6]. We have next to speak of Refutation. An argument may be refuted either by a counter-syllogism or by bringing an objection. As to 2 the counter-syllogism, it can evidently be constructed from the same topics. Our syllogisms are taken from popular beliefs; and there are many such beliefs contrary to each other.

---

[1] τὸ μὲν εἰκὸs, *i.e.* the defence that the man did not do it *because it was sure to be suspected*, is analogous to saying that it is probable that improbable things will happen. We go merely on the general ground that, as the man was likely to do it, it is likely that he did not do it, because man's estimate of likelihood is often wrong. In the other case,—when we say that his strength makes it likely—this is more than ἁπλῶs εἰκόs,—it is an εἰκόs *in the proper sense*—a general illustration applied to the *particular* circumstances of this case. Most men who commit assaults are strong: *this* man is strong. See the definition of εἰκόs in I ii [5, where it is said to be οὕτωs ἔχον πρὸς ἐκεῖνο πρὸς ὃ εἰκόs, ὡς τὸ καθόλου πρὸς τὸ κατὰ μέρος. When we say 'the improbable is probable,' the εἰκόs is so, not in reference to τὸ κατὰ μέρος, to any particular case, but to that which is itself general, viz. the other εἰκόs. This is what he here calls ἁπλῶs or καθόλου εἰκόs, as opposed to τὶ εἰκόs (R. C. J.).

[2] 'In the way that has been already stated,' *i.e.* under the conditions and circumstances before mentioned (Cope).

[3] Cicero, *Brutus*, 30.

[4] ἐδυσχέραινον. Cp. Eur. *Med.* 580 f; Arist. *Nub.* 889–1104; Plato, *Apol. Socr.* 19 B.

[5] Plato, *Protag.* 319 A.

[6] The rest of the chapter is held to be spurious by Professor J. Cook Wilson (*Trans. Oxford Philol. Soc.* 1883–4, p. 4 f), who is opposed by Susemihl in Bursian's *Jahresb.* xlii 38 f.

3 The mode of bringing objections—as has been shown in the *Topics*[1]—is fourfold.

Either the adversary's enthymeme furnishes it from itself; or it is taken from an analogous case; or from an opposite case; or from previous decisions.

4   1.   As an example of the first case, suppose the enthymeme

1402 b to argue that love is good.   The objection can be brought in two ways: either generally, by saying that all want is an evil; or particularly, by saying that there would be no such proverb as ' Kaunian love,'[2] if there were not some bad loves.

5   2.   As an instance of objection from the opposite, suppose the enthymeme to have been—'The good man does good to all his friends.'   We object—'No, the bad man does not do evil to all his enemies.'

6   3.   It would be an objection from analogy—supposing the enthymeme to be that men who have been ill-used always hate—to say ' No, men who have been well treated do not always feel friendship.'[3]

7   4.   The Decisions available are those of well-known men[4]. Suppose the adversary's enthymeme to have been, ' We must make allowances for drunken men, as they err unwittingly,' our objection is—' Then Pittakos[5] is not praiseworthy, or he would not have enacted greater penalties for an error committed in drunkenness.'

---

[1] Not the special treatise of this name (says Schrader), but the dialectical art in general (see further in Cope's *Comm.* ii 323).   *Top.* VIII 10, p. 157, speaks indeed of a fourfold division, but not in the same sense.   There it is (1) complete λύσις, (2) πρὸς τὸν ἐρωτῶντα, (3) πρὸς τὰ ἠρωτημένα,—the *form* of the adversary's question, (4) πρὸς τὸν χρόνον.   The really parallel place is *Anal. Pr.* II 26, where we have the four in the text, only that (1) ἐξ ἑαυτοῦ has no specific name, and (4) is ἐκ τοῦ κατὰ δόξαν (R. C. J.).

[2] The incestuous passion of Byblis for her brother Caunus, Ovid, *Met.* ix 453.

[3] A bad example, because it does not mark the difference between the ἔνστασις ἐκ τοῦ ὁμοίου and that ἐκ τοῦ ἐναντίου.   The analogous thing, τὸ ὁμοῖον, is here another case in which a certain kind of usage does not uniformly produce a certain failing.   Ill-treatment, it is argued, always produces hatred : good-treatment, it is answered, does not always produce friendliness.   Take this instance :— 'Men are always grateful to those who help them to pay their debts.'   Objection :— ' Men are not always grateful to those who defend them when they are slandered ' (R. C. J.).

[4] Objections founded on authority, on the previous decision of weighty judges.

[5] Of Mytilene (651–569 B.C.).   Cp. *Politics*, II xii.

Enthymemes[1] are taken from four things; these are 8
(1) Probabilities; (2) Examples; (3) Infallible Signs; (4)
Fallible Signs.

They are taken from Probabilities, when they are concluded from some general rule, real or seeming. They use
Examples when they proceed by induction[2] from an analogy
in one or more cases—the speaker assuming a universal rule,
and thence reasoning on the particular case. They are wrought
by the Infallible Signs, when they turn on something necessarily true; by the Fallible Signs, when they depend on a
statement, general or particular, which may or may not be
true.

Now, as the Probable is that which happens generally but
not invariably, it follows that Enthymemes from Probabilities
may always be refuted by bringing an objection, though this 9
objection may be apparent and not always real; since the
objector refutes the conclusion, not as being improbable, but
as being unnecessary. Thus, an unfair advantage may always 10
be gained by this fallacy,—more easily, however, in defence
than in accusation. The accuser proves his case by probabilities. To refute a conclusion as improbable, and to refute it
as unnecessary, are two different things. A conclusion from
what generally happens is always open to objection; else it
would not be a probability[3] but a constant and necessary
truth. Yet, if the conclusion is shown to be unnecessary[4],
the judge fancies that it is not probable, or that he must not consider it as probable;—reasoning falsely, as we said; for he
ought not to judge merely on grounds of necessity; he ought
to judge also on grounds of probability—this is the meaning

---

[1] Here = αἱ ἐν αὐτῷ τῷ λόγῳ πίστεις, including 'examples.'

[2] Spengel (followed by Roemer) brackets δι' ἐπαγωγῆς, Victorius thinking that
either these words or the διὰ before τοῦ ὁμοίου must go. But Spengel presently
adds that Victorius has shown the words δι' ἐπαγωγῆς to be right, from *Anal. Pr.*
II xxiv. Every use of 'example' implies an inductive process (R. C. J.).

[3] Vahlen, followed by Roemer, adds <ὡς ἐπὶ τὸ πολὺ καὶ> to the sentence
translated in the text, οὐ γὰρ ἂν ἦ <ὡς ἐπὶ τὸ πολὺ καὶ> εἰκὸς ἀλλ' ἀεὶ καὶ ἀναγκαῖον.

[4] For the impossible manuscript reading ἂν οὕτως ἐλύθη, Bekker substitutes εἰ
οὕτως ἐλύθη, while Spengel (followed by Roemer) would prefer ἂν οὕτω λυθῇ, and
Cope ἂν οὑτωσὶ λυθῇ.

of 'using his best discretion.'[1]   Hence it is not enough if
the defendant shows that the charge is not necessarily true ;
he ought to show that it is not probable.   This latter thing
will be achieved, if his objection agrees better with what
11 generally happens.   The objection may be of this kind in two
ways—(1) in respect of the time : (2) in respect of the facts[2]:—
1403 a it will be most effective, if it is such in both respects :—for, if
a majority of instances are on our side[3], this makes a stronger
probability.

12   Fallible Signs, again, and the enthymemes which employ
them, can be refuted, even though the facts are real—as was
said at the beginning[4]; for we see from the *Analytics*[5] that no
13 Fallible Sign can lead to a strictly logical conclusion.   The

---

[1] κρίνειν, Spengel prefers κρινεῖν. Cp. I xv 5.

[2] ἢ τῷ χρόνῳ ἢ τοῖς πράγμασι. A stronger probability may rest on either of two grounds.
      I. *First Interpretation* :—(1) τῷ χρόνῳ = 'frequency' (Victorius) ; *a majority of instances* may be against our opponent. (2) τοῖς πράγμασιν. The majority of apparently similar instances may be on his side ; but there may be something in the special facts of this case which distinguishes it from these cases. (How can this be called μᾶλλον ὡς ἐπὶ τὸ πολύ?) The superior probability will be most firmly established if *both* arguments are on our side ; *i.e.* if we can show (1) that the thing *usually* happens as we say, not as he says ; (2) that the special circumstances of the case are against his story.
      II. *Second Interpretation.* The adversary makes a statement of facts. Suppose I cannot dispute his facts ; I may, however, be able to show that, *at the time* to which he refers, some conditions were present, which altered the significance of these facts. Thus, he says : 'I am accused of being lukewarm in the cause of the democracy ; but, five years ago, I subscribed three talents for the public defence.' This may be quite true ; the πράγματα may be as he states them. But I may be able to show that, *at that time*, three talents was a very small sum, though, now that the State has been impoverished, it seems a large sum. This would be refuting his argument τῷ χρόνῳ—'by a consideration of the time.' Cp. the 5th topic in c. xxiii, ἐκ τοῦ τὸν χρόνον σκοπεῖν. This is my own view. The clause εἰ γὰρ τὰ πλεονάκις οὕτως refers to τοῖς πράγμασιν. If it can be shown, not only that the *time* affects his case, but that experience is against his account of the facts, so much the better.
      III. Cope (*Introd.* p. 274) understands τῷ χρόνῳ of the time which the speaker assigns to the facts alleged by the adversary. The adversary says—this or that happened in 1872. I may dispute the facts, or I may admit them, but refer them to 1871.—The ἔνστασις πρὸς τὸν χρόνον in *Top.* VIII 10, p. 161 *a* 10, means merely 'an objection to gain time.' (R. C. J.)

[3] εἰ γὰρ τὰ πλεονάκις οὕτως. Roemer, following the *scholium* and Victorius, prints εἰ γὰρ τὰ <πλείω καὶ> πλεονάκις οὕτως, as in § 13.

[4] I ii 18.   [5] II 27.

mode of solution which applies to Probabilities applies also to enthymemes of Example. If we have one[1] contrary instance, the conclusion is refuted as being unnecessary, though a majority of instances or the ordinary course of things is against us. If the majority of instances and the ordinary course of things are against us, we must contend that the present case is unlike, or has conditions which are unlike, or at least presents some difference.

Infallible Signs, and the Enthymemes taken from them, 14 will not admit of refutation on the ground that the reasoning is not strict :—this, again, we see from the *Analytics*[2]. It remains to show that the alleged fact does not exist. If it is shown that it *does* exist, and that it is an Infallible Sign, then there is no further possibility of refutation ; for this amounts to a manifest demonstration.

xxvi.   Amplification and Depreciation do not constitute

Supplementary criticisms.   merely an elementary form of enthymeme ; (by 'elementary form' I mean the same thing as a 'commonplace'—that being an 'elementary form' or a 'commonplace,' under which several enthymemes fall.) Amplification and Depreciation are *enthymemes*[3]—tending to show that a thing is great or small ; just as there are enthymemes to show that a thing is good or bad, just or unjust, or the like—in short, 2 that it is any of those things with which syllogisms and enthymemes are concerned. If these several enthymemes are not commonplaces of enthymemes, neither are Amplification and Depreciation.

Nor are Destructive Enthymemes a different species from 3 Constructive[4]. Evidently we refute a conclusion by a Demonstration or by an Objection ; and what we demonstrate[5] is the

---

[1] ἔχωμεν <ἕν> τι Vahlen, Roemer. The punctuation of the rest of the sentence is that of Vahlen and Spengel, which is adopted by Cope and Roemer.

[2] II 27.

[3] ἐνθυμήματα, omitted in one MS, and by Muretus, Spengel, and Roemer.

[4] ἄλλο τῶν κατασκευαστικῶν omitted in the Paris MS and the old Latin translation, and bracketed by Spengel and Roemer.

[5] ἀνταποδεικνύουσιν : ἀνταποδείκνυσιν, supported by the scholiast and the Latin translation, is preferred by Spengel.

opposite of that conclusion.   Thus, if the adversary showed that the thing *has* happened, we show that it has *not* happened ; or *vice versa*.   This, then, cannot be the difference.   The same instruments are used on both sides : enthymemes are

4 brought to show that the thing is or is not.   As to the Objection, it is not an enthymeme[1]; as we said in the *Topics*[2], it means stating some popular principle from which it shall appear that the adversary has not reasoned strictly or has made a false assumption.

5   There are three departments of Rhetorical inquiry.   This may be taken as a sufficient account of Examples, Maxims, Enthymemes, and generally of the *Inventive* province—of the

1403 b way to find arguments and the way to refute them.   It remains to discuss *Diction* and *Arrangement*[3].

APPENDIX ON BOOK II, CHAPTER XIX.

On ' Topics' in Aristotle's Rhetoric.

The Enthymeme is a syllogism from likelihoods and signs, that is, from general statements and from particular statements, in regard to such contingent things as human action can influence.

These general and these particular statements are drawn

I. *εἴδη*.

chiefly from a store of popular knowledge which the rhetorician must possess. This store of *popular* knowledge is divided into departments corresponding

---

[1] ἡ γὰρ ἔνστασις κτλ.   *An. Pr.* II 27, 'An objection is a proposition opposed to a proposition, but differing from a proposition in that it may be particular (ἐπὶ μέρους), whereas a proposition either cannot be particular at all, or at least not in *general* syllogisms' (R. C. J.).

[2] This follows from *Top.* VIII 10, p. 157, though it is not expressly said there (R. C. J.).

[3] § 5.   ἐπεὶ δὲ δὴ τρία—λέξεως καὶ τάξεως.   Spengel thinks that Aristotle wrote περὶ μὲν οὖν παραδειγμάτων κτλ.—εἰρήσθω τοσαῦτα, and that λοιπὸν δὲ—τάξεως, the last clause in this Book, is a false addition ; for (1) it is contrary to his usage to place εἰρήσθω τοσαῦτα in the protasis, and (2) he has nowhere promised to treat λέξις and τάξις.   In II xviii 5, τὰ λοιπὰ προσθέντες may refer to the πίστεις only ; and ἡ ἐξ ἀρχῆς πρόθεσις may mean 'the purpose to treat them' (R. C. J.).   Vahlen would even omit the words καὶ ὅλως τῶν περὶ τὴν διάνοιαν (see further in Cope's *Comm.* ii 333 f).

to the departments of *scientific* knowledge, the most important of these being the Ethical and Political. Each of these departments of the rhetorician's knowledge must be stocked with a certain number of facts and propositions available as premisses in argument. These facts, relative to different special branches of knowledge, are called εἴδη, or more strictly τόποι τῶν εἰδῶν; also, ἴδιαι προτάσεις—'propositions peculiar to this or that subject' (II xxii 1 ; I ii 22).

But, besides this classification of the *materials* of the enthymeme, it will help the memory to have also a rough classification of the *forms* in which the enthymeme can be built.

II. τόποι ἐνθυμημάτων.

To supply this, Aristotle enumerates in II xxiii twenty-eight such forms. These are, in the proper sense, τόποι τῶν ἐνθυμημάτων. The word τόπος means *the* place in which a thing is to be looked for in the memory. The propositions about special subjects are ἴδιοι τόποι—places in the memory where *special materials* for the enthymeme are to be looked for. The τόποι τῶν ἐνθυμημάτων are places in the memory where certain forms or types of enthymematical argument are to be looked for ;—genera or classes of enthymemes.

Further, besides these special materials and these forms, are there any general notions with which all Rhetoric and all Dialectic necessarily deals, and towards dealing with which the rhetorician ought to have some formulas ready?

III. The κοινοὶ τόποι.

Aristotle answers that there are four such general notions. (1) A speaker may wish to argue that a thing would be desirable, if only it was possible; but it is impossible. It will be a help to him if he has fixed in his memory some general grounds on which anything may be argued to be possible or impossible:—if there is in his mind, a place, a region of arguments about the possible or impossible. This then is our first universal topic—the topic of the possible or impossible. (2) Next, a speaker may wish to contend that a certain thing *has* happened or *will* happen. He should be prepared with some general principles by which the probability in each case may be measured. The second universal topic is that of fact past and fact future. (3) Again, he may wish to argue that though *this* is good, *that* is better; though *this* is strong, *that* is stronger. He ought therefore to have some principles of comparison : there should be in his mind a place, a topic, of *degree*. Here (in c. xix 26 f) Aristotle explains that, if the rhetorician knows what is a *good* and a greater *good*, or is *just* and more *just*, what is *noble* and more *noble*, he will *practically* be sufficiently armed. There is no practical use in his studying the abstract principles of a comparative estimate as such.

Lastly (4) the speaker may have to show that this is a *great* deed, a *great* man, a *small* deed, a *small* man : he may want to magnify, or to lower, depreciate. The fourth topic is that of amplification and depreciation ; or more correctly, of *great* and *small*. For in c. xxvi (*ad init.*) he says that αὔξειν καὶ μειοῦν is not the *topic* merely of an enthymeme ; not merely one of those moulds into which an enthymeme may be cast ; but is itself an enthymeme. To amplify—to depreciate—are enthymemes to show that a thing is great or small; just as there are other enthymemes to show that a man is *good* or *bad*, *just* or *unjust*. We do not call the proving of a man to be just or unjust a separate *class* of enthymeme : the class of the enthymeme depends on the arguments used to prove the man just or unjust. No more, then, can we say that the proving of a thing to be great or small is in itself a separate *class* of enthymeme. It is an enthymeme which may be built on any argument, but which always deals with the general conception of great and small. Now, as the rhetorician deals not with abstract greatness, but with great *good*, great *justice*, great *honour*, it is no more necessary in this case, than in the case of μᾶλλον and ἧττον, to have *abstract* principles. Knowing what is a *good*, we shall know what is a great good.

Thus, then, of the four κοινοὶ τόποι, it is only two—the possible and impossible, fact past or future—which need special treatment in a rhetorical treatise. The other two are worth mentioning, because they serve to remind the rhetorician of two general ways in which his special knowledge may be used (R. C. J.).

BOOK III

i. THERE are three subjects of rhetorical inquiry,—first, as regards the sources of the proofs,—secondly, as regards the style,—thirdly, as to the order in which the parts of the speech are to be placed.   We have spoken of the proofs, and of their several sources, showing that these are three in number[1],— showing, too, of what kind they are, and why their number is not larger,—viz. because all men are persuaded either by some affection of their own minds, when they are the judges, or by conceiving the speakers to be of a certain character, or by a demonstration.

Enthymemes, also, have been spoken of, and the sources from which they must be provided,—these being, on the one hand, the special commonplaces of enthymemes, on the other, the general commonplaces[2].

We have next to speak of Diction; for it is not enough to 2

Diction, or Style.

know *what* we are to say ;—we must say it in *the right way* :—this contributes much toward determining the character of the speech.   The first subject of our 3 inquiry was naturally that which comes first in nature—as to the means by which persuasiveness shall be given to our facts.   The second question is how to dispose these in language ; the third is one of the greatest importance, but one, with

Delivery.

which it has not yet been attempted to deal— regarding the art of delivery.   It was long before this art was applied even to tragic or epic recitation ; for the earliest poets used to act their own tragedies.   Now it is plain that delivery concerns rhetoric, just as it concerns

---

[1] I ii 3.   [2] Books I and II.

poetry ; and a few writers—Glaukon of Teôs among the rest—
4 have treated it. The art of Delivery[1] is concerned with the
voice : it is the art of knowing how to use it for the expression
of each feeling; of knowing, for instance, when it should be
loud, low, or moderate ; of managing its pitch, shrill, deep, or
middle ;—and of adapting the rhythm to the subject. These
are the three things, which speakers have in view—volume,
harmony and rhythm. The honours of dramatic contests fall,
as a rule, to the actors ; and, just as, on the stage, the actors
are at present of more importance than the poets, so it is,
owing to the vices of society[2], in the contests of civil life.
5 The rules of delivery have not yet been reduced to an art—
indeed, the art of Diction itself was of late development; and,
1404 a properly viewed, the subject is thought vulgar. As, however,
the whole discipline of rhetoric aims at appearance, we must
give our attention to this subject, considered as necessary, not
as desirable in itself; for, strictly speaking, our sole aim in our
language should be to give neither pain nor pleasure ; our
facts ought to be our sole weapons, making everything superfluous which is outside the proof ; owing to the infirmities of
the hearer, however, style, as we have said, can do much.
6 (At the same time, style has necessarily a certain small value
in every kind of exposition; the mode of expression chosen
makes some difference to the clearness,—not such a very great
difference, however ; it is all imagination and relative to the
hearer ; thus, no teacher commends geometry by graces of
style.)
7   When the Art of Delivery comes to us, it will perform the
function of the actor's art ; hitherto, but slight progress has
been made towards treating it, as by Thrasymachos in his
work *on Pathos*[3]. The dramatic faculty is a gift of nature
rather than of Art; but Diction is in the province of art.
Hence those who are strong in diction gain honours in their
turn, just as do speakers who excel in delivery ; for speeches
of the literary class are stronger in diction than in thought.

[1] αὐτὴ μὲν MSS : αὕτη schol.
[2] Or, 'owing to the defects (or depravity) of our political constitutions.'
[3] Sauppe, *Or. Att.* III p. 164, 4; Spengel, *Artium Scriptores*, p. 93 f.

The first improvement in style was naturally made by the 8
poets; for words are instruments of imitation, and the voice
is the most imitative of all our organs.   Thus the arts of
recitation, the art of acting, and more besides, were formed.
And, as the poets seemed to have won their present reputation[1], 9
even when their thoughts were poor, by force of their style, the
first prose style was led to become poetical[2], like that of
Gorgias[3].   To this day, indeed, the mass of the uneducated
think that such persons are the finest talkers.   It is not so,
however; the diction of prose and the diction of poetry are
distinct.   This appears from what is happening now: the
writers of tragedies are themselves modifying their style; and,
just as they passed from tetrameter to iambic, because the
iambic measure is, of all, the most like conversation, so they
have discarded all those words which violate the ordinary
idiom, but which the earlier writers used for ornament[4], and
which to this day the writers of hexameters so use[5].   It is
absurd, then, to imitate those who have themselves dropped
the fashion; and it becomes plain that we need not enter 10
minutely into the whole question of style, but need discuss
only that style of which we are speaking.   The other style has
been treated in the *Poetics*.

ii.   These points, then, may be taken as discussed.   One 1404 b
Clearness.   virtue of Diction may be defined to be clearness.
This appears from the fact that, if our language
does not express our meaning, it will not do its work.   Again,
Appropriate-
ness.   diction ought to be neither low nor too dignified,
but suitable to the subject.   (The diction of poetry
could hardly be called 'low,' yet it is not suitable to prose.)
Diction is made clear by nouns and verbs used in their proper 2

---

[1] τὴν δὲ δόξαν Paris MS, τήνδε τὴν δόξαν other MSS; τήνδε disapproved by
Spengel and bracketed by Roemer.

[2] 'The language (of prose) first took a poetical colour' (Cope).

[3] Spengel, *Art. Scr.* p. 69.

[4] οἷς δ' οἱ πρῶτοι ἐκόσμουν : οἷς οἱ πρότερον κτλ, the Scholiast and Spengel:
οἷς [δ'] οἱ πρῶτοι κτλ, Roemer. ἀφείκασιν is bracketed by Twining, Spengel, Bekker
ed. 3, and Roemer; but retained by Vahlen, and by Bywater, *Journal of Philology*,
xvii 73 f.   [5] c. 20–22.

sense; it is raised and adorned by words of the other classes mentioned in the *Poetics*[1]. Deviation from the ordinary idiom makes diction more impressive; for, as men are differently impressed by foreigners and by their fellow-
3 citizens, so are they affected by styles. Hence we ought to give a foreign air to our language; for men admire what is far from them, and what is admired is pleasant. In the case of *metrical* composition there are many things which produce this effect, and which are in place *there*; for the things and persons concerned are more out of the common. In prose the opportunities are much fewer, the subject-matter being humbler. Even in poetry, if fine language were used by a slave, or by a very young man, or about mere trifles, it would be somewhat unbecoming; even in poetry, there is a sliding
4 scale of propriety. We must disguise our art, then, and seem to speak naturally, not artificially; the natural is persuasive, the artificial is the reverse; for men are prejudiced against it, as against an insidious design, just as they are suspicious of doctored wines. The difference is the same as between the voice of Theodôros[2] and that of other actors; *his* voice seems
5 to belong to the speaker,—*theirs*, to other men. A successful illusion is wrought, when the composer picks his words from the language of daily life; this is what Euripides does, and first hinted the way to do[3].

Language is composed of nouns and verbs,—nouns being of the various classes which have been examined in the *Poetics*[4]. Strange words, compound words, words coined for the occasion, should be used sparingly and rarely:—*where*, we will say by and by[5]. The reason of this has been given already:—the
6 effect is too odd to be fitting. Accepted terms, proper terms, and metaphors, are alone available for the diction of prose. This appears from the fact that all men confine themselves to these: all men in talking use metaphors, and the accepted or

---

[1] c. xxii.

[2] A celebrated tragic actor, mentioned in *Pol.* 1336 *b* 28, and in Dem. *De Fals. Leg.* § 274.

[3] He 'gave us the earliest glimpse of this kind of writing' (Cope); cp. Cope's *Introd.* 284 note 2.

[4] c. xxi.   [5] c. iii and vii.

proper terms for things; so it is plain that, if the composer is
skilful, the foreign air will be given, the art may be concealed,
and he will be clear. And this, we saw, is the excellence of
rhetorical language. Equivocal terms are the class of words 7
most useful to the sophist, for it is with the help of these that
he juggles; synonyms are most useful to the poet. By **1405 a**
synonyms in ordinary use I mean, for instance, 'to go' and
'to walk':—these are at once accepted and synonymous
terms[1].

The nature of each of these kinds of words,—the number
of sorts of metaphor,—and the supreme import-

Metaphor.

ance of metaphor both in poetry and in prose,
have been explained, as we said, in the *Poetics*[2]. In prose the 8
greater pains ought to be taken about metaphor, inasmuch
as prose depends on fewer resources than verse. Clearness,
pleasure, and distinction, are given in the highest degree by
metaphor; and the art of metaphor cannot be taught[3]. Our 9
metaphors, like our epithets, should be suitable. This will
result from a certain proportion; if this is lost, the effect will
be unbecoming, since the contrast between opposites is strongest
when they are put side by side. As a crimson cloak suits a
young man, what (we must inquire) suits an old man? The
same dress will not suit him. If we wish to adorn, we must 10
take our metaphor from something *better* in the same class of
things; if to depreciate, from something *worse*. Thus (opposites being in the same class) it would be an example of this
to say that the beggar 'prays' or that the man who prays
'begs'; as both are forms of asking. So Iphikrates said that
Kallias was a 'begging priest,' not a 'torch-bearer'[4]; and
Kallias replied that he must be uninitiated, or he would not call
him a 'begging priest,' but a 'torch-bearer'[5]: both are con-

[1] § 7, 'Aristotelis quidem esse videntur, sed fortasse ex ampliore exemplar
huic loco adnexa sunt' (Roemer, *Praef.* lxxx).	[2] c. xxi, xxii.

[3] Lit. 'it is impossible to acquire it from anyone else'; *Poet.* xxii 9, 'This
alone cannot be imparted by another; it is a mark of genius,—for to make good
metaphors implies an eye for resemblances' (Butcher).

[4] ἀλλ' οὐ δᾳδοῦχον, bracketed by Diels and Roemer.

[5] A hereditary office of high distinction, in connexion with the *Eleusinia*, here
described as held by Kallias, the third of that name, the son of the third
Hipponikos. Iphikrates is the self-made man of *Rhet.* I ix 31.

cerned with a god, but one is a title of honour, the other of dishonour. Some people call actors 'creatures of Dionysos,' but they call themselves 'artists.'[1] Both terms are metaphors, the one calumnious, the other complimentary. Again, pirates nowadays call themselves 'purveyors.' So we may speak of the wrong-doer as 'making a mistake,' or the erring man as 'guilty of a wrong.' We may say that the thief has merely 'taken,' or that he has 'plundered.' The expression in the Têlephos of Euripides—

> '*Ruling* the oar,
> And, having landed on the Mysian coast,'...[2]

is unsuitable, because the word 'to rule' is above the dignity
11 of the subject; so no illusion is produced. There is another fault, which may arise from the form of a word, when the sound which this symbolises is not pleasant. Thus Dionysios 'the brazen'[3] in his elegiacs calls poetry the 'scream of Kalliopê,'[4] both being sounds; the metaphor from inarticulate sounds, how-
12 ever, is unworthy. Again, the metaphors, by which we give names to nameless things, must not be far-fetched, but drawn from things so kindred, and so similar, that the affinity appears
1405 b at first sight: as in the well-known riddle—

> 'I saw a man who had glued bronze to a man with fire.'[5]

The operation has no name; but, both processes being applications, he has called the application of the cupping-instrument a 'glueing.' As a general rule, good riddles supply good metaphors; for metaphors are in the nature of riddles, and so

---

[1] The term is so used by Dem. *De Fals. Leg.* 212. Διονυσοκόλακες became proverbial, as in Diogenes Laërtius, x 418; Athenæus, 538 F; and Alkiphron, iii 48.

[2] The next line was ἐτραυματίσθη πολεμίῳ βραχίονι, 'was sorely wounded by a foeman's arm'; Fragm. 705 Nauck.

[3] A poet and rhetorician of the early part of the fifth century, who was called 'the brazen' from his having been the first to suggest the use of bronze money at Athens.

[4] Fragm. 7 Bergk, *P. L. G.* ed. 4.

[5] The next line is preserved by Athenæus, 452 C, οὕτω συγκόλλως ὥστε σύναιμα ποιεῖν, 'I saw a man who welded brass with flame upon his fellow, so closely as to bring the blood together.' The riddle is ascribed by Plutarch to Cleobulina or Eumêtis; cp. Bergk, *P. L. G., Poëtae Eleg.* vii.

of course the metaphors are happy. Also, metaphors should 13
be taken from beautiful things :—the beauty or ugliness of a
word consisting, as Likymnios[1] says, either in the sound or in
the sense. There is yet a third consideration, which answers
the sophistic argument. Bryson[2] said that there could be no
such thing as foul language, if the *meaning* is the same, whether
we use this or that term. This is false. One term may be
more appropriate than another, more in the image of our
thought, better suited to set it before the eyes. Again, this
term and that term do not describe the thing in the same
aspect—and so, on this ground also, one of them must be
regarded as fairer or fouler than another. Both words denote
the fair or foul things, but not *qua* fair or foul ; or, if so, yet
in different degrees. Our metaphors must be taken from this
quarter,—from things beautiful in sound or in significance,—
beautiful to the eye, or to some other sense. It makes a
difference whether we say, for instance, ' rosy-fingered morn,'[3]
or ' crimson-fingered,' or worse still, ' red-fingered.' In using 14
epithets, too, we may characterise an object either from its
mean or base side, as, ' Orestes, the matricide' or from its
better side, as, ' avenger of his father.'[4] Thus Simônides, when
the winner of the mule-race[5] offered him a small fee, declined
to write, on the ground that he did not like to write about
half-asses. But, when the pay was made enough, he wrote—

> ' Hail, daughters of wind-swift steeds !'[6]

(yet they were the daughters of the asses too). Then, without 15

---

[1] A pupil of Gorgias, probably identical with Likymnios, the dithyrambic
poet of Chios (c. 12 § 2). His *Art* of Rhetoric is mentioned below, in c. 13 § 5.
Cp. Plato's *Phædrus*, 267 C ; Blass, *Die Attische Beredsamkeit*, i 85 f, ed. 2.

[2] A sophist of Herakleia in Pontus ; cp. Cope in *Journal of Cl. and Sacred
Philol.* ii 143 and Natorp in Pauly-Wissowa.

[3] *Il.* i 477 etc.

[4] Eur. *Orestes*, 1587 f :—

Menelaus. ὁ μητροφόντες ἐπὶ φόνῳ πράσσει φόνον.

Orestes. ὁ πατρὸς ἀμύντωρ, ὃν σὺ προὔδωκας θανεῖν.

[5] Anaxilas of Rhêgium and Zanklê, who died in 476 B.C. ; the name of the
victor is preserved by Hêrakleides Ponticus, *Pol.* 25. Simônides died in 467, and
the race with the Chariot drawn by mules, founded in 500 B.C., was abolished in
444. Cp. Bentley's *Diss. upon Phalaris*, 156 (198 Wagner).

[6] Fragm. 7 Bergk.

changing one's word, one may extenuate it[1]. This extenuation consists in making less either of the evil or of the good : as Aristophanes in the *Babylonians*[2] jokingly uses 'coinlet' for 'coin,' 'cloaklet' for 'cloak,' 'gibelet' for 'gibe,'—'plaguelet' &c.—Both in metaphors and in epithets, however, we must be cautious and observe the mean.

iii.   Frigidities of style have four sources. First, compound words. Thus Lykophron[3] speaks of the '*many-faced* heaven (above) the *high-peaked* earth' ;— and the '*narrow-channelled* shore.'[4] Gorgias spoke of 'the *beggar-poet*[5] flatterer'; 'forsworn or *ultra-veracious.*' Alkidamas[6] has—'the soul filling with passion, and the face becoming *flame-hued*' ; 'he thought that their zeal would prove *doom-fraught*' ; he describes 'the persuasiveness of his speech' as 'end-fulfilling'[7] ; and 'the floor of the sea' as 'dark-hued.' All these phrases seem poetical, because they are composite.

Faults of style.
Compound words.

1406 a

---

[1] Similarly Spengel (who doubts the genuineness of τὸ αὐτὸ), 'ut epithetis rem maiorem vel minorem reddere licet, sic verba ipsa extenuari possunt.' This implies that τὸ αὐτὸ is the accusative after ὑποκορίζεσθαι. In Liddell and Scott, however, the verb is regarded as intransitive :—'to use diminutives'; and Cope's paraphrase is as follows :—'Further the same thing may be effected (as by epithets in the way of elevation or depreciation) by diminutives,' *lit.* 'Diminutives are, or amount to, much the same thing as epithets.' Diminutives are only a special variety of epithets.

[2] Fragm. 90 Kock.

[3] The rhetorician and sophist. Several of the following phrases may have come from a panegyric on Theseus and other Athenian heroes.

[4] A reference either to the Hellespont, or to the narrow path running along the Scironian cliffs in Megara. Cp. Blass *Att. Ber.* ii 235, and Cope's *Comm.* iii 37.

[5] or 'beggar-witted' (Cope).

[6] Alkidamas, a rhetorician and sophist of the fourth century, who was a pupil of Gorgias. He is the reputed author of two extant declamations. The first of these, *On the Sophists*, argues in favour of an aptitude for extemporaneous discourse, as contrasted with the elaborately written compositions of Isokrates. The second purports to be a speech of Odysseus attacking Palamedes, and is less likely to be his genuine work. Aristotle's quotations apparently come from a lost work in praise of philosophy and culture, and from a discourse on the *Odyssey*. See Vahlen, *S. Ber.* of the Vienna Acad. 1863, 491–528 ; Blass, *Att. Ber.* ii (1892) 345 f; and Brzoska, in Pauly-Wissowa.

[7] Shakespeare's 'thought-executing.'

This is one source of frigidity. Another is the use of 2

Archaic or rare words. strange words. Thus, with Lykophron, Xerxes is a 'mammoth man,' Skiron a 'fell wight'; Alkidamas offers a 'playful theme'[1] to poetry, and speaks of the 'distraughtness of a man's nature'—'whetted with the untempered anger of his thought.'

A third cause is the use of lengthy, unsuitable or frequent 3

Inordinate Epithets. epithets. In poetry it is fitting to say '*white* milk'[2]; but in prose such epithets are either somewhat unsuitable, or, when too abundant, they betray the trick, and make it clear that this is poetry. It is right enough to use some epithets : they relieve the monotony, and give an air of distinction to our style; but we should aim at a mean, for too much art does more harm than utter carelessness : the latter is not good, but the other is positively bad. This is why Alkidamas seems frigid ; his epithets are not the mere seasoning but the actual meat, so thickly packed and over-grown and obtrusive[3] are they. It is not 'sweat' but 'the *damp* sweat'; not 'to the Isthmian games' but 'to the *solemn festival* of the Isthmian games.' It is not 'the laws,' but 'those laws which are *the kings of the state*'; not 'with a rush,' but 'with the *impulse rushing from his soul*.' He does not say 'having taken to himself a school of the Muses,' but 'to *Nature's* school of the Muses'; (he speaks of) the solicitude of his soul as '*sullen-visaged*'; (he says) not, 'the winner of favour,' but 'the winner of *multitudinous* favour.' Again—'*dispenser* of pleasure to the hearers'; 'he hid it (not among branches, but) among the branches *of the wood*.' 'He veiled'—not his body, but—'the *shame* of his body.' He calls the soul's desire '*mirror-like*'— (this being a compound word, as well as an epithet, so that we get poetry); and, in the same way, the excess of his depravity as '*abnormal*.'[4] Hence, by using poetic language, they make their style absurd and frigid owing to the impropriety,

---

[1] ἄθυρμα 'a toy,' or 'playful and sportive theme,' a 'bagatelle'; part of the quotation below in § 4.

[2] *e.g. Il.* iv 434.

[3] ἐπιδήλοις, 'glaring'; ἐπὶ δήλοις, proposed by Bernays, is approved by Vahlen and Roemer.   [4] Or 'exotic.'

—and obscure, owing to the wordiness; for, when the speaker reiterates what is already understood, he overclouds and darkens the sense.   People generally use compound words, when there is no name for a thing, and when the compound is easy,—as '*pastime*'; but, if this is carried too far, it becomes

1406 b distinctly poetical.   Thus, compound words are most useful to writers of dithyrambs,—the dithyramb being sonorous;— rare words to epic poetry, since the rarity has grandeur and boldness; metaphor, to iambic verse,—iambic verse being, as we have said, the present metre of tragedy[1].

4   The fourth and last source of frigidity is metaphor. Meta-
                phors, too, may be unsuitable, either from their
Metaphors.
                absurdity (comic poets have their metaphors), or from an excess of tragic grandeur:—they are obscure, when they are far-fetched.   Thus Gorgias spoke of events being 'fresh, with the blood in them still'; 'you sowed this shameful seed, and have reaped this evil harvest.'   This is too poetical.   Again, Alkidamas calls philosophy 'a fort planted on the domain of the laws,' and the *Odyssey* 'a fair mirror of human life.'   He speaks of 'offering no such playful theme[2] to poetry.'   All these phrases fail to be winning, for the reasons just given.   The address of Gorgias to the swallow, which had polluted his head in its flight, is a masterpiece of the tragic style.   'Nay,' he said, 'this is unseemly, Philomêla.' The act would not have been unbecoming in a bird, but was unbecoming in a girl.   It was a judicious reproach, then, to call her what she *was*, and not what she *is*.

iv.   The Simile, too, is a metaphor; the difference is but
                small.   When the poet says of Achilles, 'He
Similes.
                sprang on them like a lion,'[3] this is a simile.   When he says 'The lion sprang on them,' this is a metaphor; for, as both the animals are brave, he has transferred the name of

2   'lion' to Achilles.   The simile, too, is available in prose; rarely, however, as it is poetical.   Similes must be used like metaphors; for they *are* metaphors, differing in the point stated.

---

[1] i 9.   [2] § 2 *supra.*
[3] ὡς δὲ λέων ἐπόρουσεν.   Cp. *Iliad* xx 164, ὦρτο λέων ὥς.

The following are examples of similes. Androtion said of 3
Idrieus[1] that he was 'like curs which have been unchained—
they rush on one, and bite;—and so Idrieus, freed from his
bonds, is savage.' Theodamas said that 'Archidâmos was
like Euxenos,—without his knowledge of geometry,'—and,
vice versa, Euxenos will be 'an Archidâmos, who knows
geometry.'[2] In Plato's *Republic*[3], those who strip the dead
are compared to 'curs who bite the stones, while they do not
touch the thrower'; the people are likened to 'the captain of
a ship, who is strong but a little deaf'[4]; the verses of poets to
'persons, who have bloom, without beauty'[5]; these seem
different, when their prime is passed, and similarly with
verses, when resolved into prose. Perikles said of the **1407 a**
Samians[6] that they were 'like children who took the sop, but
cried'; and of the Bœotians, that they were 'like oaks; for
an oak is shattered by an oak, so are the Bœotians by their
wars with each other.' Demosthenes[7] compared the people to
'sea-sick voyagers'; Demokrates[8] compared public speakers
to 'nurses who swallow the morsel, and, in doing so, just
touch the children with the saliva.'[9] Antisthenes[10] said that
the lean Kêphisodotos[11] was 'like incense—his consumption
gives pleasure.' All these may be used either as similes, or
as metaphors. Metaphors, which have gained applause, will,
of course, serve as similes too; and similes, with the explanation omitted, will be metaphors. A 'Proportional' 4

---

[1] The Athenian orator and Atthidographer, Androtion, was sent as envoy to
Mausôlus, prince of Caria (377–351), who was succeeded by his brother Idrieus.
Nothing is known of the imprisonment of the latter, which must have preceded
his accession.

[2] Of these three persons nothing is known.

[3] 469 D. [4] 488 A. [5] 601 B.

[6] After the final reduction of the island by Perikles, 440 B.C.

[7] Supposed by Victorius and others to be the Athenian general, *sine causa*
says Spengel.

[8] Notorious for his bitter and offensive sayings. Two of the name are
mentioned in Isæus and Demosthenes respectively, but nothing worth mentioning
is known of either.

[9] Cp. Arist. *Eq.* 715–8.

[10] Almost certainly the Cynic.

[11] The orator mentioned in Dem. *Lept.* 146, 150. Three of his sayings are
quoted below, iii 7.

metaphor[1] must always apply reciprocally to both of two things in the same class; thus, if a bowl is the shield of Dionysos, it is fitting to call a shield the bowl of Ares.

v. These then are the elements of language. The first condition of style is Purity; and this depends on
2 *Primary requisites of style, in regard to composition; idiomatic purity, dependent on (1) proper use of connecting particles.* five things. (1) First, on connecting particles, and on their use in that correspondence and natural sequence, which some of them require; as μέν and ἐγὼ μέν require δέ and ὁ δέ. This correspondence should be satisfied, while the hearer's memory is fresh; we must not have a long dependent clause, or insert a clause before that which is required for the *apodosis*; this is rarely fitting. 'I, as soon as he had told me, (for Kleon had come praying and insisting,)—went with them.' Here, clauses have been inserted before that which is to form the *apodosis*.

If what comes before the word 'went' is made
3 *(2) Use of special and not general terms.* long, the sentence is obscure. (2) The first excellence, then, depends on the connexion of clauses: the second, on the use of terms that are
4 special and not general[2]. (3) Thirdly, we must avoid am-
(3) Avoidance of ambiguity. biguous language; that is, unless we deliberately wish to be obscure—as writers wish, who have

---

[1] In the *Poetics*, xxi 4, Aristotle defines metaphor as 'the imposition of a foreign name' by means of a *transference* 'either from genus to species, or from species to genus, or from species to species, or proportionally.' Of these four kinds of 'metaphor' the first two are simply cases of *synecdoche*, as (1) the generic *vessel* for the specific *ship*, or (2) the specific *sail* for the generic *ship*. The third is *metonymy*, as 'rob' for 'cut off,' both being species of 'taking away.' It is only the fourth kind, the *proportional metaphor*, that corresponds to our use of the word. Here there are always four terms, and as *a* is to *b*, so is *c* to *d*; for example, as the *shield* is to *Ares*, so is the *bowl* to *Dionysos*. The 'shield' and the 'bowl' both fall under the same *genus*, viz. 'the characteristic badge of a deity'; and both can be reciprocally transferred. Thus, a bowl can be called the 'shield of Dionysos,' and a shield 'the bowl of Ares.' The latter phrase was actually used by the dithyrambic poet, Timotheos:—ἦτει δ' ἥρως θ' ὅπλον· φιάλην Ἄρεως κατὰ Τιμόθεον, Athen. 433 D. Similarly, as the 'evening' is to the 'day,' so is 'old age' to 'life'; hence we may call evening the 'old age of the day,' and old age the 'evening of life' (*Poet.* xxi 6). Cp. Cope's *Introd.* 290 f, 374 f.

[2] So Cope, in *Comm.* III 57.

nothing to say, but pretend that they mean something. Such persons express themselves in poetry, as Empedoklês did; for the comprehensive language mystifies by its vagueness[1], and the hearers are affected, as people are ordinarily affected by soothsayers, to whose ambiguous utterances they assent in either sense:—

'Crœsus will destroy a great empire by crossing the Halys.'[2]

Soothsayers speak of their subject in general terms, because as a rule the mistake will be less. As, in the game of odd or 1407 b even, one is more likely to be right in saying 'even' or 'odd,' than in guessing the *exact* number; so it is safer to say a thing *will be* than to say *when*; and, for this reason, sooth-sayers do not trouble themselves to define the *when*. All these cases of ambiguity are alike; and so, when we have no such object as that mentioned, we should avoid ambiguity.

(4) Observance of gender   (4) The fourth point concerns the *genders* of 5 nouns, as distinguished by Protagoras into mas-culine, feminine and neuter. These, too, must be properly given :—' Having come and spoken (*feminine participles*), she went away.'

(5) The fifth condition is the observance of grammatical 6 and (5) number.   *number* :—' Having come (*plural participle*), they struck me.'

In every case a composition should be easy to read, or, what is the same thing, easy to deliver. This quality is *not* present, where clauses are multiplied, or where punctuation is difficult, as it is in the writings of Hêrakleitos. Hêrakleitos is troublesome to point, from its being doubtful to which of two clauses, the former or the latter, a word belongs; as, at the beginning of his treatise, where he says—

'To grasp that philosophy which is needful ever slow are men.'[3]

It is not clear with which clause we are to take 'ever.'— Further, a solecism may arise from a neglect of symmetry, if 7 with two words you couple another, which suits only one of

---

[1] 'this circumlocution deludes us by the accumulation of words' (Cope).
[2] Herodotus, I 53, 91.
[3] Fragm. 11, ed. Bywater.

them. Thus suppose a sound and a colour to be in question : '*see*' will not apply to both, but '*perceive*' will.

Obscurity is caused by not stating your meaning at the outset, when you have many details to insert. Thus—'I *meant*, after speaking to him to this effect, in this way, &c. ; —to go' ; instead of—'I meant to go, after speaking to him ; then this or that happened thus or thus.'

vi. Dignity of style is assisted by these rules. (1) To use
<small>Dignity of style.</small> the description instead of the name : as by saying, not,' Circle,' but 'A plane surface, every point on the circumference of which is equally distant from the centre.' With a view to conciseness, on the contrary, we must use the

2 name instead of the description.   If there is anything ugly or unseemly in the idea, we should use the *name*, when this ugliness resides in the description,—the *description*, when it

3 resides in the name. (2) To express our meaning by meta-
4 phors and epithets—avoiding a poetical colour. (3) To use the plural instead of the singular, as the poets do. Thus, *one* harbour being in question, still they say, 'to Achaian harbours.'[1] Again—'Here are the tablet's folds with many

5 doors.'[2] (4) To use the Article with each of two words, instead of connecting them with one Article :—as τῆς γυναικὸς τῆς ἡμετέρας. For conciseness, the reverse—τῆς ἡμετέρας

6 γυναικός. (5) To use a conjunction (and other connectives); or, in concise writing, to write without connectives, but not with-
1408 a out connexion[3]. Thus—'having gone and spoken'; or 'hav-
7 ing gone, I spoke.' (6) Also the device of Antimachos[4] is useful—to describe an object by the qualities which it does *not* possess—as he does in the case of Teumêssos[5] :—

'There is a little breezy hill.'[6]

---

[1] *Fragm. Adesp.* 83 Nauck.

[2] 'Here are the many-leaved folds of the tablets' (Cope); Eur. *Iph. Taur.* 727.

[3] Cope, *Comm.* III 67.

[4] The epic poet of Klaros, an elder contemporary of Plato, and the author of a prolix poem, the *Thebaïs*, on the expedition of the Seven against Thebes.

[5] A village in the Theban plain, standing on a low hill of the same name.

[6] In the original the description was expanded by the addition of all the characteristics that did *not* belong to it. The context, which is lost, was well known in Strabo's time, p. 409.

This mode of amplification may be applied to any extent. It is applicable either to such good qualities, or to such bad qualities, as the object does *not* possess, according as may be convenient. From this topic the poets take such epithets as 'stringless,' or 'lyreless' song,—which they derive from the negation of qualities. This device is effective in 'proportional' metaphors, as when we say that the trumpet is a 'lyreless song.'[1]

vii. Style will have *propriety*, if it is pathetic, charac-
Propriety. teristic, and proportionate to the subject. This 2
proportion means that important subjects shall not be treated in a *random* way, nor trivial subjects in a *grand* way ; and that ornament shall not be heaped upon a commonplace object ; otherwise the effect is comic, as in Kleophôn's[2] writing ; for some of his phrases were as if one should say 'Venerable fig-tree.'[3] Passion is expressed, when an outrage 3 is in question, by the language of anger ; when impious or shameful deeds are in question, by the language of indignation and aversion ; when praiseworthy things are in question, by admiring language ; when piteous things, by lowly language —and so in the other cases.

The appropriateness of the language helps to give prob- 4 ability to the *fact*; the hearer's mind draws the fallacious inference that the speaker is telling the truth, because, where such facts are present, men are thus affected ; the hearer

---

[1] The 'proportion' is, as the trumpet is to the sound of the trumpet, so is the lyre to μέλος, the proper term for the sound of the lyre. Hence, if you wish to express the 'sound of the trumpet,' you may substitute the fourth term, μέλος, for the second, but you must make the latter applicable to the trumpet by the use of a negative epithet, ἄλυρον, showing that you are in the present case not applying the word to the lyre. As examples of the use of these 'limiting epithets' in Greek tragedy, we have κῶμον ἀναυλότατον (*Phœn.* 818), θίασον ἀβάκχευτον (*Or.* 319), μηνυτῆρος ἀφθέγκτου, ἀπτέροις πωτήμασιν (*Eum.* 245, 250), ἀρδις ἄπυρος, Ζηνὸς ἀκραγεῖς Κύνες, Διὸς πτηνὸς κύων (*P. V.* 822, 888, 1024), κίσσινον βέλος, μοχλοῖς ἀσιδήροις (*Bacch.* 25, 1104).

[2] Identified by Cope with Kleophôn, the supposed tragic poet mentioned in *Poet.* ii and xxii ; but here regarded as an unknown orator by Tyrwhitt, with whom Spengel agrees. The opinion of Robortello, Dacier, and Ritter, that he was an epic poet, is supported by Bywater in *Journal of Philology,* xii 19–21.

[3] or 'sovran fig'; here the poetic word πότνια, 'lady,' is applied to a commonplace object.

thinks, then, that the case stands as the speaker says, whether
it does so stand or not[1], and invariably sympathises with the
5 passionate speaker, even when he is an impostor. Hence
speakers often confound their audience by making a noise.
6   This representation of facts by means of appropriate signs
is also 'characteristic,' since each class of men, and each disposition, has a style suited to it. 'Class' may represent a
difference of age, as between boy, man, and old man; or the
difference of sex; or the difference between Laconian and
Thessalian. By dispositions I mean those things which give
a definite character to a man's life; not every disposition
7 gives such a character. Now, if the speaker's words are
appropriate to the disposition, he will represent the character;
for the educated man would not use the same words, nor use
them in the same way, as the boor. (An impression may be
made on hearers by a trick which speech-writers use to nauseous
excess:—'Who does not know this?', 'All men know it!'[2]
The hearer allows it from sheer shame, in order to be even
with the rest of the world.)
8   The difference between a seasonable and unseasonable use
1408 b affects all the special rules of propriety. The corrective for
9 every excess is the notorious one—to censure oneself at the
same time[3]: the thing seems to be true, since at all events
10 the speaker knows what he is doing. Again, the conditions
of just proportion should not *all* be observed at the same
time; in this way an illusion is wrought on the hearer.
Suppose, for instance, that our *words* have a harsh sound;
we must not make our voice harsh, and our features harsh,
and have everything else in keeping; else, each several detail
is seen to be an artifice: whereas, if some of them are appropriate and some not, the artist does the same thing unnoticed.
(Of course, if soft words are said in a harsh voice or *vice versa*,

---

[1] εἰ καὶ μὴ οὕτως ἔχει ὡς ὁ λέγων, bracketed by Vahlen and Bekker, in ed. 3.
ὡς ὁ λέγων is awkwardly used for ὥς φησιν ὁ λέγων. ὡς alone is bracketed by
Roemer.

[2] Frequent in Isokrates, and in Macaulay.

[3] προσεπιπλήττειν, the manuscript reading retained by Bekker, Spengel and
Roemer. προεπιπλήττειν, suggested by the quotation in Quintilian, viii 3 37, is
preferred by others, including Cope.

persuasiveness is lost.)—Compound words, epithets in tolerable   11
number, and foreign words, are most suitable to the language
of passion; an angry man may be excused for saying that a
wrong 'cries to heaven' or calling it 'colossal.' Or such words
may be used, when the speaker has got hold of his audience,
and has worked them up to enthusiasm with praise or blame,
anger or kindness: as Isokrates does at the end of his *Panegyricus*[1], with his 'fame and name,' and 'they who had the
heart, &c.'[2] Men use such language, when they are enthu-
siastic, and therefore allow it, of course, when they are so
affected. Hence it has been found to suit poetry; for poetry
is an inspired thing. Such language, then, should be used
either thus, or in irony, as Gorgias used it, and as it is used in
the *Phædrus*[3].

viii. The *form* of our composition should be neither metrical, nor devoid of rhythm; the first is not per-
Rhythm. suasive, for it has an artificial air, and at the
same time distracts the attention, for it makes us look for the
recurrence of the cadence:—just as children chime in, when
the herald asks—'whom does the freed man choose as his
patron?'—'Kleon.'[4] On the other hand, that which has *no*   2
rhythm is as the illimitable; and a limit we must have, though
not a *metrical* limit; for the infinite, being beyond our grasp,
is unpleasing. It is number which gives definiteness to all
things; and that number which belongs to the form of com-

---

[1] § 186, φήμην δὲ καὶ μνήμην καὶ δόξον πόσην τινὰ χρὴ νομίζειν ἢ ζῶντας ἕξειν
ἢ τελευτήσαντος καταλείψειν τοὺς ἐν τοιούτοις τοῖς ἔργοις ἀριστεύσαντας; In Aristotle's
text all the MSS have φήμη δὲ καὶ γνώμη, first corrected by Victorius.
[2] οἵτινες ἔτλησαν, 'in that they *brooked*, etc.' The prosaic phrase οἵτινες
ἐτόλμησαν is the manuscript reading in Isokr. *Paneg.* § 97, where it has been
corrected with the aid of the text of Aristotle, Isokrates' own quotation in *De
Perm.* (shortly before p. 332), and the quotation in Dionysius, *Dem.* c. 40.
[3] 231 D; 241 E.
[4] Cope implies that the great demagogue is meant: 'Can it be that the custom
had been handed down from generation to generation for a century or so after
Cleon's death? If so, it is a very remarkable fact.' (*Comm.* iii 84.) But Kleon
may mean any demagogue or popular προστάτης of the day. The *Index Aristotelicus* recognises only one historical reference to Kleon in Aristotle, and classifies
all the other ten under the heading of *nomen usitatum ad significandum quemlibet
hominem*, as here and in *Rhet.* II ii 2, III v 2, *Poet.* XX 11.

3   position is *rhythm*, of which *metres* are sections[1]. Prose must
therefore have *rhythm*, but not *metre*[2]; for then it will be
poetry. This rhythm, however, must not be precise; and
precision will be avoided, if it is carried only to a certain
point.

4   One kind of rhythm is the heroic; this is grand, and
remote from the measure of common conversation[3]. The
iambic, on the other hand, is the very cadence of common
talk; hence men use iambics in conversation more than any
other kind of metre. But we must have majesty; we must
carry our hearers away. The trochee, again, is too much
1409 a   akin to the comic dance,—as appears in the tetrameter, which
has a tripping rhythm. There remains the pæan, which
rhetoricians began to use from the time of Thrasymachos[4],
though without being able to say what it was.

The pæan is the third rhythm, and closely connected with
those just mentioned. It is as three to two; of the others,
one is as one to one; the other, as two to one. Between these
two last ratios the ratio of 1½ to 1 is intermediate; and such
5   is the pæan[5]. The other rhythms, then, must be dismissed,

---

[1] τμητά MSS : τμήματα Bywater.   [2] Cicero, *Orator*, 228.

[3] σεμνὸς καὶ λεκτικῆς ἀρμονίας δεόμενος, the suggestion made by Tyrwhitt on
Poët. iv 19, is adopted in the texts of Spengel and Bekker (ed. 3) and by Cope.
Vincentius Madius, *i.e.* Maggi, in his ed. of *Poet.*, 1550, had already proposed
σεμνὸς ἀλλὰ λεκτικῆς ἐστὶν ἀρμονίας δεόμενος, which is adopted by Roemer, with the
sole omission of ἐστὶν. The MSS have σεμνὸς καὶ λεκτικὸς καὶ ἀρμονίας δεόμενος,
where the statement that the heroic measure is 'deficient in harmony' is untrue.

[4] Thrasymachos of Chalkêdôn, who was born about 457 B.C. and is represented as a man of mature years, as compared to Lysias, in the *Republic* of Plato,
marked an epoch in the history of prose style in Greece. His style was
intermediate between the elaborately artificial style of Thukydides and the plain
style of Lysias (Dion. Hal. *Dem.* init.). Cicero, *Orator*, 175, describes him as the
inventor of rhythmical prose. The *Panegyric, Busiris* and *Amartyros* of Isokrates
begin with the first pæan, *e.g.* πολλάκις ἐ|θαύμασα, and the *De Bigis* and
Trapeziticus with the fourth pæan, *e.g.* περὶ μὲν οὖν.

[5] Cp. Cicero, *Orator*, 188. 'Pes enim, qui adhibetur ad numeros, partitur in
tria, ut necesse sit partem pedis aut aequalem esse alteri parti aut altero tanto aut
sesqui esse maiorem. Ita fit aequalis dactylus, duplex iambus, sesquiplex paean.'
The ratio between the two parts of the foot is 1 : 1 in the case of the dactyl (or
spondee); 2 : 1 in the case of the iambus or trochee; and the mean of these two,
3 : 2, in the case of the pæan, which consisted of three short syllables combined
with one long syllable, the long syllable being either at the beginning or the end, or
in the second or third place. Two short syllables count as equivalent to one long.

for the reasons just given, as well as because they are metrical ;
the pæan must be adopted, since it is the only one of the
rhythms above-named, which does not constitute metre, and
so it attracts least notice. At present the same form of pæan
is used both at the beginning and at the end of sentences ; but
the end ought to be distinguished from the beginning. And 6
there are two opposite kinds of pæan, one of which suits the
beginning, where the present usage places it ; this is the
pæan which begins with a long syllable and ends with three
short ones, as Δᾱλŏγĕνĕς, | εῑτĕ Λῠκῐ|αν, or χρῡσĕŏκŏμ|ᾱ ῞Εκᾰτĕ, |
παῖ Διός¹. The other pæan, on the contrary, begins with
three short syllables and ends with a long one : μĕτᾰ δĕ γᾱν |
ῠδᾰτᾰ τ᾽ ὠκ|ĕᾱνŏν ῆ|φᾰνῐσĕ νῠξ². And *this* pæan forms a con-
clusion ; for the short syllable mutilates the rhythm by its
incompleteness³. The period ought to be broken off by a
long syllable, and the end ought to be marked, not merely by
the copyist or by a marginal note⁴, but by the rhythm.

ix. We have seen, then, that our composition must be
rhythmical and not unrhythmical ; we have seen what
rhythms, and what arrangement of them, make it so.

Further,—the style must be either *running* and unbroken
in its chain, like the preludes of dithyrambs, or
compact, like the ' strophê ' and ' antistrophê ' of
the old poets. The *running* style is the ancient 2
one, as—' This is the setting forth of the inquiry
of Herodotos of Thurii.' In earlier times it was universal,
though now it is used only by a few. By a ' running ' style I
mean one which has no end in itself, until the sense comes
to an end. It is unpleasing on account of this indefiniteness ;
for everyone wishes to descry the end. This is the reason
why men gasp and become exhausted only at the goal⁵ ; they

*The running
style, con-
trasted with
the compact.*

¹ Simonides, fragm. 26 *b* Bergk, ed. 4.   ² *ib.* Cp. *Orator*, 214, 218.
³ Cp. *Orator*, 192–5 ; Cope, *Comm.* iii 88 f ; Marx, *Neue Jahrb.* Apr. 1908.
    ⁴ A short dash below the first word of the line in which the sentence is about
to close. Examples may be found in the British Museum *papyrus* of the Funeral
Oration of Hypereides. *Orator*, 228, ' interductu librarii.'
    ⁵ ἐπὶ τοῖς καμπτῆρσιν, the *turning-point* of the δίαυλος, is here the *goal* of the
στάδιον or single race (Cope, *Comm.*).

do not grow weary before, because they have the end in view.
3 This, then, is the *running* species of style. The *compact* style
is that which is in periods ; and by a period I mean a sentence
which has a beginning and an end in itself, and is of a size to
1409 b be taken in at one view[1]. Such a style is pleasing and easy
to follow ; pleasing, because it is the reverse of indefinite, and
because the hearer always fancies that he has grasped something, and has got something defined ; whereas it is unpleasant
to foresee nothing, and to get nothing done. The style is easy
to follow, because it is easy to remember ; and this, because
periodic composition involves number, the easiest of all things
to remember. Hence all men remember verse more easily
than unfettered prose ; for verse has a number, which is its
4 measure. The period must also contain a complete sense ; it
must not break off in the middle—as in the lines of Sophokles

'Lo, this is Kalydôn, of Pelops' land....'[2]

Such a break may suggest a meaning the opposite of the true
one : thus, in the instance just given, one might suppose that
Kalydôn was in the Peloponnesus.
5   A Period is either of several 'members' or simple. The
period of several 'members' is a sentence complete in itself,
with distinct parts, and such that it can be comfortably delivered—not with the aid of an arbitrary division, as in the
case of the period just quoted, but as a whole structure. A
'member' is one part of this period ; by a simple period I
6 mean that which consists of one 'member.' 'Members,' as
well as periods, must be neither curt nor long. Brevity often
trips up the hearer ; for, when he is still straining forward to
that measure, of which he carries a definition in his own mind,
and then is violently checked by the cessation of the sentence,
it necessarily happens that he stumbles, as it were, from the
revulsion. Long sentences, on the other hand, leave the

---

[1] 'Of a size to be taken in at a glance' (*Attic Orators*, i 35, ed. 1876).
[2]   Καλυδὼν μὲν ἥδε γαῖα, Πελοπίας χθονὸς
        ἐν ἀντιπόρθμοις πεδί' ἔχουσ' εὐδαίμονα.
These are the opening lines, not of any play of Sophokles, but of the
Meleager of Euripides, Fragm. 515 Nauck. Kalydôn, so far from being part of
the Peloponnesus, is on the opposite side of the strait, as shown by the fact that
Πελοπίας χθονὸς in the first line is the gen. after ἀντιπόρθμοις in the second.

hearer behind; just as people, who turn beyond the ordinary limit, leave behind the companions of their walk. In the same way the period which is too long becomes a speech in itself, or something like the prelude of a dithyramb, and the result is expressed by the joke of Dêmokritos of Chios[1] against Melanippides[2] for having written such preludes instead of antistrophic dithyrambs :—

'A man contrives ill for himself when he contrives it for another ; and the long prelude is worst of all for its maker.'[3]

This may fittingly be said of the users of long periods too. On the other hand, the period, of which the 'members' are too short, is not properly such at all; and so it sends the hearer headlong.

The period of more than one 'member' is either simply 7 divided, or antithetical. Simply divided, as in this example: —'I have often wondered at the holders of solemn assemblies, and the founders of athletic contests.'[4] Antithetical, when, in each of the two 'members,' opposite is balanced by opposite, or when two opposites are linked under the same word. Thus, 1410 a 'They served both classes—both those, who had stayed behind, and those, who had followed them ; for the latter, they acquired a new territory larger than their own home-land ; to the former, they left land enough at home.'[5] Here the opposites are 'staying at home—following,'—'enough—more.' And so—'both those, who want to get money, and those, who wish to enjoy it';[6]—where enjoyment is opposed to acquisition. Again—'it often happens, in such enterprises, that the prudent fail, and the foolish succeed.'[7] 'At the time, they were crowned with the prize of valour ; and, not long after, they got the empire of the sea.'[8] 'To sail through the mainland and march through the sea, bridging the Hellespont and cleaving Athos.'[9] 'Though citizens by nature, they were

---

[1] A musician contemporary with his namesake, Dêmokritos of Abdêra.

[2] Melanippides of Mêlos, the most famous master of dithyrambic composition in the earlier half of the Peloponnesian war.

[3] Mullach, *Fragm. of Demokritos*, p. 91. The second line is a parody of Hesiod's *Works and Days*, 266, ἡ δὲ κακὴ βουλὴ τῷ βουλεύσαντι κακίστη.

[4] *Paneg.* § 1, immediately followed (as it happens) by a regular *antithesis*.

[5] *ib.* § 35.   [6] *ib.* § 41.   [7] *ib.* § 48.   [8] *ib.* § 72.   [9] *ib.* § 89.

deprived of their city by law.'¹ 'Some of them perished
miserably, and others were saved shamefully.'² 'In our
private capacity, to receive barbarians to dwell with us, while,
in our public capacity, we endure to see many of our allies in
slavery.'³ 'To enjoy in life, or bequeath after death.'⁴ Take,
again, what was said in a law-court of Peitholaos and Lyko-
phrôn⁵:—' These men *sold* you, while they were at home, and
now they have come to you and *bought* you.'

All these expressions have the contrast above mentioned.

8 This mode of expression gives pleasure, because opposites are
most striking; and are still more easily recognised, when put
close beside each other; also because the antithesis resembles
a syllogism; for the refutative syllogism consists in bringing
opposites together.

9 This, then, is the nature of Antithesis. 'Parisôsis' is when
the 'members' are equal; 'Paromoiôsis' when each 'member' has the extremes alike⁶. This must be either at the
beginning, or at the end. At the beginning, the likeness
must always be between whole words; and at the end, it may
be in the final syllables of words, or inflexions of the same
word, or in the repetition of a word. Thus, at the beginning
—ἀγρὸν γὰρ ἔλαβεν ἀργὸν παρ' αὐτοῦ⁷.

δωρητοί τ' ἐπέλοντο παράρρητοί τ' ἐπέεσσιν⁸.

At the end—ᾠήθησαν αὐτὸν παιδίον τετοκέναι, ἀλλ'
αὐτοῦ αἴτιον γεγονέναι. ἐν πλείσταις δὲ φροντίσι καὶ
ἐν ἐλαχίσταις ἐλπίσιν. Or, with inflexions of the same
word—ἄξιος δὲ σταθῆναι χαλκοῦς, οὐκ ἄξιος ὢν χαλκοῦ;⁹

---

¹ *Paneg.* § 105. ² *ib.* § 149. ³ *ib.* § 181. ⁴ *ib.* § 186.
⁵ Brothers of Thêbê, the wife of Alexander of Pheræ, apparently the
defendants in some cause of which nothing more is known. Someone on the side
of the plaintiff says:—'These are the men who, in their own Thessalian home, at
Pheræ, *sell* your fellow-countrymen as slaves, and, now that they have entered
your court, have *bought* and bribed you.' (Cp. Cope's *Comm.* iii 103.)
⁶   ἀντίθεσις = contrast of sense.
     παρίσωσις = parallelism of structure.
     παρομοίωσις = parallelism of sound.
This last is subdivided into ὁμοιοκάταρκτον, ὁμοιοτέλευτον and παρονομασία,
according as the 'parallelism of sound' affects the beginning, the end, or the
whole, of the two contrasted words.
⁷ Aristophanes, i fragm. 649 Kock. ⁸ *Il.* ix 526.
⁹ Spengel and Roemer regard this as a question. 'Is he worthy to have a
bronze statue, when he is not worth a brass farthing?'

Or, with the same word—σὺ δ' αὐτὸν καὶ ζῶντα ἔλεγες κακῶς
καὶ νῦν γράφεις κακῶς. Or, with one syllable,—τί ἂν ἔπαθες
δεινόν, εἰ ἄνδρ' εἶδες ἀργόν; The same sentence may unite 1410 b
all these things, and have at once ' Antithesis,' ' Parison,' and
' Homoioteleuton.' (The possible beginnings[1] for periods have
been pretty well enumerated in the Theodekteia[2].) There 10
are also false antitheses, such as Epicharmos[3] used to make—
' There was a time, when *I* was in their house ; and there was
a time, when their roof was over *me*.'

x. These points having been settled, we have to speak of
the sources of those smart sayings which win
applause. To invent such, is for the clever or
practised man : the business of this treatise is to
draw attention to their use. We must then explain 2
and classify these means ; and we may start from this principle.
All men take a natural pleasure in learning quickly ; words
denote something ; and so those words are pleasantest which
give us *new* knowledge. Strange words have no meaning
for us; common terms we know already ; it is
metaphor which gives us most of this pleasure.
Thus, when the poet calls[4] old age 'a dried stalk,'[5] he gives
us a new perception by means of the common *genus* ; for both
the things have lost their bloom. Now poets' similes have 3
the same effect ; hence, when they are good, they have this
sprightliness. A simile, as has been said before[6], is a metaphor

The means of giving vivacity and winning applause.

Metaphor.

---

[1] ἀρχαί MSS: Rose's suggestion ἀρεταί is accepted by Roemer.

[2] Cope infers from this passage of the *Rhetoric*, that Aristotle in the earlier
part of his career, probably whilst he was still carrying on his rhetorical school,
composed a work upon this subject, mainly devoted to style and composition and
arrangement, the contents *in extenso* of the third book of his extant *Rhetoric*, to
which therefore the latter would naturally refer for fuller details. To this he gave
the name of his friend Theodektes, himself a proficient in the art, and also the
author of a treatise on it (*Introd.*, 1867, p. 57). Diels sums up his opinion thus:—
' *Die Kunst des Theodektes* nur eine Ausgabe der Aristotelischen Rhetorik (und
zwar die älteste) darstellt' (*Abhandlung* of Berlin Acad., 1886, *Ueber das dritte
Buch der Aristotelischen Rhetorik*, p. 12).

[3] Fragm. 49, p. 273 Lorenz.   [4] ὅταν γὰρ εἴπῃ, as in iv 1.

[5] *Od.* xiv 213, ἀλλ' ἔμπης καλάμην γέ σ' ὀίομαι εἰσορόωντα | γιγνώσκειν.

[6] iv 1.

with a preface ; for this reason it is less pleasing because it is more lengthy ; nor does it affirm that *this* is *that* ; and so the
4 mind does not even inquire into the matter.   It follows that a smart style, and a smart enthymeme, are those, which give us a new and rapid perception.   Hence superficial enthymemes are not popular—meaning by ' superficial ' those which are obvious to all, and which demand no inquiry— nor, again, those which, when stated, are not understood ; but either those which convey knowledge, as soon as they are uttered, though this knowledge was not possessed before ; or those, behind which the intelligence lags only a little[1]; for here there is a sort of acquisition : whereas, in the other cases,
5 there is neither sort[2].   In respect to *sense*, then, these are the popular enthymemes.   In respect to *style*, the popular *form*

Antithesis.

is the antithetic, for example,—' regarding the peace, which the rest of the world enjoys in common, as a war upon their private interests,'[3] where war is
6 contrasted with peace.   The popular *words* are the meta- phorical,—the metaphor being neither remote, since this is hard to see at a glance, nor trite, for this excites no emotion. The third condition is, that the thing should be set before the

Actuality.

eyes ; for the hearer should see the action as present, not as future.   We must aim, then, at these three things,—Metaphor, Antithesis, Actuality[4].

7   Metaphors are of four kinds,—the most popular being
1411 a those ' from analogy.'[5]   Such was the saying of Perikles that the youth, who had perished in the war, had vanished from the city in such sort as if the spring were taken out of the year[6].   And so Leptines said in reference to the Lace- dæmonians that we ' must not suffer Greece to lose one of her two eyes.'[7]   When Chares[8] was anxious to give account of his conduct in the Olynthiac war, Kêphisodotos[9] expressed

---

[1] II xxiii 30.
[2] Neither immediate nor slightly subsequent acquisition of knowledge.
[3] Isokrates, *Philippus*, § 73.
[4] Or 'Vividness'—but this is ἐνάργεια (R. C. J.).
[5] Cp. note on iv 4.   [6] Cp. I vii 34.
[7] The other 'eye' being of course *Athens, the eye of Greece.*
[8] Commander of mercenaries in the Olynthiac war, 349 B.C.   [9] III iv 3.

indignation, saying that Chares proposed to give his account ' while his grasp was upon the people's throat.'[1] On another occasion, when he was urging the Athenians to make an expedition to Euboea, he said that ' they must go out with the decree of Miltiades for their commissariat[2]. The Athenians having made truce with Epidauros and the sea-board, Iphikrates expressed his irritation by saying that ' they had been stripped of their stores for the campaign.'[3] Peitholaos described the Paralos[4] as ' the people's cudgel,' and Sêstos[5] as ' the meal-shop of the Peiræus.' Perikles urged the removal of that ' eyesore '[6] of the Peiræus, Ægina. Mœrokles[7] said he was no worse than such an one—naming a respectable citizen ; that person was a scoundrel for 33⅓ per cent., he for ten per cent. Or, take the iambic line of Anaxandrides[8] about the delay of his daughters to get married—

> 'The bridals of my girls are *overdue.*'[9]

Or the saying of Polyeuktos[10] about a certain apoplectic Speusippos[11],—that he ' could not keep quiet, although fortune

---

[1] εἰς πνῖγμα τὸν δῆμον ἔχοντα MSS ; ἀγαγόντα Dionysius ; ἄγχοντα Abresch (and Bywater) followed by Roemer. This correction accounts for both the variants.

[2] All the MSS have ἐπισιτισαμένους, 'having taken for their provisions promptitude like that of the decree of Miltiades' at the time of the first Persian invasion. The future, ἐπισιτισομένους, is preferred by Victorius, Lobeck, Spengel, and Cope, who paraphrase the passage thus :—they must march out at once to the aid of Euboea, and *there* provide themselves with provisions like Miltiades' decree; they were to lose no time in making provision *at home.* This hurried expedition belongs to the year 358 B.C., Dem. *Androt.* 14, Εὐβοεῦσιν ἡμερῶν τριῶν ἐβοηθήσατε.

[3] Epidauros was a weak neighbour which could be plundered with impunity.

[4] The swift State-galley sent to apprehend public offenders. Demosthenes, *Chers.* 29, names the *Paralos* as one of the three instruments of State-punishment.

[5] Sêstos, on the Hellespont, one of the emporia for the corn imported from the Kimmerian Bosporos and other parts of the Euxine coast.

[6] An annoying obstacle to the happiness of Athens.

[7] An anti-Macedonian contemporary of Demosthenes. He was inclined to exaction in money-matters (*Fals. Leg.* 293), and here uses a metaphor from money to describe his own view of his comparative respectability.

[8] A poet of the Middle Comedy ; Com. Fr. II fragm. 68 Kock.

[9] Or 'my daughters' marriage-bonds have passed their date'; ὑπερήμεροι, a metaphor from a delinquent who has failed to pay a legal due by the proper date.

[10] An Attic orator on the same side as Demosthenes.

[11] The tone of the reference shows that this was an unimportant person who bore the same name as Plato's successor, who, curiously enough, was also a paralytic (Diog. Laërt. IV i 3, 4).

and his disease had put him in the pillory.' Kêphisodotos called triremes, 'painted mills'[1]: and Diogenes[2] described taverns as 'the public messes of Attica.' Æsion[3] spoke of their 'having poured the city into Sicily';—this is a metaphor, and puts the thing before the eyes. 'So that Hellas *cried aloud*'[4]—this is, in a way, metaphorical and vivid. Again, Kêphisodotos[5] warned the city not to have too many *concourses*[6]. Isokrates used the same term in reference to the 'concourse' at the festivals[7]. In the *Funeral Oration*, it is said that 'Greece might well cut off her hair at the grave of those who fell at Salamis, deeming her freedom buried with their valour.'[8] The saying that 'Greece might well mourn, since her valour *was buried in that grave*,' is a vivid metaphor; while the juxtaposition of *valour* and *freedom* gives a certain antithesis. Again, Iphikrates said—'the path of my speech

1411 b

[1] Instruments of grinding oppression against the tributaries of Athens, differing from ordinary mills, in being gaily painted. ποικίλους is here a 'privative' or 'limiting' epithet; cp. III iv 4 *supra*.

[2] Diogenes the Cynic had already left Athens. There is nothing in the text to show that he was already dead. He is said to have died in 323, and an attempt has been made to place the date of the *Rhetoric* between Midsummer 323 and the death of Aristotle in Midsummer 322. The date of the death of Diogenes is itself doubtful (see Diels in *Rhein. Mus.* xxxi 14), and Aristotle mentions in his treatise (II xxiv) Dêmades and Demosthenes, both of whom were still alive (Diels, Berlin *Abhandlung*, 1886, p. 10 f).

[3] An Athenian orator contemporary with Demosthenes, whose speeches he regarded as reading better than those of his precursors, Plutarch's *Dem.* c. 11.

[4] βοᾶν is metaphorically used of inanimate things by Demosthenes, *Fals. Leg.* 93; *Ol.* i 2.

[5] Kêphisodotos, an author of pointed sayings already mentioned in iv 3 and x 6.

[6] ἐκκλησίας bracketed by F. A. Wolf and Roemer.

[7] *Philippus* § 12.

[8] 'Lysias,' *Epitaphios*, § 60, ὥστ' ἄξιον ἦν ἐπὶ τῷδε τῷ τάφῳ τότε κείρασθαι τῇ Ἑλλάδι καὶ πενθῆσαι τοὺς ἐνθάδε κειμένους, ὡς συγκαταθαπτομένης τῆς αὐτῶν ἐλευθερίας τῇ τούτων ἀρετῇ. This *Epitaphios* was delivered over those who died at Ægospotami towards the end of the Peloponnesian war. Hence ἐν Σαλαμῖνι was omitted by Dobree, *Adv.* i 13, approved by Schoell. A friend of Babington's (Hyp. *Epit.* 29) proposed to alter those words into ἐν Λαμίᾳ, thereby introducing a reference to a Funeral Oration shortly after the death of Aristotle. This is accepted by Sauppe (*Ausg. Schr.* 356), who regards this passage as a later addition to the text. The whole clause ἐπὶ τῷ τάφῳ—τελευτησάντων is omitted by Diels, Berlin *Abhandl.* 1886, 5–8. Wilamowitz, *ib.* 35–37, would retain the clause, and assign the passage to the *Epitaphios* of Gorgias.

lies through the midst of the deeds of Chares'[1]; this is a metaphor of proportion, and the phrase 'through the midst' is graphic.   Again, to speak of 'summoning dangers to the rescue of dangers'[2] is a vivid metaphor[3].   Lykoleôn said in defence of Chabrias[4]—'They did not revere even his symbol of supplication, the brazen statue'; this is a metaphor for the time, but not for all times; it serves, however, to give vividness; it is when he is in danger, that his statue is a suppliant, —that (of course) lifeless image of life, the record of public services[5].   'In every way studying to be spiritless';—a metaphor, since 'studying' implies *increasing* something[6].   And 'God has *kindled* intellect to be a light in the soul'[7]; both intellect and light *show* something.   'We are not composing but *postponing* our wars'[8]:—both things are of the future,— postponement, and the kind of peace in question.   It is a metaphor to say 'this treaty is a *trophy* much nobler than those won on battlefields; these commemorate small things and a single issue; the treaty is a monument of the whole war'[9]:—for both 'trophy' and 'treaty' are tokens of victory. Or—'Cities render heavy accounts to the censure of mankind'[10]:—the account being a sort of just penalty.

xi.   We have seen, then, that smartness depends on 'proportional' metaphor, and on 'setting things before the eyes.'   We must now explain what we mean by 'setting things before the eyes,' and by what methods this is effected.   This is 2 my definition—those words 'set a thing before the eyes,' which describe it in an active state.   For instance,

Those words 'set a thing before the eyes' which describe it in an active state.

---

[1] Said by Iphikrates in his prosecution of Chares in 355 B.C.   Cp. II xxiii 7.

[2] The author is unknown.

[3] πρὸ ὀμμάτων <καὶ> μεταφορά is proposed by Thurot, and accepted by Roemer.

[4] On the occasion of his trial in 366 B.C.   Cp. Grote, c. 79.   Nothing more is known of Lykoleon.

[5] The statue represented Chabrias *obnixo genu scuto proiecta hasta*; Nepos, *Chabrias*, 1.

[6] Isokr. *Paneg.* 151.   [7] The author is unknown.

[8] Isokr. *Paneg.* 172.   [9] *ib.* 180.

[10] The author is unknown.   There is a parallel passage in Isokr. *De Pace*,'120.

to say that a good man is 'four-square'[1] is a metaphor, since both the man and the square are complete ; but it does not describe an active state.   This phrase, on the other hand, '*in the flower of* his vigour'[2]; or this, 'at large, like a sacred animal,'[3]—are images of an active state.   And, in the verse—

'From thence the Greeks, then, *darting* with their feet,'[4]

the word 'darting' gives both actuality and metaphor—for it

3 means swiftness.   Or, we may use the device, often employed by Homer, of giving life to lifeless things by means of metaphor.   In all such cases he wins applause by describing *an active state* : as in these words—

'Back again plainward rolled the *shameless* stone.'[5]
'The arrow *flew*.'[6]
'The arrow *eager* to fly on.'[7]

1412 a   'The spears stuck in the ground *quivering* with hunger for the flesh.'[8]
'The spear-point shot *quivering* through his breast.'[9]

In all these cases the thing is shown in an active state by being made alive ;—'to be shameless,' 'to quiver,' &c., are active states.   These terms are applied with the help of a proportional metaphor ;—as the stone is to Sisyphos, so

4 is the shameless man to the victim of shamelessness.   This, again, is among his admired images for lifeless things—

'Curved, white-crested—some in front, and more behind—.'[10]

All such expressions make the thing moving and living—and an active state is movement.

5   Metaphors, as has been said before, must be taken from appropriate but not obvious things ; just as in philosophy acuteness is shown by discerning resemblance between things apart ; as Archytas[11] said that 'an arbitrator and an altar were

---

[1] Simonides, Fragm. 5 Bergk ed. 4.   [2] Isokr. *Philippus*, 10.
[3] Isokr. *Philippus*, 127.
[4] Eur. *Iph. Aul.* 80, τοὐντεῦθεν οὖν Ἕλληνες ᾔξαντες δορί, quoted ποσίν by Aristotle.   The manuscript reading in the *Rhet.* τοὐλεύθερον δ', was corrected by Victorius into τοὐντεῦθεν οὖν.
[5] *Od.* xi 598, αὖτις ἔπειτα πέδονδε (here quoted as ἐπὶ δάπεδόνδε) κυλίνδετο λᾶας ἀναιδής, 'Downward anon to the valley rebounded the boulder remorseless.'
[6] *Il.* xiii 588.   [7] *Il.* iv 126.   [8] *Il.* xi 574.   [9] *Il.* xv 541.
[10] *Il.* xiii 799, 'The waves of the bellowing ocean ; bending their heads foam-crested, they sweep on, billow on billow.'
[11] The Pythagorean philosopher and mathematician of Tarentum.

the same thing'—for each is a refuge for injured innocence. Or, one might say that 'an anchor and a swing¹ were identical'; for each is the same sort of thing, with the difference between 'above' and 'below.' To speak of States having been 'put on the same level'² is to use the same phrase of things which are far apart, equalisation being here the point in common between a superficies and political resources.

Now smartness, too, is given, as a rule, by means of meta- **6** phor³, with the addition of a deception. The fact that the hearer has learned something is made plainer by its contrast with his expectation ; the mind seems to say—'Indeed ! So I was wrong.' The smartness of apophthegms, too, depends on a meaning beyond the mere words—as when Stêsichoros says, 'the grasshoppers⁴ will sing to themselves on the ground.' Good riddles are pleasing for the same reason ; there is a new perception and there is a metaphor. The like is true of what Theodôros⁵ calls 'novelty' in style. This happens when the thing is a surprise, and, as he says, does not answer to our presentiment ; like those words, formed by a change, which comic writers use. Jokes which depend on the change of a letter have this effect : they deceive. And so in verse ; the hearer is disappointed by the line,—

'Statelily stept he along, and under his feet were his—chilblains'⁶:

one expected 'sandals.' (This kind of point, however, must be obvious on the instant.) The verbal joke depends on a meaning which is not proper to the word, but twists it ; for instance, the saying of Theodôros about Nikon the citharaplayer—' θράττεισε'⁷ : he affects to mean,—θράττει σε,—and

---

¹ κρεμάθρα, a hanging basket.

² ὠμαλίσθαι, Victorius' correction for ἀνωμαλίσθαι. Aristotle has in mind the passage in Isokr. *Philippus*, 40, οἶδα γὰρ ἅπασας (τὰς πόλεις) ὠμαλισμένας.

³ He has said, at the beginning of § 5, that *metaphor as a rule* is from οἰκείων καὶ μὴ φανερῶν. That kind of metaphor which gives 'smartness,'—that *also* involves a surprise (R. C. J.).   ⁴ Or 'cicalas'; cp. II xxi 8.

⁵ The rhetorician of Byzantium, already mentioned in II xxiii 28.

⁶ The author of the original is unknown.

⁷ Meineke proposed Θρᾷττ' ἦσε; Cope regarded the phrase as a play of words between θράττει, 'you are confounded,' and Θρᾷττ' εῖ, 'you are a Thracian maidservant'; Cobet suggested Θρᾴττης εῖ; Susemihl, Θρᾳττίζει, 'he is playing the Thracian' (the 'other meaning,' according to Jebb), or Θρᾳττίζει σε, 'it makes you play the Thracian.'

deceives us; for he has another meaning.   So, when this is

1412 b perceived, it gives pleasure (of course, if the hearer does not
understand that Nikon is a Thracian, he will see no point in

7   it).   Or this—'you want him to find his Mede.'[1]   (Both kinds
of smartness[2] must be used seasonably.)   Of the same sort
are such pleasantries as saying that, 'for the Athenians the
ἀρχὴ θαλάττης was not the ἀρχὴ κακῶν—they benefited by it:
or that, as Isokrates[3] said, the ἀρχή *was* an ἀρχὴ κακῶν for the
city.   In each case the thing said is unexpected, and, at the
same time, its truth is recognised.   In the latter case, there
would be no point in saying that ἀρχή *is* ἀρχή, were there not
a double meaning; in the former case, the ἀρχή which is the
subject of the negation has a different sense from that first

8   named.   In all such instances, however, the merit of the pun,
or of the metaphor, depends on its fitness.   Thus, in saying
that Ἀνάσχετος is οὐκ ἀνασχετός[4], there is a pun with the
negative; but it is fitting only if Anaschetos is disagreeable.
Again:—

'Thou canst be too much our stranger-friend';[5]

[or][6] 'Thou canst be too much,' &c., is equivalent to saying,
'The stranger must not always be a stranger'[7]; for this same
word ξένος means 'alien.'[8]   Of the same kind is the admired
saying of Anaxandrides,[9]

'Well is it to die ere one has done a deed worthy of death,'[10]

for this is equivalent to saying—'It is a worthy thing to die,
without being worthy to die,' or 'without doing deeds worthy

9   of death.'   The species of diction is the same in all these
cases; but, the more compact and the more antithetical the

---

[1] Some play of words between πέρσαι (for πέρθω) and Πέρσαι is apparently
intended; but the point is not clear.

[2] *i.e.* the 'surprise' and the 'joke that depends on the letter.'

[3] *Philippus*, 61; *Paneg.* 119; *De Pace*, 101.

[4] 'There is no bearing Baring.'

[5] Com. Fragm. iii 209 Kock.   [6] Bracketed by Spengel.

[7] Bekker, followed by Roemer, omits ξένος after the iambic line above quoted.
Vahlen, approved by Cope, would read:—οὐκ ἂν γένοιο, μᾶλλον ἢ ξένος ξένος ἢ οὐ
μᾶλλον ἢ σε δεῖ.   τὸ αὐτὸ καί· οὐ δεῖ κτλ.

[8] Or 'this too is again of a different kind' (Cope).

[9] III x 7 *supra.*

[10] Or, ''Tis well to die ere doing a deed deserving death.'

expression, the greater the applause. The reason is, that our
new perception is made clearer by the antithesis, and quicker
by the brevity. Further, the saying must always have, either   10
a personal application, or a merit of expression, if it is to be
striking as well as true. It may be true and yet trite ; thus,
' one ought to die innocent ' is true, but not smart. ' Wife and
husband should be well matched '—this is not smart. Smartness depends on having both qualities : thus ' it is worthy of a
man to die, while he is unworthy of death.' The greater the
number of conditions which the saying fulfils, the greater
seems the smartness ; as, for instance, when the words are
metaphorical, and the metaphor of a certain kind,—with antithesis, parallelism of structure, and actuality.

Similes, also, of an effective kind, as has been said above[1],   11
are in a sense metaphors[2] ; for, like the ' proportional ' metaphor, they always involve two terms. For instance, a shield
(we say) is ' the goblet of Ares,'[3]—a bow is a ' chordless lyre.'[4]
Thus stated, it is not a *simple* metaphor ; it would be a *simple*   1413 a
metaphor to say that the bow is a lyre, or the shield a goblet.
There are similes, also, of this simple kind,—as the comparison   12
of a flute-player to an ape, or of a shortsighted man to a
sputtering lamp (since both wink). But the happy simile is   13
where there is a ' proportional ' metaphor :—as one may compare a shield to a ' goblet of Ares,' a ruin to the ' rag of a
house,' or say that Nikêratos is a ' Philoktêtês stung by
Pratys,'—to use the comparison of Thrasymachos, when he
saw Nikêratos defeated in recitation by Pratys, and with long
hair and still squalid[5]. It is in these things that poets are
most hissed for failure, or most applauded for success—as
when they make it come just right thus—

' Curly as stalks of parsley are his legs.'

---

[1] c. iv and c. viii.

[2] The sense is in favour of following the scholiast and Spengel and Roemer by
reading εἰσὶν δὲ καὶ αἱ εἰκόνες...αἱ (for ἀεὶ) εὐδοκιμοῦσαι κτλ.

[3] Timotheos, Fragm. 16 Bergk, ed. 4.   [4] iv 4 *supra*.

[5] Thrasymachos compares the rhapsode Nikêratos, defeated by Pratys, to the
hero Philoktêtês bitten by the serpent,—Soph. *Phil.* 267, πληγέντ' ἐχίδνης ἀγρίῳ
χαράγματι. The point of the comparison is heightened by the fact that Philoktêtês
led the life of an unkempt hermit during his ten years on the island of Lêmnos.

'Just like Philammon struggling with the sand-bag.'[1]

All things of this kind, too, are similes ; and that similes are metaphors has been often said.

14   Proverbs, again, are 'metaphors from species to species.' Suppose for instance that one introduces something in the expectation of profiting by it himself, and then is injured, he says 'This is like the Carpathian and the hare'[2];—since both he and the Carpathian have had the fate in question.

The sources and the theory of smartness in style may now
15 be considered as explained.   It may be added that hyperboles of the most popular kind are also metaphors ;—as the hyperbole about the man with the black eye—'You would have taken him for a basket of mulberries':—the bruise being something purple; but the *quantity* of the purple makes the exaggeration.   The formula, '*like* so or so,' may be a hyperbole differently stated. '*Like* Philammon struggling with the sand-bag'—otherwise—'You would have thought that he was Philammon boxing with the sand-bag.' 'With legs curling *like* parsley'; otherwise—'You would have thought he was not on legs, but on stalks of parsley, so curly are they.' Hyperbole is boyish, for it expresses vehemence.   Hence it is most used by angry people :—

'Not if his gifts to me were as the sand or the dust : I will not marry the daughter of Agamemnon son of Atreus, never, though she should vie in beauty with golden Aphroditê, and in skill with Athênê.'[3]

1413 b   (Hyperbole is most used by the Attic orators.)   For the reason given above, it does not suit an elderly speaker.

xii.   It must not be forgotten that each branch of Rhetoric
General types   has its fitting style.   There is a difference between
of style.   the literary and the agonistic style; and, in the latter, between the parliamentary and the forensic style.   It

---

[1] τῷ κωρύκῳ.   A sack filled with bran or sand, used for practising boxing, the *follis pugilatorius* of Plautus, *Rudens,* 722.   The names of the authors of the last two quotations are unknown.   The athlete Philammon is mentioned in Dem. *De Cor.* 319.

[2] A proverbial reference to the Carpathian, who imported a pair of rabbits into the island between Crete and Rhodes, and lived to see the island overrun and devastated by their progeny.

[3] *Il.* ix 385 f.

The style of
literature and
that of debate. is necessary to know both styles. A knowledge of the agonistic style means simply the power of speaking good Greek ; a knowledge of the literary style means not being tongue-tied, when one wants to impart something to the world at large, which is the case with those who have no skill in composition. The literary style is the 2 most accurate ; the agonistic is the best adapted to delivery. This fitness depends upon one of two things ; expression of character, or expression of emotion. Hence actors seek plays, and poets personages, of these types. (The poets who write to be read have a circulation[1], however,—as Chærêmôn[2],— who has all the finish of a professional speech-writer—and, among dithyrambic poets, Likymnios[3]. On a comparison, the speeches of the literary men seem thin in actual contests ; while speeches by orators, which were well delivered[4], seem unworkmanlike when they are read. The reason is that their style is suitable only in the arena of debate. For the same reason, devices suited to delivery, when not helped by delivery, seem silly because they are not doing their proper work. Thus *asyndeta* and reiterations of the same word are rightly reprobated in the literary style, but not so in the agonistic style,—indeed public speakers use them, for they are dramatic. But when we reiterate, we must also vary,—an art, which is, 3 as it were, introductory to the whole art of delivery. ' *This* is the thief in your midst—*this* is the knave—*this* is he who finally sought to be a traitor.' Philêmôn, the actor, illustrated this by his delivery of the passage about Rhadamanthys and Palamêdês in the *Gerontomania* of Anaxandrides[5], and by his pronunciation of ' I ' in the prologue to the 'Good Men ':

[1] βαστάζονται, lit. 'are carried about in the hands.'

[2] The tragic poet already quoted in II xxiii 29. His elaborate finish is exemplified by his enumeration of all the flowers in a garland, Athen. 679 F.

[3] III ii 13 *supra*.

[4] εὖ λεχθέντες (understanding λόγοι) comes from the scholiast, εὖ μὲν λεχθέντες. The MSS have ἢ τῶν λεχθέντων or εὖ λεχθέντων, 'who have been well spoken of.' The sense requires something like λεχθέντες εὐδοκιμοῦντες, 'though highly esteemed, when delivered.'

[5] Athen. 614 c, 'Anaxandrides in the *Gerontomania* even describes Rhada-manthys and Palamedes as inventors of jests, writing thus': καίτοι πολλοί γε πονοῦμεν | τὸν ἀσύμβολον εὗρε γελοῖα λέγειν 'Ραδάμανθυς καὶ Παλαμήδης.

indeed, if one is not dramatic in such repetitions, it becomes
4 a case of 'the man who carries the beam.' So it is, too, with
asyndeta. 'I came—I met him—I made my petition': one
must *act* this,—not say it as if it was a single clause, with
unvarying sentiment and tone. *Asyndeta* have this further
property—a greater number of things seems to have been
said in an equal time; for it is the connecting particle which
makes one of many, and so, if the connecting particle is
removed, of course many will be made out of one. Hence
asyndeton serves to amplify:—'I came, I spoke to him, I
1414 a besought' (these seem *many* things); 'he disregarded all
that I said.'[1] This is what Homer[2] wishes to do in the
passage :—

> 'Nireus, again, from Symê—
> 'Nireus, son of Aglaia—
> 'Nireus, fairest of all—.'

A person of whom *much* is said must needs be mentioned
often; if, then, he is mentioned *often*, it seems as if *much* were
said; a fallacy which has enabled the poet to make Nireus
important by a single mention, though nowhere does he say
a word about him afterwards.

5   The Deliberative style, then, is exactly like rough fresco-
painting[3]:—the larger the audience, the more distant the
spectacle ;—in both, then, minute touches are superfluous,
and are seen at a disadvantage. The Forensic style is more
finished ; most so, when the cause is heard by a single judge[4];
for then it depends least upon rhetorical artifices[5]; the relevant
and the irrelevant are then more easily seen in one view, and
the turmoil is absent, so that the judgment is serene[6]. Hence
the same speakers are not brilliant in all these different kinds ;
where there is most room for declamation, there finish is least

---

[1] Reading, with Spengel and Roemer :—" ἦλθον, διελέχθην, ἱκέτευσα "· πολλὰ δοκεῖ· "ὑπερεῖδεν ὅσα εἶπον."

[2] *Il.* ii 671 f.   [3] Or 'like scene-painting' (Cope).

[4] ἡ < ἐν > ἑνὶ κριτῇ Spengel and Roemer.

[5] ἐλάχιστον γάρ ἐστιν ἐν ῥητορικοῖς inferior MSS;...ἐν ῥητορικῆς Paris MS; ἔνεστι ῥητορικῆς Spengel; < ἑνὶ > ῥητορικῆς (*sc.* ἐνὶ κριτῇ) Vahlen. We may also suggest ἐλάχιστον γὰρ ἔνι (=ἔνεστι) ῥητορικῆς. ἐστιν in the MSS may have arisen from an explanation of ἔνι as equivalent to ἔνεστι, but this use of ἔνι is very rare in Aristotle.

[6] Or 'unclouded' (R. C. J.).

in place; and this is where voice, especially loudness of voice, has scope.

The Epideiktic style is the best suited to writing; for it is 6 doing its own work when it is being read;—next, the Forensic.

A further classification of style, according to its need to be 'sweet' or 'magnificent,' is unnecessary. Why these, rather than 'temperate,' 'liberal,' or any other note of moral virtue? 'Sweet,' of course, it will be made by the qualities above mentioned,—assuming the excellence of style to have been rightly defined[1]. With what other object is it to be 'clear,' and 'not grovelling,' but 'suited to the subject'? If it is diffuse, or if, again, it is curt, it will not be 'clear': the fitting thing is plainly the mean. Sweetness will be given to style by the happy mixture of the things aforesaid—the familiar and the foreign, and the rhythm, and that persuasiveness which comes of propriety.

xiii.   Style has now been discussed, both generally[2] and in relation to each branch of Rhetoric[3]. It remains
Arrangement.   to speak of Arrangement. The speech has two parts:—it is necessary to *state* the matter which is our subject, and to *prove* it. We cannot, then, have a statement without a demonstration, or a demonstration without a previous statement; for the demonstrator must demonstrate something, and the expositor set a thing forth, in order to prove it. One of these processes is Statement, the other Proof:—just as 2 one might divide Dialectic into Problem and Demonstration. The division now in use is absurd. 'Narrative' belongs, I 3 presume, to Forensic speaking only. In Epideiktic or in Deliberative rhetoric, how can we have Narrative in their sense, or Refutation of the adversary, or Epilogue to the 1414 b argument? Again, 'Proem,' 'Contrast,' 'Review,' have a place in Deliberative speaking, *only* where there is a personal controversy. Accusation and Defence, also, are often present in such a speech, but not *qua* Deliberative speech. The Epilogue, again, is not essential even to a Forensic speech— as, when the speech is short, or the matter easy to remember;

[1] c. ii 1.   [2] c. ii–xi.   [3] c. xii, note.

4 for the advantage of Epilogue is abridgment[1]. The *necessary* parts of the speech, then, are Statement and Proof. These are proper to all. The greatest number that can be allowed is four—Proem, Statement, Proof, Epilogue. 'Refutation' comes under the head of Proof; 'Contrast' is a way of amplifying one's own argument, and is therefore a part of Proof, since he who does this, is demonstrating something. This is not true of the Proem, nor, again, of the Epilogue, 5 which merely refreshes the memory. If, then, we are to follow Theodôros[2] in taking into our division such terms as the above, we shall have 'Narrative Proper' distinguished from 'Supplementary' or 'Preliminary Narrative'—'Refutation' from 'Supplementary Refutation.' Now a new term should be brought in, *only* where there is a distinct kind of thing to differentiate; otherwise, it is empty and nonsensical, like the terms used by Likymnios[3] in his Art—'Speeding on'— 'Aberration'—'Ramifications.'

xiv. The Proem is the beginning of the speech,—analogous to the Prologue in poetry and the Prelude
The Proem.
in flute-playing. All these are beginnings, and pave the way, as it were, for what follows. The musical Prelude is most like the Epideiktic proem. Flute-players begin by playing anything that they can execute brilliantly; and then knit this on to the key-note of their theme[4]. The same kind of composition suits epideiktic rhetoric. The speaker should start by saying whatever his fancy prompts

---

[1] συμβαίνει γὰρ τοῦ μήκους ἀφαιρεῖσθαι, 'contingit enim e longa magnaque re partem abscindere' (Victorius). 'For what happens (in an ordinary epilogue) is a subtraction from the length'—not the brevity of a speech; *i.e.* an epilogue is appropriate to a long speech, not a short one (Cope). 'E longa oratione licet delibare quibus peroremus' (Spengel). We may suggest συμβαίνει γὰρ τοῦ μήκους ἀφαιρεῖσθαι <ἕνεκα>, 'for the epilogue exists for the very purpose of subtracting from the length of the speech.'

[2] xi 6 *supra*. The superfluous subdivisions of Theodôros are noticed in Plato's *Phædrus*, 266 D.

[3] A rhetorician, as well as a dithyrambic poet, xii 2 *supra*.

[4] τῷ ἐνδοσίμῳ, 'the actual opening, preliminary note, of the subject, which gives the tone to the rest' (Cope). τὸ ἐνδόσιμον is defined by Hesychius as τὸ πρὸ τῆς ᾠδῆς κιθάρισμα. See p. 182 n. 1 *infra*.

—then strike his key-note, and knit his proem to his theme: and this is just what they all do. Take, for instance, the proem to the *Helen*[1] of Isokrates;—there is nothing common between the Eristics and Helen. And here, even if the speaker passes into a foreign region, it is fitting, rather than that the speech should be monotonous. The proems of epideiktic 2 speeches are taken from topics of praise or blame,—as by Gorgias in his *Olympiakos,*—'Ye deserve the admiration of many, Hellênes'—where he is praising the founders of the great festivals;—as Isokrates[2], on the other hand, censures them for having crowned athletic excellence, but assigned no prize to mental prowess. Another topic is from advice;—as 3 that 'we *ought* to honour the good,'—and, accordingly, the speaker himself[3] lauds Aristeides;—or that 'we should honour men, who are not popular, nor yet unworthy[4],—who are good, but unrecognised'—as Paris son of Priam. Such a speaker 1415 a is giving us *advice*. Another topic is borrowed from forensic 4 proems,—namely from the appeal to the hearer to be indulgent, when our subject is paradoxical, difficult, or trite. Thus Chœrilos—

'But now, when all the spoil has been divided.'[5]

The proems of Epideiktic speeches, then, should be from one of these topics—praise, blame, adhortation, dehortation,

---

[1] §§ 1–13.

[2] *Paneg.* §§ 1, 2.   [3] The speaker is unknown.

[4] Probably from the *encomium Alexandri*, already quoted in II xxiii 5, 8, 12; xxiv 7, 9.

[5] From the exordium of Chœrilos' epic poem on the Persian war. The context, preserved by the scholiast, and quoted by Victorius, Gaisford, Spengel and Cope, is as follows:

ἆ μάκαρ, ὅστις ἔην κεῖνον χρόνον ἴδρις ἀοιδῆς,
Μουσάων θεράπων, ὅτ᾽ ἀκήρατος ἦν ἔτι λειμών·
νῦν δ᾽ ὅτε πάντα δέδασται, ἔχουσι δὲ πείρατα τέχναι,
ὕστατοι ὥστε δρόμου καταλείπομεθ᾽, οὐδέ πῃ ἔστι
πάντῃ παπταίνοντα νεοζυγὲς ἅρμα πελάσσαι.

Oh! the bards of olden ages, blessed bards in song-craft skill'd,
Happy henchmen of the Muses, when the field was yet untill'd.
All the land is now apportion'd; bounds to all the Arts belong;
Left the last of all the poets, looking keenly, looking long,
I can find no bright new chariot for the race-course of my song.
History of Classical Scholarship, i 40, ed. 1906.

appeals to the hearer; the key-note of the piece[1] may be either foreign, or proper to its subject.

5   As to the Proems of Forensic rhetoric, one must grasp the fact that they are equivalent to the prologue of drama and to the introduction of an epic poem—as the dithyrambic prelude is analogous to the epideiktic proem :

'For thy sake,—for thy gifts and for thy trophies.'[2]

6   But, in drama[3] and in epos, the introduction is an indication of the subject, in order that the hearers may know it beforehand, and that their thoughts may not be in suspense;—for the indefinite bewilders ;—so that he who puts the opening (as it were) into the hand of the listener, makes it immediately easy[4] for him to follow the story.   Hence

'Sing the anger, goddess.'[5]
'Tell me, Muse, of the man.'[6]
'Lead me forth on another story, how from Asia a great war came to Europe.'[7]

In the same way the tragic poets explain the action; if not directly, as Euripides does, at all events somewhere in a prologue : as Sophokles—

'My father was Polybos....'[8]

And so in Comedy.   This, then, is the essential and proper task of the proem,—to explain the object of the work ; hence, if the subject is plain and short, there is no need for a proem.

7   All other applications of the proem are merely remedial and are common to all three branches[9].   They are derived (1) from the speaker ; (2) from the hearer ; (3) from the subject; (4) from the adversary.   From (1) the speaker and (4) the

---

[1] (1) *i.e.* the topic, which links the proem on to the treatment of the subject, may be immediately connected either with the proem or with the subject.   This is indifferent, so long as the ἐνδόσιμον serves the purpose of a link.   Or (2) ἐνδόσιμα may here be loosely used for προοίμια; so Cope, *Introd.* 339, *Comm.* iii 167 (R. C. J.).

[2] Bergk's *P. L. G.* iii 728, frag. anon. 124.

[3] Reading τοῖς δράμασι (with Susemihl), for τοῖς λόγοις (R. C. J.).   τοῖς προλόγοις is the text of the scholiast and the Latin translator.   ἐν δὲ τοῖς [λόγοις καὶ] ἔπεσι is the text of Spengel, who suggests ἐν δὲ τοῖς < δικανικοῖς > λόγοις.

[4] ἐχόμενον, 'immediately easy'; or (with Cope) 'supplies him with a clue, as it were, *by which he may hold,* so as to enable him to follow the story.'

[5] *Il.* i 1.   [6] *Od.* i 1.

[7] Part of the exordium of Chœrilus' epic on the Persian war (cp. 181 n. 3 *supra*).

[8] *Œdipus Tyrannus*, 774 f.   [9] Or 'general' (R. C. J.).

adversary, when they are concerned with allaying or exciting a prejudice. There is, however, this difference. The defendant must *begin* by answering hostile insinuation : the accuser must place his hostile insinuation in the *epilogue.* The reason is plain enough : the defendant, when he wants to have his innings[1], must first remove the hindrances, and must therefore begin by doing away with the prejudice against him; the man who has evil to suggest, must suggest it in the epilogue, in order that people may remember it the better.

(4) Appeals to the hearer have for their object to make him friendly to us or angry with the adversary :—*sometimes* to make him attentive, or the reverse.   Sometimes ; for it is not *always* expedient to make him attentive ; and hence speakers often try to move their hearers to mirth. The whole art of proem may be summed up, if you like, in this—making the hearer docile, and making yourself seem estimable ; for estimable people are heard with more attention. (3) Men are **1415 b** attentive to important subjects, to those which concern themselves, to the marvellous, to the pleasant; therefore the speaker must instil the notion that his subjects are of this kind. If he wishes to render them inattentive, he must say that the subject is trifling, unimportant for them, or painful. It must not be forgotten, however, that all such topics are 8 beside the question : they are addressed to an infirm hearer, who listens to what is irrelevant ; for, if the hearer is *not* of this kind, there is no need for a proem, except in the sense of stating the subject summarily, in order (so to say) that the body may have a head. The task of making the hearers 9 attentive belongs, it may be added, to any part of the speech, when the need arises ; indeed the hearer relaxes his attention everywhere more than at the beginning. It is absurd, then, to fix this at the beginning,—the point at which everyone listens with most attention. So, wherever there is occasion, we must say, 'Attend to me : it is as much your concern as mine' : or

‘I will tell you that, the like of which you never yet’[2]

[1] ‘When he is about to introduce his own case,’ Cope.
[2] From an unknown tragic poet.

heard for terror, or for wonder. This means the rule of Prodikos, in fact:—'Whenever the audience are drowsy, throw in a flavour of the fifty-drachm.'[1] Plainly these appeals are made to the hearer, not simply as set hearer of a cause.

10   Everyone seeks to instil prejudice, or to remove misgivings, in his exordium:—

> 'King, I will not say that it was in haste—'[2]
> 'Why dost thou use preface?'[3]

In particular, preface is used by those who have, or are thought to have, a bad case; it is better for them to dwell on anything rather than on their case itself. Hence slaves do not answer the questions put them, but talk round about them, and use preface. The mode of inspiring the hearer with good will, and all similar feelings, has been explained[4]. It is well said

11

> 'Grant that I may come to the Phæacians with a claim on their *love* and their *pity*.'[5]

These, then, are the two things at which we should aim.

In the Epideiktic proem, the hearer should be made to think that the praise applies to himself, or to his family, or to his pursuits, or is shared by him in some other way; for it is a true saying of Sokrates in the *Epitaphios*, that 'it is not hard to praise Athenians among Athenians, but only among Lacedæmonians.'[6]

12   The proems of the Forensic speech furnish those of the Deliberative:—in which, however, it is naturally rarest. The subject is one which is known already, and which requires no preface, unless (1) on account of the speaker himself, (2) on account of his opponents, or (3) because the hearers make either more or less of the matter than one wishes. Hence we

---

[1] τῆς πεντηκονταδράχμου, sc. ἐπιδείξεως, 'the fifty-drachm *discourse*,' Prodikos' most famous, and interesting, and expensive lecture. Cp. Plato's *Cratylus*, 384 B, τὴν πεντηκοντάδραχμον ἐπίδειξιν (Cope).

[2] Sophokles, *Antigone*, 223 f. For σπουδῆς ὕπο, in Aristotle's quotation, the MSS of Sophokles have τάχους ὕπο, retained by Jebb on the ground that 'Aristotle's quotations seem to have been usually made from memory, and his memory was not infallible' (see note on *Ant.* 223).

[3] Euripides, *Iph. Taur.* 1162.

[4] II iv and viii.   [5] *Odyss.* vii 327.

[6] Plato, *Menexenus*, 235 D; I ix 30 *supra*.

must either (1) seek to raise a prejudice, or (2) to clear ourselves, or (3) to amplify, or (4) to make less of the subject[1]. These, then, are the objects of the proem, or else its object is ornament; since, without a proem, the speech seems slovenly 1416 a —like the encomium of Gorgias on the Eleans; where, without so much as squaring his elbows,—without any preliminary sparring—he begins at once with 'Elis, happy city.'

xv. In dealing with a calumny[2], one topic may be derived

Proem, continued.

from the means by which one would clear oneself from any unpleasant suspicion; it does not matter whether the suspicion has been *uttered* or not; and this topic is universal.

A second topic consists in meeting the issues actually 2 raised; either by denial of the fact; or by saying that it is not injurious, or not injurious to the complainant; or not so great as stated; or no wrong, or only a small wrong; or not dishonourable; or of no importance. The controversy always turns on some such point;—as when Iphikrates said, in answer to Nausikrates, that he had done what Nausikrates alleged, and had done a harm; but had done no wrong. Or, if the speaker is wrong, he may strike a balance, urging that, if the deed is hurtful, at all events it is honourable :—if it is painful, at least it is advantageous,—or something of that kind.

A third topic is to show that the thing was a mistake, or a 3 misfortune, or unavoidable. Thus Sophokles said, that he was not trembling for the reason given by his calumniator— namely, that he might *seem* an old man—but of necessity; it was not by his own choice that he was eighty years old. Or, we may substitute a different motive for the motive alleged : —thus : 'He did not mean to do a harm, but to do *this*' : 'he did not mean to do that, with which he was slanderously charged,—it was an accident that injury was inflicted.' 'It would be just to hate me, had I acted with a view to this result.'

---

[1] These four points are arranged in two pairs: (i) raising or rebutting a prejudice, (ii) amplifying or minimising the subject.

[2] περὶ διαβολῆς = περὶ τοῦ ἀπολύεσθαι διαβολήν (R. C. J.).

4   There is a fourth topic, when the calumniator, or anyone nearly related to him, is or has been involved in the charge.

5   A fifth topic is, when other persons are involved, who are generally acknowledged not to be liable to the charge; thus it may be argued—' If he is an adulterer because he is neat in his person¹, then so-and-so is an adulterer too.'

6   A sixth topic is when the calumniator, or another, has brought the same charge against other persons; or when, without being expressly accused, they were suspected as the speaker is now; and have proved innocent.

7   A seventh topic consists in recrimination. 'It is absurd, if belief is to be given to the statements of one who is himself untrustworthy.'

8   It is an eighth topic when there has been a previous decision. Thus Euripides in the exchange-case answered Hygiænôn's contention, that he was impious for having written a verse which encourages perjury—

'My tongue is sworn—my soul is unsworn.'²

'It is unjust of him,' said the poet, 'to bring before a lawcourt points already decided in the Dionysiac contest. In the theatre I have rendered my account for these—or will yet render it, if he likes to accuse me.'

9   A ninth topic is to denounce calumny,—to show how great an evil it is,—how it raises false issues,—how it means distrust of one's real case.

The topic from tokens is common to accuser and apolo-
1416 b gist. Thus, in the *Teukros*³, Odysseus says that Teukros is a near relation of Priam, Hêsionê being Priam's sister. Teukros answers that his father, Telamôn, was a foe to Priam; and that he himself did not betray the (Greek) spies.

10   An eleventh topic, proper to the accuser, consists in praising some small merit at length, and then expressing a weighty censure concisely; or, first noticing many merits of the adversary, and then blaming in him some one thing, which is of

---

¹ εἰ ὅτι καθάριος ὁ <δεῖνα> μοιχός Richards (Roemer), or, simply, εἰ ὁ καθάριος μοιχός. Cp. II xxiv 7, καλλωπιστής.
² *Hippol.* 608, 'My tongue has sworn; my mind remains unsworn.' See Cope's *Comm.* iii 183.   ³ Of Sophokles.

paramount significance for the issue. Such accusers are the most artistic, and the most unfair : they try to hurt a man through his merits, by mixing these with evil.

A device common to accuser and to apologist depends on 11 the possibility of several different motives for the same act. The accuser must adopt a malignant and disparaging construction : the apologist must take the better construction. Take for example the preference of Diomêdês for Odysseus[1]. One speaker must ascribe it to a belief that Odysseus was the best man. The other, denying this, must ascribe it to the fact that Odysseus alone was so worthless as to be no rival for Diomêdês.

xvi. This may suffice in regard to the art of exciting prejudice.

In Epideiktic speeches the Narrative must be not continuous, but broken up. We have to relate the
Narrative. actions, on which the speech is founded. The speech is composed of two elements ;—first, the inartificial, since the speaker is in no way the author of the actions ; secondly, the artificial,—which consists in proving that the fact is so, if it be hard to believe,—or that it is of a certain character[2], or of a certain importance ;—or in proving all these things. Hence it is sometimes undesirable to relate all 2 our facts continuously, since this mode of exposition tasks the hearer's memory. Rather—' *These* facts show that our hero is brave '; '*these* facts show that he is wise or just.' This kind of statement is simple : the other is intricate and lacks plainness. Well-known facts should be merely recalled to the 3 memory ; hence[3] most people require no narrative—as when your purpose is to praise Achilles ; everyone knows his actions —you have only to *use* them. If Kritias, on the contrary, is your subject, narrative is needed—for not many people know[4].

An absurd rule is current to the effect that narrative 4 should be rapid. When the baker asked whether he was to

---

[1] *Il.* x 242 f; cp. II xxiii 20, 24 *supra*.
[2] Corresponding to (2) and (3) in c. xvii 1.
[3] διό, 'since the facts *are* well-known' (R. C. J.).
[4] On the *lacuna* at this point, cp. Cope, *Introd.* 349, *Comm.* iii 188.

make the cake hard or soft, his customer asked—'Why cannot you make it *right*?' Just so here. Our narrative ought not to be lengthy, any more than our proem or the statement of our proofs; here, again, excellence lies neither in rapidity nor in brevity, but in the mean; that is, in saying just so much as will explain the matter; or, as will establish the fact, the injury, or the wrong,—or, so much as you wish to establish:

1417 a

5 —the adversary's aim being to negative this. And you should bring into your narrative anything that tends to show your own worth, or the adversary's worthlessness: 'Meanwhile, I was always urging him to the right course,—not to abandon his children to danger; but he answered that, wherever he might find himself, there he would find new children';—as Herodotus[1] says that the Egyptian rebels answered. Anything, too, may be brought in which will please the judges.

6   For the defendant, narrative is less important. His contention is either (1) that the fact has not occurred; or (2) that it was not harmful; or (3) that it was not unjust; or (4) that it was not of the importance alleged. He ought not to waste his time, then, on any admitted fact, unless this has some bearing on his own contention;—as on a contention that, admitting the act, it was not an unjust act. Again, he should

7 give only a summary of past events, unless an account of them, as actually passing, tends to move pity or indignation. For instance, the story of Alkinoös[2], when told to Pênelopê, is comprised in sixty lines[3]. Such, too, is the treatment of the Epic Cycle by Phayllos[4], and the prologue in the *Œneus*[5].

8   Further, the narrative should have an ethical colour. The condition of effecting this is to know what gives *êthos*. One way, then, is to make the moral purpose of action clear, the quality of the *êthos* being determined by the quality of this purpose, and the quality of the purpose by the end. Hence mathematical discourses have no moral character, since they have no moral purpose, for they have no moral end. But

---

[1] ii 30.   [2] *Od.* ix–xii.
[3] *Odyss.* xxiii 264–284, 310–343 (fifty-five lines).
[4] Of Phayllos nothing whatever is known (Cope).
[5] Eur. frag. 558 f Nauck.

the Sokratic discourses have such a character, since they deal
with moral subjects. Different moral traits go with each 9
character. Thus :—' As he was talking, he strode on '—this
suggests the type of rowdy and boor. Then, one should speak,
not (as it were) from the intellect, as is the fashion now, but
from the moral purpose :—' However, I wished it to be ' ;—
' Yes, it was my deliberate intention ' ; ' Well, though I gained
nothing by it, it is better thus.' One course would have
shown a prudent man ; the other shows a good man : the
prudent man shows himself in the pursuit of advantage, the
good man in that of honour. And, if any such trait seems incredible, then add the reason, as Sophokles does :—for instance
in the *Antigone*, where she says that she cared more for her
brother than she could have cared for husband or children.
The latter, if lost, could have been replaced ;

> ' But, now that sire and mother are with Death,
>   No brother's life could bloom for me, again.'[1]

Or, if you have no reason to give, show at least that you are
conscious of the statement being hard to believe ;—' Such,
however, is my nature ' :—for the world does find it hard to
believe in any motive except self-interest.

   Use, too, in your narrative the traits of emotion,—the 10
symptoms of it which are familiar to all, or which are
peculiarly characteristic of yourself or of your adversary. ' He
left me with a scowl ' ; or,—as Æschines[2] said of Kratylos 1417 b
—' hissing and shaking his fists.' These touches are persuasive, because the things which the hearers know become
tokens to them of things which they do *not* know. Many
similar touches may be borrowed from Homer :—

> ' So she spake, and the old woman covered her face with her hands ' :—[3]

(expressive), since people who are on the point of weeping
put their hands to their eyes.

   Present yourself in a definite character from the very
outset, in order that the hearers may view you, as contrasted
with your opponent, in this light ; only, hide your art. How

---

[1] *Ant.* 911 f, where the MSS have κεκευθότοιν for Aristotle's βεβηκότων, 'a mere
slip of memory'; cp. note on xiv 10, p. 184 n. 2 *supra*.
[2] Supposed by Victorius to be Æschines Socraticus.   [3] *Od.* xix 361.

easy it is to do this, may be seen from the case of people bringing us news[1] :—though we have no idea what the tidings are, we get a foreboding.—The narrative should be distributed over the speech ; and in some cases there should be none at the beginning.

11   In Deliberative Rhetoric there is least room for narrative, for no one can narrate the future. When, however, there *is* a narrative, its object will be merely to refresh the hearer's memory of the past, in order that he may judge better of the future. Or the object may be to excite a prejudice, or to praise. But, in narrating, the deliberative speaker is not doing his own work.

If a statement is incredible, the speaker must make himself responsible for the fact, and give the explanation at the outset, and marshal his reasons in a way acceptable to the hearers[2]. Thus, the Iokastê of Karkinos, in his *Œdipus*, goes on giving her word in answer to the inquiries of the man who is seeking her son ; and so the Hæmon of Sophocles[3].

---

[1] How much the drama of modern life has lost in the extinction of the messenger! (R. C. J.)

[2] Reading διατάττειν ὡς βούλονται, for διατάττειν οἷς βούλονται, which is probably corrupt. The application of the examples in the text appears to be as follows :—(i) Iokastê tells the inquirer things about her son which he finds it hard to believe. She meets his unbelief by *pledging her word* for the facts. (ii) Kreon knows that Hæmon is in love with Antigone, and Hæmon thinks her sentence unjust. Kreon finds it 'incredible' that Hæmon should be at the same time dutiful to himself, but Hæmon explains the reason (*Ant.* 701-4). Cope (*Introd.* 354), who (like the scholiast) would omit τε after ὑπισχνεῖσθαι, appears to understand it thus:—'if the statement is incredible, the speaker must promise both to assign the cause, and to set forth his reasons in the terms his hearers desire.' He thinks that ὑπισχνεῖται, said of Iokastê, means 'promising to satisfy the questioner'; and he holds that Αἵμων is corrupt (similarly in *Comm.* iii 197). I object
(i) to his omission of τε, and to his way of taking ὑπισχνεῖσθαι,
and (ii) to his version of οἷς βούλονται.
Victorius' explanation (as quoted by Cope) is : 'the speaker must promise to assign the reason, and to *refer the matter* (διατάττειν) to those whom the hearers approve.' But διατάττειν cannot mean *committere* ; nor do I understand his explanation about Hæmon, unless he means (1) the thing 'incredible' to be Hæmon's defence of Antigone; (2) the 'promise,' his promise of obedience (R. C. J.).
διατάττειν οἷς βούλονται is translated *vadiare quibus volunt*, which suggests διαιτᾶσθαι or διαιτηταῖς (as observed by Roemer), or, possibly, διαιτηταῖς ἐπιτρέπειν οἷς, βούλονται.

[3] *Antigone*, 701-4.

xvii.   Our proofs must be demonstrative.   There are four
possible issues ; our demonstration must have
reference to the issue.   Thus, (1) if one disputes
a *fact*, this negative is the first thing which one has to prove
in court ; (2) if one says, ' I have done no harm,' that must be
proved ; (3) if one says ' I have not done so much harm,' or
(4) ' I have done it justly,' then the truth of *this* becomes the
issue.

It must not be forgotten that the issue of the *fact* is the 2
only one, under which it may happen that one of the two
parties is *necessarily* a knave.   It may be impossible to plead
ignorance,— as it is possible, when the justice of an act is the
point at issue.   Hence, *in this case*[1], we should dwell (on this
topic)[2] ; but not so in the other cases[3].

In Epideiktic speaking, the greater part of the argument 3
(as that certain things are honourable or advantageous) is
amplification ; the facts must be taken upon trust ; it is but
rarely that the speaker attempts demonstration of the facts
themselves, only when they are incredible, or when he has
some other special reason.

In Deliberative speaking, one may contend either (1) that 4
certain things will not happen, or (2) that these things will result
from our adversary's policy, but are unjust, (3) inexpedient,
or (4) will result in a less degree than he says.   We must see,
too, whether he makes any false statement outside his immediate subject; for such statements seem to justify the inference
that he is misrepresenting his subject itself.   Examples are 5
better suited to Deliberative speaking, Enthymemes to **1418 a**
Forensic speaking :—Deliberative Rhetoric is concerned with
the future, and so we must have examples from the past ;
Forensic Rhetoric is concerned with the existence or non-
existence of facts, and here rigorous demonstration is more
possible ; for the past has precision.   Our enthymemes ought 6
not to be given in a string, but worked in here and there ;

---

[1] *i.e.* where *fact* is in question (R. C. J.).

[2] viz. that the adversary is *necessarily* a knave (R. C. J.).

[3] Or, as Spengel, p. 444 : Hence the speaker ought to dwell *on this point* (illa
iudicatione : does Spengel mean the question of *fact*, or the argument that the
adversary is necessarily a knave ?), not on the others (R. C. J.).

otherwise they hurt each other's effect. There is a limit of quantity :

'Friend, since thou hast said as much as a prudent man would say—'[1]

7 'as much as'—not '*such* things as.' Nor ought we to look for enthymemes on *all* subjects, else we shall do what some of the philosophers do, who apply demonstration to things which are better known, and more easily taken on trust, than their

8 premisses. When you are trying to move feeling, use no enthymeme ; it will either expel the feeling, or will have been used in vain ; for simultaneous motions tend to expel each other ; and either each destroys the other, or one overpowers the other. Nor should an enthymeme be sought, when you are seeking to make your speech ethical; for there is neither

9 *êthos* nor moral purpose in a demonstration. Maxims, however, should be used both in narrative and in proof; for a maxim is ethical. Thus :—"I have given him this, and have given it, though I know the maxim, 'Trust no man.'" Or, if it is to be pathetic :—' Nor do I repent, though I have been injured :—the gain accrues to him, the sense of just conduct to me.'

10 Deliberative speaking is naturally more difficult than Forensic, since it concerns the future ; the other concerns the past, which is already known, even to soothsayers, as Epimenides of Crete said. His divinations used not to concern the future, but only the dark things of the past. Again, in forensic speaking, we have the law for our theme; and, given a starting-point, it is easier to find our demonstration. Then, Deliberative speaking offers few topics, on which we can pause by the way, such as that of attack upon the adversary, discourse about oneself, or appeals to feeling ; it admits these less than any branch of Rhetoric, unless the speaker leaves his proper ground. If, then, one is at a loss for topics, one must do like the Athenian orators and Isokrates ; Isokrates brings accusation into his deliberative speeches ; as accusation of the Lacedæmonians into his *Panegyricus*[2], and accusation of Chares into

11 his *Speech about the Social War*[3]. An Epideiktic speech should be interwoven with laudatory episodes, in the manner

---

[1] *Od.* iv 204. [2] §§ 110–114. [3] *De Pace,* § 27.

of Isokrates, who is always bringing some one in[1]. This is what Gorgias meant by saying that matter of discourse never failed him. When, in speaking of Achilles, he praises Peleus, and then Æakos, and then the god, and valour, and this or that,—he is using the device in question.

When you have means of demonstration, you should use both the ethical and the demonstrative styles; if you have *no* enthymemes, the ethical style only; and, indeed, it better befits an estimable man that his character should appear in a good light than that his speech should be closely reasoned. Refutative enthymemes are more popular than Demonstrative, because in all refutative processes, the strictness of the conclusion is more evident, since opposites are more striking when set side by side.

Refutation of the adversary is not a distinct department of proof; his arguments are to be broken down, either by objection, or by counter-syllogism. Both in Deliberative and in Forensic speaking we should begin by bringing our own proofs, and then meet the arguments on the other side, refuting them and pulling them to pieces by anticipation. If, however, the adversary's case has a great number of points, we should begin with these, as Kallistratos did in the Messenian assembly, when he first disposed of the arguments about to be used against him, before he stated his own. The speaker who is replying should first address himself to his adversary's speech in the way of refutation and counter-syllogism— especially if the adverse arguments have gained applause ; for the mind rejects a speech, against which it is prepossessed, just as it rejects a man, supposing the adversary to have made a good impression. It is necessary, then, to make room in the hearer's mind for the coming argument. This room will exist, if you remove the obstacles. Hence you should begin by combating the adverse arguments—all of them, or the chief, or the plausible, or those which are easy to refute—and then establish your own arguments.

12

1418 b

13

14

15

---

[1] Episodes on Theseus in the *Helena* §§ 22–38, and on Paris, *ib.* 41–48 ; on Pythagoras and the Egyptian priests in the *Busiris*, 21–29; on the poets, *ib.* 38–40; and on Agamemnon in the *Panathenaicus*, 72–84 (Spengel).

'First I will come to the defence of the goddess......
Now I do not think that Hera...'[1]

Here he has laid hold first of the weakest point.

16   So much of argumentative proof. As to ethical proof[2], seeing that there are some things, which it is invidious to say of ourselves, or which expose us to the charge of tediousness or to contradiction, or which, if said of another, suggest that we are abusive or ill-bred, we must put these things into the mouth of some other person,—as Isokrates does in the *Philippos*[3], and in the *Antidosis*[4],—and as Archilochos does in his satire. Thus it is the father, whom he introduces speaking of the daughter in the verse :

'Nothing is beyond hope, against nothing should men make a vow';[5]

and thus he uses Charon the carpenter in the verse beginning

'Not Gyges' wealth......'[6]

Thus, too, in Sophokles, Hæmon pleads for Antigone with
17 his father as it were in the words of others[7].   Enthymemes

---

[1] Eur. *Troades*, 969, 971.

[2] It will be convenient to recall here the several connexions in which Aristotle has used *êthos* in relation to rhetorical persuasion. (1) 'Ethical proofs' proper are equivalent to 'proofs inherent in the *êthos* of the speaker' (I ii); this is further explained in II i. (2) In II xii 13 the *êthê* proper to youth, manhood, old age, noble birth, wealth, power, etc. are described. The advantage of knowing these is that we shall be able to give our speech the *general* colour or tone acceptable to the audience. They are really subservient, then, to the treatment of *pathê*,—to the exciting of certain feelings in the hearer's mind. (3) In III vii he says that 'style will have Propriety, if it is, first, *pathetic*; secondly *ethical*; thirdly, proportional to the subject.' By 'pathetic' he means, if the speaker appears to be himself affected in a way suitable to the facts which he is relating. 'Ethical style' he defines as "the representation of facts by means of appropriate signs,' *i.e.* the presentation of the persons introduced, as speaking or acting in a characteristic way—with the marks or traits proper to their age, condition, etc. This has nothing to do with 'ethical proof' proper, *i.e.* the production in the hearer's mind of a good impression about the speaker's character. Nor has it anything to do with the *êthê* of II xii 13, which help us to come into a general sympathy with our hearers. It is merely a precept for effectiveness of style,—one of the characteristics essential to vivid, graphic description. (4) The *êthos* of III xvii is the '*êthos* of the speaker.' The special rule given is meant to guard us against spoiling our 'ethical proof' by seeming egotistic, abusive, or illbred (R. C. J.).

[3] §§ 4–7.   [4] §§ 132–9, 141–9.

[5] Fragm. 74, Bergk, ed. 4.

[6] οὔ μοι τὰ Γύγεω τοῦ πολυχρύσου μέλει, Frag. 25, Bergk, ed. 4.

[7] *Antigone*, 688–700.

should sometimes, too, be thrown into the form of maxims ;—
for instance, ' Sensible men ought to make up their quarrels
when they are prosperous—for so they will gain most.'[1] Put
in the form of an enthymeme, this would be :—' If men ought
to adjust their differences at the moment when it is most
beneficial and gainful to do so, then they ought to do so when
they are prosperous.'

xviii.   As to Interrogation, it is opportune to interrogate,
first of all, when the adversary has already made **1419 a**

Interrogation. one admission, so that, when one more question
has been asked, the absurdity is complete. Thus Perikles
questioned Lampôn about the mode of celebrating the rites of
the Saving Goddess ; Lampôn said that no uninitiated person
could be told of them; Perikles asked—'Do *you* know them?'
' Yes,' said Lampôn.—' How, if you are uninitiated ? '

The second case is when one premiss is already obvious, 2
and it is plain that the conclusion will be granted by the adversary when we put it to him. We ought to put the other
premiss in the form of a question, suppressing the obvious
premiss, and then put our conclusion. Thus Sokrates, when
Melêtos accused him of believing in no gods, (asked)—' Do
you recognise such a thing as the dæmonic ? '[2] Melêtos said

---

[1] Cp. Isokrates, *Archidamus*, 50.

[2] εἴρηκεν εἰ δαιμόνιόν τι λέγοι, ὁμολογήσαντος δὲ ἤρετο is the text of the inferior
MSS and the scholiast, followed in Bekker's third ed.   The perfect εἴρηκεν, ' has
said,' cannot be right ; we want ἤρετο, ' asked.' I cannot find any instances of
λέγειν as equivalent to νομίζειν or ἡγεῖσθαι ; but it might easily have the sense
' mention in ordinary conversation,' ' have often on one's lips.'

εἴρηκεν ὡς ἂν δαιμόνιόν τι λέγοι, ἤρετο is the text of the Paris MS, rendered in
the Latin translation :—*dixit, ac si dæmonium aliquid diceret, interrogabat*.   This
is retained by Spengel, who adds ' *Meletus de Socrate* εἴρηκεν ὡς ἂν δαιμόνιόν τι
λέγοι.'   This then must be a quotation : Sokrates (said), ' He (Melêtos) has said
that he (Sokrates) believed in a δαιμόνιον.'   This will not do.   Clearly the only
corruption is in εἴρηκεν (R. C. J.).   Spengel's text is retained by Roemer, while
Kayser omits εἴρηκεν and alters the ὡς ἂν of the Paris MS into ὡς δέ.   Madvig
proposes : Σωκράτης, Μελήτου οὐ φάσκοντος αὐτὸν θεοὺς νομίζειν εἰρηκότος δὲ ὡς
δαιμόνιόν τι λέγοι, ἤρετο κτλ.   Melêtos had himself charged Sokrates with introducing
ἕτερα καινὰ δαιμόνια, thus implying that Sokrates believed in certain δαιμόνια.
Sokrates infers that one who believes in the existence of δαιμόνια, must believe in
the existence of δαίμονες.   The text of the passage in Plato's *Apol*. 27 C runs as
follows :—ἔσθ' ὅστις δαιμόνια μὲν νομίζει πράγματ' εἶναι, δαίμονας δὲ οὐ νομίζει;
Οὐκ ἔστιν...οὐκοῦν δαιμόνια μὲν φῂς με καὶ νομίζειν καὶ διδάσκειν εἴτ' οὖν καινὰ εἴτε

'Yes.' Then Sokrates asked—'Are not the dæmons either children of the gods, or sharers of some divine nature?' Melêtos admitted it. 'Then, is there anyone,' said Sokrates, 'who believes in children of the gods, but denies gods?'[1]

3   A third case is when we purpose to show that the arguments of the adversary are inconsistent or paradoxical.

4   The fourth case is when the adversary cannot refute us, except by an answer which has a sophistical air. If he answers in this fashion—'Yes and No'—'In some cases, not in others' —'In one sense, not in another'—the hearers think that he is puzzled[2], and applaud us.

Under any other circumstances, it is better not to attempt interrogation:—for if the adversary brings an objection, a victory seems to have been gained over us;—the infirmity of the hearer makes it impossible to put a long chain of questions. For the same reason, our enthymemes ought to be packed as closely as possible.

5   In replying, if the adversary's terms are ambiguous, they should be regularly[3] defined, and this not too concisely. If there is a suspicion that we are contradicting ourselves, our explanation should be given in our first answer, before the adversary has put his next question or drawn his conclusion; —it is not hard to foresee what is the point of his argument. This, however, and the art of refutation generally, may be

παλαιά· ἀλλ᾽ οὖν δαιμόνιά γε νομίζω κατὰ τὸν σὸν λόγον καὶ ταῦτα καὶ διωμόσω ἐν τῇ ἀντιγραφῇ. The text of Aristotle is thus paraphrased in the Fragm. περὶ ἐρωτήσεως :—λεγόντων γὰρ τῶν κατηγόρων ὡς Σωκράτης θεοὺς οὐ νομίζει καὶ καινὰ δαιμόνια εἰσάγει, ἀνήρετο αὐτοὺς περὶ τῶν δαιμόνων, εἰ μὴ θεοὺς ἢ θεῶν παῖδας ἡγοῦνται αὐτούς· ὡς δὲ συνέφησαν, Ἔστι δὲ ὅστις θεοὺς οὐ νομίζει, θεῶν παῖδας νομίζων; παρέλιπε γὰρ τὸ αὐτόθεν ὁμολογούμενον, ὅτι ὁ δαιμόνια νομίζων θεοὺς νομίζει.

[1] The enthymeme is :—'The dæmons are children of the gods; Those who believe in the existence of the children believe in the existence of the father (this is φανερόν, and is not expressed by the questioner); therefore, Those who believe in dæmons believe in gods' (R. C. J.).

[2] θορυβοῦσιν ὡς ἀποροῦντος, the correction proposed by Spengel and Schneidewin. As an alternative, Spengel suggests ἀποροῦντα, the Paris MS having ἀποροῦντας. The inferior MSS, followed by Bekker, have ἀποροῦντες. It is not the *audience*, however, but the person under interrogation, that is perplexed. The Fragm. περὶ ἐρωτήσεως has, πρὸς γὰρ τοὺς οὕτω ἀποκριναμένους οἱ ἀκροώμενοι θορυβοῦσιν ὡς ἀποροῦντας καὶ οὐκ ἔχοντας ἀντειπεῖν.

[3] λόγῳ, 'with a full explanation' (R. C. J.).

taken as known from the *Topics*[1]. Again, when the adversary's 6
conclusion is being drawn, and when this conclusion is in the
form of a question, we should justify our answer. Thus when
Sophokles[2] was asked by Peisandros whether he had voted for
the same course as the other *Probouloi*[3]—namely for establishing the 'Four Hundred'—he said 'Yes.' 'How,' asked
Peisandros, 'did you not think this a wicked course?' 'Yes.'
'And so you did this wickedness?' 'Yes,—for there was
nothing better to do.' So, too, the Lacedæmonian, under
examination for his conduct in the ephoralty, was asked
whether he thought that his colleagues had been justly put
to death. 'Yes,' he said. 'And were not *you* responsible
for the same measures?' 'Yes.' 'Then would not *you*, too,
be justly put to death?' 'No indeed, *they* acted thus for
money; *I* did not, but on conviction.' Hence[4], it is better
not to put any more questions after drawing our conclusion,
nor to express the conclusion in the form of a question, unless **1419 b**
the truth of our case is triumphantly clear.

Jokes seem to be of some service in debate; Gorgias said 7
that we ought to worst our opponent's earnest with mockery,
and his mockery with earnest; a good saying. The various
kinds of jokes have been analysed in the *Poetics*. Some of
these befit a free man and others do not: one must take care
then to choose the kind of joke that suits one. Irony is more
liberal than buffoonery; the ironical man jokes on his own
account, the buffoon on some one else's[5].

---

[1] VIII iv.   [2] The statesman and orator (not the poet). Cp. I xiv 3.
[3] A board of ten, appointed in 413 B.C. to devise measures for the public
safety, after the failure of the Sicilian expedition, Thuc. VIII 1.
[4] *i.e.* in view of this danger (R. C. J.).
[5] *Note on the bearing of cc. xvii–xviii.* The term πίστις has two senses:—
(I) the large sense, including ἄτεχνοι and ἔντεχνοι πίστεις (I ii), the ἔντεχνοι being
equivalent to (1) ἠθική, (2) παθητική, and (3) λογική πίστις. (II) The special
sense, = λογική πίστις, proof effected by direct reasoning, answering to the
ἀπόδειξις of Dialectic. Now the ἠθική and παθητική πίστις do not belong to any
one division of the speech. They may be involved in the Proem, the Narrative,
and the Epilogue, as well as in the Argumentation. All the four parts of the
speech are here successively treated by Aristotle, in connexion with τάξις, and he
marks the narrower sense in which πίστεις are dealt with here by saying at the
outset, ἀποδεικτικάς. He is not telling us here the *method* of such proof; he has
told us this already. He has explained its two *instruments*:—Enthymeme and

xix. The epilogue has four elements :—(1) the attempt
to dispose the hearer favourably towards ourselves, and unfavourably towards the adversary ;
—(2) amplification and extenuation; (3) the attempt to excite
certain feelings in the audience; (4) recapitulation.

    Epilogue.

(1) After we have proved our own truthfulness and the
falseness of the adversary, the next thing is naturally to praise
ourselves, vituperate him, and clinch our case. We must aim at
proving either relative or absolute goodness on our part, and
either relative or absolute badness on his part. The means of
presenting people in either light—the topics, that is, by which
they are to be made out good or bad—have been stated[1].

2   (2) The facts having been proved, the next thing in the
natural order is to make much of them, or to make little of
them. The facts must be admitted before one can discuss their
magnitude; as the growth of the body implies something
preexisting. The topics of amplification and extenuation
have been set forth already[2].

3   (3) Next—the quality and the magnitude of the facts
having been ascertained—we have to inspire the hearer with

Example; he has classified the materials to which these instruments have to be
applied in each of the three branches, and (in Book II) the chief moulds or types
into which the arguments themselves may be thrown. Here he is speaking of the
way to *marshal* those proofs, which he has already shown us how to *construct*.
C. xvii is a collection of general rules and remarks on this subject : (1) the πίστεις
must bear, of course, on the point at issue between ourselves and our opponent or
our audience. Those issues are four. (The first of these offers us, he remarks in
passing, this advantage—that *sometimes* we can insist on the *necessary* immorality
of our opponent.) (2) These issues are most distinct in *Forensic* Rhetoric. But
they can also be distinguished in *Deliberative* Rhetoric, while, in *Epideiktic* Rhetoric,
there is seldom any need of ἀπόδειξις. (3) It is useful to watch 'whether he
makes any false statement outside his immediate subject.' (4) Enthymemes suit
Forensic Rhetoric best ; Examples, Deliberative. (5) Our Enthymemes 'should
not be given in a string' etc. General rules and remarks of this kind occupy the
chapter to the beginning of § 16:—'So much of argumentative proof.' He then goes
on :—'As to ethical proof' etc. The particular precept which comes next does not,
however, belong specially to the third division of the speech. 'Ethical proof'
may come in anywhere. But it was convenient to give it under this head.

    C. xviii, or Interrogation, is specially connected with the subject of 'argumen-
tative proofs,' for it is often a special way of gaining a *logical* victory. 'Jokes,'
again, considered as a means of *overthrowing* the adversary, come in here, § 7.
(R. C. J.)

[1] I ix.   [2] II xix.

certain feelings;—namely, with pity or indignation or anger
or hatred or envy or emulation or pugnacity.   The topics for
these, too, have been stated before[1].

(4)   There remains, then, recapitulation.   This should be 4
managed *here* in the way commonly, but wrongly, recom-
mended for the proem ; we are advised to repeat our points
over and over again, in order that they may be easily seized.
Now, in the proem, we ought to state our subject, in order
that the general issue may not be unknown ; in the epilogue,
we ought to state summarily the arguments by which our case
has been proved.   The starting-point should be the remark, 5
that we have performed our undertaking ; and then we may
state *what* we have said, and *why*.   One mode of doing this is
by contrasting our own case with the adversary's ; either by
comparing what he and you have said on the same point, or
without this direct comparison.   ' This was *his* account of the
matter, here is *mine* ; and *my* reasons are these.'   Or ironically: 1420 a
—' *He*, you know, spoke thus, and *I* thus.'   Or ' What airs
would he give himself, if he had proved all this, instead of
merely proving *this*? '   Or Interrogation may be used :—
' What has not been proved ? '   Or ' What has *he* proved ? '—
The recapitulation, then, may either take this form of direct 6
contrast, or follow the natural order of the statements,—
taking first our own ; then, if we like, the adversary's separately.
An *asyndeton* is in place at the end of a speech, making the
ordinary sentence into a true epilogue : ' I have spoken—you
have heard ; you have them ;—judge.'[2]

---

[1] II i–xi.

[2] This illustration is doubtless a reminiscence of the epilogue of the speech of
Lysias against Eratosthenes, Or. xii, παύσομαι κατηγορῶν· ἀκηκόατε, ἑωράκατε,
πεπόνθατε· ἔχετε, δικάζετε.   'The speech for the prosecution must now close ; I
have appealed to your ears, to your eyes, to your hearts ; the case is in your hands ;
I ask for your verdict.'

INDEX

Index

speech-writers, II xi 6 n.; III vii 7;
xii 2
Speusippos, III x 7
'spring,' 'the year has lost its,' I vii
34; III x 7
Stasinus, I xv 14 n.; II xxi 11
statements, topic from joining separate
or dividing composite, II xxiv 3
Stêsichoros, II xx 5; xxi 8; III xi 6
stock-subjects of Athenian declaimers,
II xxii 6
Strabax, II xxiii 17
strange words, III iii 2
style, III i 5 f; points of excellence in,
ii; purity, v; dignity, vi; propriety,
vii; smartness, xi 6, 14; sweetness,
xii 6; characteristic style, vii 1, 6;
pathetic, vii 1, 3; proportionate, vii
1 f; two kinds of style, III ix 1-3;
general types of style, xii 1-6; faults
of style, III iii. Cp. *actuality* and
diction
surprise, point given by a touch of, III
xi 6
suspicion, removal of, II xxiii 24
symmetry of results, topic from, II
xxiii 17; neglect of symmetry in
style, III v 7
synonyms, III ii 7

taste, faults of, III iii 1
tetrameters, trochaic, III i 9; viii 4
Teumêssos, III vi 7
Theagenes of Megara, I ii 19
Thebes, II xxiii 6, 11
Themistokles, I xv 14
Theodekteia, III ix 9 ult.; p. xviii
Theodektês, II xxiii 3, 11, 13, 17,
20, 24; xxiv 3
Theodôros, (1) the actor, III ii 4;
(2) the rhetorician, II xxiii 28; III
xi 6; xiii 5; p. xiv
Thirty, the, II xxiii 23, 25; Thirty
Tyrants, II xxiv 3
Thracian, III xi 6
Thrasybulos, II xxiii 25, 29; xxiv 3
Thrasymachos of Chalkêdôn, II xxiii
29; III i 7; viii 4; xi 13; p. xiv
time, argument from considerations of,
II xxiii 6
Timotheos, the dithyrambic poet, III
iv 4 n.; xi 11

topics, universal or special, I ii 22;
topic of degree, III xix 2; topics of
the emotions, xix 3; Appendix on
'topics,' pp. 142-144
torture I xv 26
tragedies once acted by their authors,
III i 3
tragic poet anon., quoted, II x 5; xxi
6; xxiii 5, 20; III vi 4; xiv 9
travel, books of, I iv 13
trochaic tetrameters, III i 9; viii 4
'two sides to every question,' II viii 4
tyranny, I viii 4 f
tyrants and body-guards, I ii 19

universal classes of argument, II xviii f;
arguments from universal consent,
II xxiii 12

virtue and vice, analysis of, I ix 1-31;
virtues, II i 7
vivacity of style, III xi 1, 10
voice, III i 4; vii 10

war and peace, I iv 9
ways and means, I iv 8
wealth, I v 7; II xvi
wealthy, characteristics of the, II xvi
well-born, character of the, II xv
wines, doctored, III ii 4
wisdom, practical, I ix 13
witnesses, I xv 13-19
wonder, the origin of learning, I xi 21
word, topic from various senses of a,
II xxiii 8; beauty of words, III ii;
compound words, III iii 1; rare
words, *ib.* 3
wrong-doers and their victims, characters of, I xii
wrong-doing, I x, xi, xii, xiii, xiv; III
xv 3

Xenophanês, I xv 29 f; II xxiii 18, 27
Xenophon, *Hellen.*, II xxiii 3 n., 12 n.;
Mem., II xx 4 n.;
Xerxes, II xx 3; III iii 2

youth, characteristics of, II xii 3-16

Zeno (of Elea?), I xii 10

For EU product safety concerns, contact us at Calle de José Abascal, 56–1°,
28003 Madrid, Spain or eugpsr@cambridge.org.

www.ingramcontent.com/pod-product-compliance
Ingram Content Group UK Ltd.
Pitfield, Milton Keynes, MK11 3LW, UK
UKHW010337140625
459647UK00010B/658